Helping Schoolchildren Cope with Anger

A Cognitive-Behavioral Intervention

SECOND EDITION

Jim Larson
John E. Lochman

Foreword by Donald Meichenbaum

THE GUILFORD PRESS
New York   London

Printed in the United States of America

This book is printed on acid-free paper.

Last digit is print number: 9   8   7   6   5   4   3   2   1

Library of Congress Cataloging-in-Publication Data

Larson, Jim, 1942–
    Helping schoolchildren cope with anger : a cognitive-behavioral intervention / Jim Larson,
John E. Lochman ; foreword by Donald Meichenbaum. — 2nd ed.
        p. ; cm.
    Includes bibliographical references and index.
    ISBN 978-1-60623-973-5 (pbk. : alk. paper)
    1. Anger in children—Treatment.   2. Oppositional defiant disorder in children—
Treatment.   3. Cognitive therapy for children.   4. School mental health services.   I. Lochman,
John E. (John Edward)   II. Title.
    [DNLM: 1. Anger. 2. Child. 3. Aggression—psychology. 4. Child Psychology—
methods.   5. Cognitive Therapy—methods.   6. School Health Services.   WS 105.5.E5]
    RJ506.A35L37 2011
    618.92′89—dc22
                                                                                2010035211

About the Authors

Jim Larson, PhD, is Professor of Psychology and Director of the School Psychology Program at the University of Wisconsin–Whitewater. He is also a member of the Scientific Board of the Melissa Institute for Violence Prevention and Treatment, headquartered in Miami, Florida. Formerly a school psychologist with the Milwaukee Public Schools and the lead psychologist in the school system's Violence Prevention Program, Dr. Larson's major research interests are the treatment of anger and aggression in children and youth and programming for the prevention of school violence.

John E. Lochman, PhD, ABPP, is Professor and Doddridge Saxon Chair of Clinical Psychology at the University of Alabama and Director of the University's Center for the Prevention of Youth Behavior Problems. Dr. Lochman has conducted extensive research and published widely on family, peer, and neighborhood risk factors; social-cognitive processes; and intervention and prevention with aggressive children. He is the recipient of awards including the International Collaborative Prevention Research Award from the Society for Prevention Research, and is Editor-in-Chief of the *Journal of Abnormal Child Psychology.*

Foreword

I was asked to write the foreword to the first edition of *Helping Schoolchildren Cope with Anger* and did so with much enthusiasm. When the second edition was being prepared, the request to provide another foreword was forthcoming. Once again, I was eager to obtain an update and review the contributions of two major researchers in the field of anger management training with students. In this edition, Jim Larson and John Lochman have provided a detailed, clinically sensitive, theoretically and empirically based treatment manual for working with aggressive youth. Focused on a group intervention, the book is designed for use with 8- to 12-year-olds and employs an array of cognitive-behavioral procedures.

Before I describe the valuable features of the book's comprehensive presentation, let me first highlight the urgency of this work. Students who have emotional and behavioral disturbances, especially evident in the form of anger regulation and aggressive behavior (some 6–16% of boys and 2–9% of girls), are at a high risk of academic failure, poor peer relationships, dropping out of school, and later psychiatric disturbances and trouble with the law. The individual and societal costs of such a developmental trajectory are substantial. Just consider that every high school dropout, over the course of his or her lifetime, will earn $290,000 less and pay $100,000 less in taxes than students who graduate from high school. Or consider that a 1% increase in those who graduate from high school in the United States would save $1.4 billion in taxes or $2,100 per student per year (Moretti, 2007).

Surely, there are many entry points to alter this developmental course. Larson and Lochman have provided a thoughtful description of the Anger Coping Program (ACP) and a more extensive Coping Power Program that involves parent training as one way to alter this trajectory. Both training programs are based on the social information-processing model of aggressive behavior offered by Kenneth A. Dodge and his colleagues.

The ACP addresses the core difficulties and deficits that students have with emotional self-regulation, including anger management, cognitive deficits, and distortions in perspective taking, attribution making, and social problem solving. In a detailed manner, Larson and Lochman walk group leaders through session-by-session descriptions, and they use case examples to illustrate the intervention steps.

Here is a list of the impressive strengths of this new edition:

1. Theory driven and evidence based, with impressive follow-up data for up to 3 years.
2. Ecologically based, focusing on how to integrate the ACP into a school-oriented approach that includes a consideration of schools' mission statements, codes of conduct, classroom management, and teacher and administrative collaboration.
3. Highlights generalization activities that facilitate behavior change across settings, time, and response classes. The authors provide a detailed critical discussion of how to go beyond a "train-and-hope" approach. Their discussion should be studied, no matter what skills you are training.
4. Discusses how to involve parent training in any student-based intervention program.
5. Considers how to alter interventions for girls versus boys (e.g., see the discussion of the SNAP [Stop Now and Plan] program). Also considered is the role of cultural differences and the "code of the streets" in the implementation of the ACP.
6. Provides a detailed Intervention Integrity Checklist and a discussion of ways to evaluate the efficacy of ACP so data-driven decisions can be made.
7. Considers possible negative aggregation effects of conducting group versus individualized ACP.
8. Explores ways to disseminate the ACP and related programs.

As the authors continue to collect data and refine the ACP, I look forward to a third edition. Given the personal and societal costs of working with children with emotional and behavioral disturbances, the need for effective interventions is critical. The field is indebted to Jim Larson and John Lochman for their leadership, scholarship, clinical perspicacity, cultural and gender sensitivity, and practical "know how."

Any "race to the top," as advocated by the present U.S. Secretary of Education, Arne Duncan, needs to ensure that *all* children, including those with behavioral and emotional problems, are included. The support of programs such as ACP and others reviewed in this valuable book should be funded and fully evaluated.

DONALD MEICHENBAUM, PhD
Distinguished Professor Emeritus, University of Waterloo, Ontario;
Distinguished Visiting Professor, School of Education, University of Miami;
Research Director, Melissa Institute for Violence Prevention and Treatment

REFERENCE

Moretti, E. (2007). Crimes and the code of criminal justice. In C. Belfield & H. M. Levin (Eds.), *The price we pay: Economic and social consequence of inadequate education.* New York: Brookings Institution.

Preface

Why did we originally choose to write a book about treating angry and aggressive children in the schools? Because, while *homicide* among students is on the decline, *interpersonal physical aggression* among them is not. Data from a combined report by the U.S. Department of Education and Department of Justice revealed that approximately 36% of high school students reported that they engaged in a physical fight during the past year, with 12% of these on school property (National Center for Education Statistics, 2009). Not all children who are aggressive in the elementary schools go on to become adolescent fighters and victimizers, but early chronic aggression is enough of a risk factor to warrant its being taken very seriously. The collaboration that has resulted in this book is a reflection of our understanding of that seriousness.

The plan for this book resulted from a meeting the two of us held at the National Association of School Psychologists in Chicago in the mid-1990s. Research on the Anger Coping Program had been under way for well over a decade; yet, it was clear to us that this potentially important intervention was still the domain of only a small circle of researchers and very few practitioners. In our work with school systems, we were aware that most counselors and school psychologists were eager to help address the problem of school violence but were uncertain as to what skills to use to meet the treatment needs of aggressive students. Both of us had done training workshops around the country, but clearly the need went well beyond our limited capacities. We decided to link our Anger Coping Program with our combined experience and scholarship to create a convenient and reliable resource for practitioners.

In this second edition of *Helping Schoolchildren Cope with Anger: A Cognitive-Behavioral Intervention*, we have produced what we believe to be an even more "practitioner-friendly" book on how to intervene effectively with angry, aggressive children. This is a book for school psychologists, counselors, and other helping professionals who work with 8- to 12-year-old children in school or school-like settings. With certain adaptations, mental health professionals in residential or other clinical settings will also find it particularly useful.

Group treatment with aggressive externalizing children can be a considerable challenge, particularly for those who lack experience. Therapeutic techniques and procedures are rarely addressed comprehensively at the preservice level, so most practitioners are left to acquire the skills on their own. As a result, these children may be left completely unserved or—as is often the case—inadequately served with efforts better designed for less challenging children. The treatment procedures described in this book are empirically based and arise out of both authors' controlled research and years of clinical experience with aggressive children. An effort has been made in this second edition to combine the extensive body of research with more practical clinical experiential acumen: procedures, hints, and suggestions that have proven themselves useful over the years. We are enthusiastic about the improvements in this new edition and believe that with its publication the field has an excellent bridge from relevant research to the practitioner.

Chapters 1 and 2 provide a solid foundation in the many issues associated with the development of aggression and a guiding theoretical orientation for the Anger Coping Program. These chapters will be particularly useful for readers having little or no instructional background in aggression or cognitive-behavioral theory and will serve as a helpful refresher for more experienced practitioners. The careful study of these two chapters is an important prerequisite to the more "hands-on" chapters that follow.

In Chapter 3 we place the Anger Coping Program within the larger context of a truly functional whole-school behavioral support plan. The ultimate effectiveness of small-group or individual anger management skills training depends greatly on its proper placement within the larger context of schoolwide and classroom-level behavioral supports. With the growing influence of response to intervention and positive behavioral supports, skills training interventions need to be more clearly articulated within this wider effort.

Chapter 4 guides the practitioner through the essential practical steps required to screen and identify those children who will benefit most from enrolling in the Anger Coping Program. Unlike some other counseling approaches, the Anger Coping Program is truly a schoolwide collaboration that must actively involve the most influential adults in the child's life, such as teachers, administrators, and parents. The intervention is "multisystemic" in that it encompasses the schoolwide systems of counseling, teaching, and discipline in attempting to effect long-term skills acquisition and generalization. The critical role that each system plays and the suggested techniques for involving interested adults are explained in detail in Chapters 5 and 6.

Prior to our presenting the actual treatment manual itself, Chapter 7 reviews the empirical evidence for the effectiveness of the Anger Coping Program. The need for practitioners to understand and utilize empirically based interventions in their work with all children cannot be overstated. Schools in particular are ideal locations for effecting positive therapeutic and behavioral change—but only if the efforts to do so are grounded in "what works." The available time in the school day is too short, the personnel costs too high, and the risks to the children too great to engage in unsupported "train-and-hope" procedures.

In Chapter 8 readers will find the complete step-by-step treatment manual for the Anger Coping Program, newly formatted and updated for this edition. Additional reproducible forms and suggested practitioner scripts combine to make a much more "user-friendly" training curriculum.

The last section of the book contains important new chapters on working with girls as well as with children from diverse cultural backgrounds, a discussion of emerging research in peer-to-peer deviancy effects, and recommendations on how best to use the Anger Coping Program one-on-one with individuals. Also new to this edition, the final chapter explores useful procedures for monitoring students' progress and evaluating the program.

In closing, we again pause to applaud those practitioners who have chosen to undertake the often daunting task of teaching aggressive children the skills they need most in order to change bad habits. In our public schools, there are groups of children with very arguably comparable needs for mental health services who may present a somewhat lesser challenge in the small-group setting. Yet, it is hard to imagine that there are children whose risks of negative outcomes later in life are greater. In these times when schools and the mental health community are constantly under fire to "do something" about violence in society, practitioners who choose to take up this challenge deserve special recognition.

JIM LARSON
JOHN E. LOCHMAN

Acknowledgments

I wish to express my appreciation to all of my students and the many school practitioners over the past 20 years who have demonstrated through their work with the Anger Coping Program that even the children highest in risk deserve all we have to offer. Special appreciation and thanks go to Sarah Beckman for her tireless research assistance on this edition and to school psychologist Jamie Kupkovits for her many insights on the treatment of aggressive girls. I also wish to recognize Byron and Judy McBride for their always helpful support, Donald Meichenbaum, Lynn, Michael, Trish, Frank, Susan, and all the wonderful people at the Melissa Institute for Violence Prevention and Treatment for their compassionate and determined efforts to make the world a better place for all children. My sincere thanks, of course, to John Lochman, a true man of science, for making this whole endeavor possible. Finally, love and appreciation go out to my mother, Dorothy; the memory of my late father, James; my son, Jeremy; and Wendy Walsh for their welcome inspiration and encouragement.

JIM LARSON

I deeply appreciate Mike Nelson's collaboration with me in the development of an anger control program in 1978 that grew out of our early training in cognitive-behavioral interventions at our respective graduate school programs. The idea of fusing anger management, using cognitive control strategies and social problem-solving skills, into one intervention for angry aggressive children was the result of this collaboration. This early pilot of a school-based group intervention subsequently evolved into the Anger Coping Program described in this book. I am indebted to the assistance of Louise Lampron, John Curry, and Peter Burch in the refinement and further development of the Anger Coping Program, and to John Coie, Karen Wells, and numerous other collaborators (including Tammy Barry, Caroline Boxmeyer, Thomas Dishion, David FitzGerald, Nicholas Ialongo, Melissa Jackson, Melissa Kuhajda, Lisa Lenhart, Wendy Mager, Walter Matthys, Terry McCandies, Desiree Murray, Nicole Powell, Lisa Reiter, Karen Salekin, Sue Smith-Scott, Janet Whidby, and Michael Windle) for the extension and continued development of directly related social skills and Coping Power intervention programs.

My work on the continued development of these programs has also been enriched in meaningful ways by my colleagues in the Conduct Problems Prevention Research Group (Karen Bierman, John Coie, Kenneth Dodge, Mark Greenberg, Bob McMahon, and Ellen Pinderhughes) as we have developed and evaluated the Fast Track program over the past two decades. The contributions of graduate students (including Sonja Schoenwald, Susan Craven-Williams, Deborah Levy, Elizabeth Wagner, Vanessa Nyborg, Mesha Ellis, Dustin Pardini, Thomas Magee, Heather McElroy, Nancy Clanton, Khiela Holmes, Annie Deming, Laura Young, Anna Yaros, Mary Wojnaroski, Rachel Baden, Haley Ford, Alberto Jiminez, Sara Stromeyer, Jessica Minney, Meaghan Kelly, Liz Adams, and Jill Rosenbaum), interns, school counselors, school psychologists, special education teachers, mental health clinicians, and the children themselves in the continued adaptation of this series of related programs have been instrumental in making these programs flexibly work with a range of children with aggressive behavior problems.

I acknowledge the support of research grants from the National Institute of Mental Health, the National Institute on Drug Abuse, the Center for Substance Abuse Prevention within the Substance Abuse and Mental Health Services Administration, the U.S. Department of Justice, and the Centers for Disease Control and Prevention in the intervention research evaluating these related programs. I express my deep appreciation to Jim Larson, who had the vision and persistence over a decade ago to take the initiative in preparing a book about the Anger Coping Program that would make it more widely accessible for dissemination and use by practitioners in school and clinic settings. Finally, I acknowledge the memories of my supportive parents; my wife, Linda; and my children (Lisa Kristianson, Kara Sair, and Bryan Lochman) and their families, including my stimulating grandchildren (Garrett, Audrey, Jonathan, and Lori), who help me rediscover the interesting nuances of positive child development.

JOHN E. LOCHMAN

Contents

HELPING SCHOOLCHILDREN
COPE WITH ANGER

CHAPTER 1

The Development of Aggression

Scene 1

Seven-year-old Robert W took his place in line at the school doorway off the playground, preparing to re-enter the building following recess. He held the classroom's basketball under his arm while he poked his finger into the back of the girl in front of him, hoping to provoke a little rise. Casey R, standing behind Robert, sensed an opportunity for fun and snatched the basketball from Robert's grasp, giggling loudly. Robert whirled, faced the laughing Casey, and threw himself upon him. Both boys crashed to the pavement, with Casey's head banging hard against the blacktop, opening a bloody gash. Robert straddled the wailing child and pummeled him in the face with both fists until the supervising teacher managed to pull him off.

Scene 2

Steven C worked the combination lock for his locker, relieved that another day in the sixth grade was finally over and he could head for home. The 15 minutes he'd spent discussing his social studies project after the bell had allowed much of the school to empty, and the third floor hall was uncommonly quiet. Opening the locker door, he reached for his new NBA warm-up jacket and suddenly felt a presence beside him.

He turned and stood face to face with another sixth-grade student, Brian K. Brian was well known among the sixth graders, especially the smaller ones. He was big, intimidating, and mean, and he hung out with a small crowd of equally detestable bullies. Before Steven could react, Brian's right hand lashed up and gripped him by the neck, knocking his head back against the locker.

"The jacket is just my brother's size. I think I'll take it." Brian gripped Steven's neck tighter as he pulled the jacket from the locker, a blank, almost calm, look on his face.

"Tell anyone and you're dead meat," he growled, banging Steven's head hard against the locker for emphasis.

1

Scenes such as these play out in schools around the world. Children and youth aggressing against one another within the school environment has become one of the most significant social concerns of the past two decades. Formerly considered "safe havens," schools in some areas of the United States often mirror the violence and danger of their hostile surrounding neighborhoods. According to the National Center for Education Statistics (2009), in 2006 students ages 12–18 were victims of approximately 1.7 million nonfatal crimes at school, and 6% of elementary school teachers reported that they had been physically threatened with injury by a student.

NEW QUESTIONS FOR SCHOOL PRACTITIONERS

Why do children act this way? How is it that kids from the same community, in the same grade, in the same classroom, can be so different?

Why can some kids take a joke and laugh, whereas other kids get angry and start swinging? Were they born that way, or did they learn it somehow? Isn't aggression among young boys normal, and won't they outgrow it?

Did the adolescent bully in the preceding vignette give us any hints when he was younger that he might be headed this way by the sixth grade? Is there some sort of a *developmental trajectory* for adolescent aggression? Once started, can this trajectory be altered in a positive direction, or is antisocial behavior ultimately inevitable? Was it simply Brian's "fate" to end up assaulting fellow students?

It has not been typical for school practitioners to ask these questions; this has been more the home turf of developmental, cognitive, and behavioral psychologists who spend their careers—and a staggering amount of private and federal grant money—trying to sort out the answers. Yet, although it has not been *typical* in the past for school personnel to investigate the theoretical and developmental psychology of aggression, it has now become *essential*.

In order to intervene effectively in the lives of aggressive children and youth, school personnel must have an understanding of what we currently know about the etiology and development of aggression. Because not all children come to aggressive behavior by the same pathway, developing informed hypotheses about each individual unquestionably aids us in creating effective interventions.

Why is aggression among school-age children of such concern? Isn't rough-and-tumble play normal among children, and won't those "mean" little boys who fight all the time just grow out of it?

Yes, rough-and-tumble play is both normal and common among school-age children, especially boys. Spend any amount of time watching an elementary school recess at virtually any school across the country and be assured.

But, no, the picture for the young fighters is bleak. In fact, there is not a strong likelihood that the children who are demonstrating nonplayful aggressive behavior at a young age will "just grow out of it." Rather, there is a stronger likelihood that this behavior is a precursor of more violent behaviors to come (Eron, Huesmann, Dubow, Romanoff, &

Yarmel, 1987; Loeber, 1990). Indeed, the *strongest single predictor* of an individual's risk of perpetrating violence as an adolescent is a history of having engaged is aggressive behavior as a child (Eron & Slaby, 1994).

HISTORICAL AND CURRENT CONCEPTUALIZATIONS OF AGGRESSION

It might be said that the "modern" era of conceptualizing aggression was ushered in by Dollard, Doob, Miller, Mowrer, and Sears (1939) in their book *Frustration and Aggression.* These authors held that it was emotional arousal influenced by externally driven events— that is, frustrating experiences or goal blocking—that caused human aggression. All aggression, they theorized, had the goal of injuring another person. The essence of what is known as the "hostile aggression" perspective is that injurious intent is a key aspect. In other words, Dollard et al. (1939) believed that every aggressive act (1) arose out of negative emotionality and (2) was designed to hurt the person or object of the aggression.

This perspective made intuitive sense. Most readers can recall at one time or another having lost their temper, usually out of frustration arising from another's misbehavior, and then either striking out at that person or wanting to. Although subsequent research has questioned the inevitability of the frustration–aggression link, Pepler and Slaby (1994) observed that the theory "succeeded in shifting attention from explanatory factors that were internal and currently unchangeable to factors that were external and potentially controllable" (p. 28).

Is all aggression, however, merely the result of emotional arousal, such as occurs when an individual is frustrated or angry? Recall the two examples of aggressive students offered at the beginning of this book. In the first example, Robert W was angry at the boy who took his basketball and set upon him aggressively. Clearly, the child was emotionally aroused. The goal of this form of aggression was to inflict harm upon the source of his anger; this action is clearly representative of *hostile aggression.*

However, in the second example, the bully had a grip on Steven's throat and banged his head against the locker with "a blank, almost calm, look on his face." Little or no emotional arousal here, yet plenty of aggression. How is that explained? In this case, the aggressor wasn't angry or frustrated, but he was motivated to acquire something. This is termed *instrumental aggression.* The goal of the bully's behavior was not his victim's pain; it was his victim's jacket. His aggression was not motivated by an internal emotional arousal; it was motivated by the potential for external reward.

Kenneth Dodge (1991) has attempted to offer a unifying theory of aggression in children and youth. Dodge refers to those acts of aggression that are more emotionally driven as *reactive aggression* and those that are more instrumentally driven as *proactive aggression.* This conceptualization can be extremely useful for school personnel, particularly as efforts are put forward for prevention and intervention. Let's look at the two more closely.

Dodge (1991) offered prototypical examples of children who are inclined toward reactive and proactive aggression. He cautioned, however, that these are very rarely pure types, except in extreme cases: "All behaviors have aspects of reaction and proaction, in that one can make guesses regarding the precipitants as well as the functions of all behaviors" (p. 206). Consider Billy, a child who uses proactive aggression:

> The first boy, Billy, is 12 years old and has been arrested four times for vandalism, theft, and similar offenses. He is reported to be a major behavior problem in school. He is a bully among his peers, in that he regularly coerces other boys into deferring to him. He teases peers, threatens them, dominates them, laughs at them, and starts fights with them (Dodge, 1991, p. 201)

Proactively aggressive children tend to be the bullies in school. Their aggression features relatively little in the way of observable emotion. They may be disliked by their peers, though they are often seen to have leadership qualities and an agreeable sense of humor. Their experience is one of positive outcomes for their own aggressive behavior and an abundance of observable violence among family members, in the neighborhood, and/or on television. Dodge (1991) also offered the case of Reid, a child inclined to reactive aggression:

> The second boy, Reid, is also 12 years old. He has been arrested for assault on his teacher. One day following her ridicule of him for failing an exam, he pulled a knife on her in the school parking lot and cut her in the arm. He is also considered highly aggressive and socially rejected among peers, but he doesn't seem to start fights so much as he escalates conflicts and can't avoid them. He overreacts to minor provocations and is viewed as volatile and short-tempered (p. 201)

Reactively aggressive children are the students with hot tempers who seem to get riled into anger and aggression at the slightest provocation. They often leave school officials scratching their heads after a blowup and asking "What was *that* all about?" They are almost universally disliked and rejected by peers. They tend to be hypervigilant for aggressive cues in their environment and routinely misinterpret the intentions of peers as hostile.

How do children gravitate to these forms of aggression? Is it biology or something in the child's inborn temperament? Is aggressive behavior learned, and, if so, how and where does this learning take place?

THE DEVELOPMENT OF AGGRESSIVE BEHAVIOR

In this section we briefly describe three major theoretical positions on the development and maintenance of aggression in children and adolescents: social learning theory, social information processing, and coercive family process. These three positions by no means exhaust the possibilities in addressing the subject. They are, however, theories well supported in the empirical literature and those that seem to have the most heuristic value for school practitioners.

Social Learning Theory

During much of the past 40 years, Albert Bandura and his colleagues (e.g., Bandura, 1971, 1973, 1983; Bandura & Walters, 1959) have explored the notion that aggressive behaviors are learned and governable, not inborn and uncontrollable: "Aggressive behavior is learned through essentially the same processes as those regulating the acquisition of any other form of behavior" (Bandura, 1973, p. 68). Just because we observe people spending enormous sums of money on fancy television and video gear is no reason to thereby conclude that such behavior is impelled by a biologically determined inner drive for television watching. The same reasoning applies to aggressive behavior. Indeed, any highly motivated behavior, whether television watching or punching an obnoxious harasser in the nose, is learned in essentially the same way.

This conceptualization of aggression is subsumed under Bandura's *social learning theory*. One may construe social learning theory as "the thinking person's behaviorism." Unlike fellow behaviorists, such as B. F. Skinner, who proposed that all behavior is externally controlled through differential reinforcement and punishment contingencies, Bandura posited that humans are "thinking organisms possessing capabilities that provide [them] with some power of self-direction" (Bandura, 1973, p. 42). In other words, human beings have minds with which to think about their behavior, to imagine new behaviors, to consider the consequences of their behavior, and to draw conclusions by watching others behave. Let us now look at the essential principles of social learning theory and how the theory explains the development of aggressive behavior.

Observational Learning

According to the social learning approach, new behaviors are learned either through experiencing the behavior directly or by observing the behavior of other people. On a daily basis, individuals are confronted with various situations that they must deal with. Sometimes they respond effectively and sometimes they don't. The more effective responses produce favorable results and remain in the behavioral repertoire, whereas the ineffectual ones are discarded (Bandura, 1973). But if we had to experience every type of situation before deciding on an appropriate response, we would progress painfully slowly in adapting to our environment! If we watched a friend walking in front us slip and fall on an icy sidewalk, we wouldn't have to keep walking and slip too before we decided to adjust our gait; we would have learned by *observing* our friend's misfortune.

Children learn aggressive behavior patterns in part by observing the consequences of aggression for others. Children reared in environments where they observe role models for whom aggression usually has positive consequences may learn that aggressive behavior can work for them too. Younger siblings who watch their brothers or sisters regularly get what they want through intimidation, coercion, or direct force—without regular negative outcomes—are more likely to choose similar strategies themselves.

Bandura and colleagues' laboratory work (see Bandura, 1983, for a review) has demonstrated the power of observational learning in regard to the aggressive behavior of young children. In numerous instances, children who viewed a model being rewarded for aggressive behavior were more likely to engage in that behavior themselves than were children who observed the model being punished for his or her aggression. Basic, simple aggressive behaviors like hitting and shoving are physically uncomplicated and require little in the way of practice to enact. A 4-year-old preschooler who wants another child's toy and who has observed the efficacy of physical aggression at home is at high risk of enacting such behavior him- or herself.

The work of Bandura and others has also demonstrated that aggressive modeling does not have to be live to have an effect on the viewer (e.g., Bandura & Barab, 1973; see Thelen, Fry, Feherenbach, & Frautschi, 1979, for a review). Excessive viewing of violent television by children at risk for aggressive behavior has been demonstrated to have significant effects (see Donnerstein, Slaby, & Eron, 1994, for a review). School personnel must be cognizant of the effects on children, who are bombarded daily with both live and media models for aggressive behavior.

Direct Experience

Aggressive behavior can also be learned through the differential reinforcement of engaging in the behavior itself. Children who are reared in environments that offer opportunities for positive outcomes following aggressive behavior may learn to use that behavior in other environments. Children who find that their desires for pleasure or control in a household are met with positive outcomes when they bully smaller children or strike out at adults may learn that such behavior "pays off." Parents who regard aggressive play or aggressive problem solving positively (e.g., Child: "Brother hit me!" Parent: "Well, hit him back!") may be unwittingly contributing to later problems at school and in the community. If such behavior has paid off at home for all their young lives, why would these children believe that it will not have similar results in kindergarten?

Conversely, children who find that their aggressive behavior in the home is met with aversive or negative outcomes—such as parental disapproval, time-outs, or other undesirable consequences—may be less likely to select that behavior in other environments. This result is particularly common in households where the child is both taught and reinforced for nonaggressive problem solving.

Self-Regulatory Influences

A central insight in social learning theory is that people have the ability to manage their own behavior by self-monitored consequences as well as or better than through consequences from external sources: "There is no more devastating punishment than self-contempt" (Bandura, 1973, p. 48). This is the power of the mind that social learning theory brings to behaviorism. Praising a child for engaging in a behavior that he or she devalues reduces the effect of the praise. For instance, Lochman, Whidby, and FitzGerald (2000) noted that chronically aggressive boys often place a high value on revenge behavior. Now, consider a child such as this who places a high value on revenge behavior, whose teacher, following an incident, praises him with "I really like the way you are just forgetting about it." As well-meaning as that praise was meant to be and as powerful as teacher approval may be in other circumstances, the child's self-evaluation that "forgetting about it is bad" will outweigh the teacher's. She may be shocked—and personally affronted—to watch him get up and start punching. Yet, later in the day the teacher may offer a reinforcer to the same child during a math lesson with the remark "I really like the way you are working hard on these problems" and find that the child's attention to the task actually increases. In this case, the child places value on "working hard," so the external reinforcer is consonant with his self-evaluation.

Most problem solving occurs in thought rather than in action (Bandura, 1973; this insight is expanded on in the section on social information processing, to follow). It is through the mental representation of possible courses of action that human beings are able to regulate their own behavior. The aforementioned child who enacted revenge upon his classmate first cognitively considered alternative actions (e.g., [1] forget about it or [2] punch him), then evaluated the possible consequences of each course of action, and subsequently executed the favored symbolic solution. In this case, though both behaviors were in his repertoire, the child considered the pain of self-contempt for not getting revenge to be more aversive than the school's consequences for fighting, and then he selected the aggressive response.

According to social learning theory, humans have the capacity for self-regulation, to select behaviors within their repertoires on the basis of anticipated consequences. The setting—or stimulus condition—has an effect on the behavior choice of the individual, as the calculated consequences differ among environments. A fourth-grade pupil out in the street with his friends who is the recipient of a nonverbal taunt from another child is more likely to select an overtly aggressive response than if he were aware of the same taunt in church or while shopping with his mother.

Different settings provide cues for the individual about what the likely consequences will be and allow him or her to adjust the response accordingly. Some children for whom the community and/or home environments provide settings that cue positive consequences for aggressive responses have an enormously difficult time making the cognitive switch once they are in the school setting.

Summary

According to the social learning theory model, aggressive behavior is acquired and maintained primarily through (1) observational learning from aggressive models, live or in the media; (2) direct experience of rewarding consequences for aggression; or (3) self-regulatory influences (e.g., applying self-reward or -punishment and differential application of cognitive feedback processes). In real life, these influences rarely act singly; instead, they interact with one another in a reciprocal process. Children whose experience has taught them to select aggressive responses at high rates learn to expect others to respond aggressively toward them. This expectation further influences the child to act aggressively. Others respond to the child with counteraggression, thus strengthening the initial expectation.

Consider the hypothetical experience of JR, a third-grade pupil. JR is a middle child in a family of five children, all under the age of 10. His home life is fairly chaotic, with the older children left to babysit while the single parent works two low-paying jobs. Lacking other child management skills, the older children control the younger children down the line through physical aggression and intimidation. The television is on constantly, unmonitored by the absent parent and tuned to the highly violent programming preferred by the dominant older child. The neighborhood is made up of other families like JR's plus an assortment of unemployed single men. The children are only casually monitored in their play with one another, which ensures frequent fights and a "might-makes-right" ethos. JR has both *observed* and *directly experienced* positive outcomes for aggression, both in his home and in his neighborhood.

One morning in school as the class was lining up for drinks at the water fountain, Terrence W, who was standing in front of JR, backed up and stepped on JR's foot.

"Oops," said Terrence, turning around to face JR with a smile and a shrug. JR's life experience was to expect others to be aggressive toward him, to expect positive outcomes from his own aggression, and to value revenge behaviors over the approval of adults in school. He shoved Terrence, knocking him into another child. Terrence came back toward JR with fists raised in a counterattack, thus confirming for JR that his expectation was accurate and his behavior warranted. The fight was on.

Social learning theory is not the *only* explanation as to how children develop the aggressive behavior patterns we see in school; however, it is an empirically supported and useful conceptualization of the process. As we shall see, numerous other factors inside and outside the child and inside and outside the school building play critical roles with some children.

Social Information Processing

We turn now to a related model that seeks to explain how various aggressive behavior patterns develop. Throughout much of the 1980s and into the 1990s, Kenneth Dodge and colleagues (e.g., Crick & Dodge, 1994; Dodge, 1980, 1986, 1991, 1993a; Dodge & Coie, 1987; Dodge & Frame, 1982) have sought to explain aggressive behavior in children through a model stressing deficiencies in social information processing. Information processing is a cognitive psychology model that uses the empirical method of laboratory experimentation to focus on the verbal learning process, with particular attention directed to short- and long-term memory. It draws heavily from human engineering in its viewpoint that we humans are information processors and decision makers with limits on how much information we can handle (Goetz, Hall, & Fetsco, 1989).

A sequential framework for competent social information processing in children has been offered by Dodge and others (e.g., Hughes & Hall, 1987). This model identifies six "steps," or cognitive operations, that a child needs to enact for competent social problem solving. The empirical basis for this model is reviewed in the next chapter because of its central role in serving as a foundation for the Anger Coping Program. As a working example of the model, think back to our little friend JR, standing in line at the drinking fountain when the fellow in front of him steps back onto JR's foot.

The *encoding process* (Step 1) occurs when an event happens in proximity to an individual and that person gathers information from his or her sensory systems and perceives the event. There is an enormous amount of information presented in the social environment at any given moment, and central to social competency is the ability to select and attend to the relevant cues (Dodge, 1986). As compared with their normally functioning classmates, aggressive children have a strong tendency to selectively attend to hostile cues at higher rates, to the exclusion of the nonhostile cues. Our little third grader, JR, attended to only the hostile cue of Terrence's foot on his, ignoring a clear cue that it was an accident ("Oops") and the gestures of nonhostility (a shrug and a smile).

After the child has selected the cue to which he or she will attend (i.e., encode it), the child needs to give meaning to it by mental representation and interpretation (Dodge, 1991). In this *representation and interpretation phase* (Step 2), the child must integrate the cue with his or her memory, looking for an understanding of the meaning of the cue. In JR's incident, he interpreted the encoded cues as being hostile even when no evidence of hostile motivation existed, which indicated a hostile attributional bias. This is what Kendall, Ronan, and Epps (1991) referred to as the "tendency to 'assume the worst' regarding the intention of peers in ambiguous (neither hostile nor benign) situations" (p. 345).

After the child has interpreted the situation to his or her satisfaction, this model hypothesizes that the child engages in a *goal selection process* (Step 3), which indicates the child's desired affective or behavioral outcomes for the social interaction (Crick & Dodge, 1994). In the example involving JR, we could hypothesize that his goal was retaliatory, in response to his biased interpretation of hostile intent. Possible parallel goals of status maintenance ("You can't get away with stepping on *my* toe!") or a felt cultural imperative defense might also be hypothesized.

In the fourth step (*response access or construction*) is seen the child's ability to summon up or generate mental representations of possible responses to the encoded and interpreted cue. For example, a child who has had her desk bumped by another pupil may generate the following response choices if she had encoded and represented the bump as accidental: "I could ignore it. I could to ask her to apologize. I could get upset and make her feel bad." JR's limited response search capabilities did not allow him mentally to generate nonaggressive responses to hostility (e.g., assertion, humor, appeal to authority), and so he generated the aggressive response.

The fifth step in the social information processing model is the *response decision process*, which asks: "Which of the possible responses shall I choose?" Dodge (1986) offered the analogy of a computer chess game. The computer responds to the human player's moves by accessing its memory and generating countermoves and evaluating the consequences of each move. The size and sophistication of the computer's memory will allow it to determine the probable consequences for one, two, three, or more moves ahead. The more complex the memory and the more sophisticated the operating system, the more competent the selected move will be. Our young friend, JR, evaluated the probable consequences of shoving Terrence for stepping on his foot as positive and judged that his skills to carry out the response were up to the task. Why didn't he consider any alternative solutions? Didn't he know he would get into trouble for that behavior? Is it that he doesn't care?

In the *behavioral enactment process* (Step 6), once the child has selected a response that he or she believes to be optimal, the child proceeds to act it out (Dodge, 1986). To be successful, the child has to have the necessary behavioral skills in his or her repertoire. For instance, a child may decide that questioning a peer's behavior is the optimal response, but if he or she does not have the verbal skills to carry it out, the enactment will not be competent (Pepler, King, & Byrd, 1991). Failure to competently enact a selected behavior creates a new cue and a loop back through the process. Because aggressive children tend to lack many of the social skills necessary to engage prosocial problem-resolution strategies, their occasional attempts are incompetently enacted. If JR had selected a nonaggressive response to Terrence, such as asking him to be careful, he would have needed the verbal skills to do it—and to do so without making it sound like a threat. Such skills involve, among others, word selection, voice tone, facial expression, and body posture. Although many students learn these social skills easily through home and school modeling and practice, others, like JR, aren't so fortunate.

Coercive Family Process

Lonnie K is 6 years old and in the first grade. He lives with both parents, a paternal grandfather, and one younger and one older brother. They all reside in the grandfather's home a few blocks from the school. Lonnie's father is currently unemployed and is on court probation for assault and criminal damage to property following an incident at a local tavern. Lonnie's mother is a hairdresser at a neighborhood shop. She was recently let go from an assistant manager position in a nearby town because of absences she blames on bouts of depression. Lonnie's oldest brother, Raymond, is in the seventh grade in a special education program for emotionally disturbed/behaviorally disordered students and has had a number of contacts with the juvenile court. There have been six calls to Social Services by neighbors over the past 10 years, primarily for suspected neglect of the children.

In his first-grade class, Lonnie presents an enormous behavior problem. He is extremely oppositional to his teacher's requests for compliance, is aggressive toward the other children, and is unable to participate regularly in group games without hitting or pushing another child. He has to be closely monitored on the playground because of his tendency to push children off swings and playground equipment rather than to wait his turn. At his best, he can be charming and funny. His teacher laments, however, that "he is growing up to be the same mean kid his older brother is."

In this section, referring to the family of 6-year-old Lonnie K as an example, we investigate the contributions of the home context to the development of aggressive behavior patterns in children. The great body of research in this area has come from Gerald Patterson and his colleagues at the Oregon Social Learning Center (e.g., Patterson, 1982; Patterson, DeBaryshe, & Ramsey, 1989; Patterson, Reid, & Dishion, 1992; Patterson, Reid, Jones, & Conger, 1975; Reid & Patterson, 1991). It was Patterson (1982) who coined the term *coercive family process* to describe a family pattern composed of the interaction between ineffective parent management skills and escalating child behavior problems. This is a family process that actually *trains* children to be aggressive and noncompliant (Patterson, 1982; Patterson et al., 1989).

Lonnie's family demographics include some of the risk factors found to be implicated in the development of aggression in the family context. Low socioeconomic status, substance abuse by parent(s), criminality of parent(s), and maternal depression have all been associated with exacerbating the coercive family process (Kazdin, 1987b; Reid & Patterson, 1991). These demographic factors, singly or together, do not cause aggressive or antisocial behavior to develop, but they do function as significant stressors that can undermine attempts at effective parenting.

It's 7:00 P.M., and Lonnie and his mother are watching a television show when 12-year-old brother Ray comes in and demands that he be allowed to watch his video. Lonnie stands and complains loudly, only to receive a shove from Ray, who then moves to insert his disc in the DVD player.

"Tell him I was here first," Lonnie demands of his mother.

"Ray," their mother finally says, looking up from her crossword puzzle. "Lonnie was watching that."

"Tough shit," returns Ray, now easily fending off wild punches thrown by Lonnie. One lands too near his genitals, and Ray boxes Lonnie on the side of his head hard. Lonnie howls in pain and screams at his mother.

"He hit me in the face!"

"Well, you were hitting him," returns his mother. "What did you expect? Now, if you both don't stop hitting, I'll get your father down here."

Lonnie ignores her and begins once again to flail away at his brother. Ray has finally had enough and wraps his arms around Lonnie's neck, squeezing.

When he finally loosens his hold, Lonnie runs from the room, shouting out his new mission to destroy some of Ray's property.

"I'll kill you if you touch my stuff!" shouts Ray, settling down in front of the set.

Their mother shakes her head and returns to her crossword.

This interaction demonstrates two key characteristics of the coercive family process, namely, ineffective parental management of aggressive noncompliant behavior and the reinforcement of coercive child behaviors. This model posits that the effectiveness with which parents manage the aggressive and noncompliant behaviors of their children plays a critical role in the course of those behaviors as the child grows. In the coercive family, as the children's aggressive behaviors grow more and more frequent and increasingly intense, the parents' attempts to manage them become increasingly inadequate (Reid & Patterson, 1991).

In the preceding example, rather than stepping in to manage the conflict, Lonnie's mother merely sits there making "parental noises." It is not uncommon to find parents—mothers especially—for whom years of ineffective parenting have led to an emotional detachment, often depression. Her vague threat about calling the father down, possibly to engage in physical aggression against the children, is ignored. Lonnie and his brother have presumably learned that she cannot physically control them herself and that her threats are rarely carried out. Consequently they now control her to a large extent. In addition, the two boys have learned that coercive behavior patterns pay off. Ray knows that he can muscle his way into the television show Lonnie and his mother are watching without serious opposition. The fact that his mother ultimately allows him to be successful only makes it more likely that he will repeat the behavior in other circumstances.

Patterson and his colleagues found that in families such as this one the effect of inept parenting practices is to permit literally dozens of daily interactions within the family in which coercive child behaviors are directly reinforced (Patterson et al., 1989). At times reinforcement comes through some form of positive regard of the parent for the coercive behavior, such as when a parent laughs at a scene of sibling bullying behavior. In addition, as in the example, instances in which the parent passively allows the child's coercive behavior to be successful (i.e., reinforced) increase the likelihood of later repetition.

The researchers found, however, that most of the reinforcement arises from escape contingencies, or what has been called an attack–counterattack positive outcome sequence. In such a sequence, when a parent intrudes with a request for compliance (e.g., *attack:* "Go to bed now"), the child learns to use aversive behaviors to escape (*counterattack:* "I ain't going, and you can't make me!"). The inept parent, believing that escaping from this aversive interaction with the child is most important, submits (*positive outcome:* "Fine, stay up and be tired all day in school. I don't care"). As an unfortunate consequence, both the child's noncompliant coercive response and the parent's escape behavior have been reinforced. The stage is set for the sequence to be repeated.

One of the features of the coercive family process is an escalation of the intensity of the coercive interactions (Patterson et al., 1989). Threats become violence, and violence becomes greater violence. With each successive interaction, the potential for either the "attack" or the "counterattack" to escalate in intensity is very real. Among family members, fear of the intensity of the interaction produces children who can control their parents and parents unwilling to discipline their children effectively.

> It is nearly 3:30 P.M., and Lonnie is returning from school. He walks through the front door of his home and into the living room. His father is in front of the TV, beer cans spread about. Lonnie is just about to begin a loud complaining script, which has successfully driven his father from the television in the past, when the man stands up from his chair. Lonnie recognizes the hostile, intoxicated look and starts to back away, but not quickly enough. His father grabs him by the front of his shirt and slaps his open palm hard against the side of Lonnie's face.
>
> "Fighting again at school? Got your damn principal callin' me at home? I'll give you all the fighting you want!" his father yells, slamming his hand once again into the struggling boy. The beating continues until Lonnie is finally able to wrest himself free and bolt out the door.

Harsh, inconsistent physical discipline is often characteristic of the coercive family process (Patterson, 1982). Ineffective parents tend to have a very narrow repertoire of discipline strategies—often limited to either verbal or physical aggression. In addition, when parental discipline is tied too closely to the parent's mood or whim, the outcome is that a certain behavior is ignored one day and punished the next. Parents who ignore (or even encourage) sibling fighting at home and then beat the child for the same behavior in school are doing more to increase the child's aggression than to eliminate it. Aggressive behavior that is punished with counteraggression and in an unpredictable, erratic fashion becomes extremely resistant to change (Park & Slaby, 1983).

Linkages from coercive family processes to the development of deviant social information-processing patterns have been noted. Dodge, Bates, and Pettit (1990) found that children who experienced physical maltreatment when they angered their parents were more likely to direct aggression toward peers who irritate them. The same children displayed more deviant processing styles, that is, they were less attentive to relevant cues, displayed hostile attributional biases, and showed poor solution-generating skills (Dodge et al., 1990; Pettit, 1997). It should come as little surprise to find that Lonnie, the youngster in the preceding coercive family example, displayed many of the information processing deficiencies common to aggressive children.

SUMMARY

As school practitioners consider intervention efforts, a knowledge of the factors involved in the onset and maintenance of chronic aggressive behavior is essential. Social learning theory provides a solid and useful cognitive-behavioral framework upon which to conceptualize the direction of treatment options. The practitioner with this knowledge understands the strength of both observational models and direct experience. Confining all the naughty and aggressive children to a single "behavior disorders" classroom, where they have only negative models, or failing to effectively reinforce prosocial problem solving runs counter to these principles.

The social information processing research of Dodge and others allows the practitioner to hypothesize the existence of both cognitive and behavioral deficits that may be responsive to treatment. Each "step" offers an opportunity for intervention. Through training in problem-solving skills (e.g., Hughes & Clavell, 1995; Lochman, Lampron, Gemmer, & Harris, 1987), children may be helped to attend to the proper environmental cues, learn to reduce tendencies toward hostile attributional bias, and increase their repertoire of nonaggressive problem-solving strategies.

The research findings of Gerald Patterson and others have demonstrated how family demographics (especially low socioeconomic status), parental characteristics such as criminality and substance abuse, coercive parent–child interactions, and ineffective parental discipline practices can all potentiate one another to create a training environment for aggressive antisocial behavior in children. Parent management training procedures offer the practitioner an intervention with considerable promise for treating the antisocial behavior of the child (Kazdin, 1987a, 1995; Larson, 1994). These procedures seek to enhance such parenting skills as nonphysical discipline strategies, child monitoring, and issuing effective compliance directives.

In the next chapter, we review the empirical basis for our model of the emotional and social-cognitive difficulties of aggressive children.

CHAPTER 2

The Empirical Foundation for a Developmental Model of Aggressive Children's Social-Cognitive and Emotional Difficulties

The occurrence of aggressive and oppositional behaviors is relatively common in mild to moderate forms during the early childhood years. However, most children develop methods of regulating their emotions and impulsive behavior during the elementary school years. Aggressive behavior only becomes more clinically significant if the behaviors are highly intense and violent, if they generate significant harm, and if they occur with high frequency (Lochman, 2000c). Seriously aggressive behavior afflicts approximately 5–10% of children, with boys exhibiting antisocial behavior outnumbering girls by roughly two or three to one (Kazdin, 1998; Lochman & Szczepanski, 1999). Rates of conduct disorder are estimated to be in the range of 6–16% for boys and 2–9% for girls (American Psychiatric Association, 1994). Children are more at risk for continued aggressive and antisocial behavior if they display aggressive behavior in multiple settings (e.g., home, school, and neighborhood) and if they develop "versatile" forms of antisocial behavior, including both overt (assaults, direct threats) and covert (theft) behaviors by early to midadolescence (Lochman, White, Curry, & Rumer, 1992; Loeber & Schmalling, 1985).

Loeber (1990) hypothesized that aggressive behavior in the elementary school years is part of a developmental trajectory that can lead to adolescent delinquency and conduct disorder. Longitudinal research has documented this evolution of behavioral problems by concluding that aggressive behavior and rejection by a child's peers are additive risk markers for subsequent maladjusted behavior in the middle school years (Coie, Lochman, Terry, & Hyman, 1992) and that aggressive behavior is a risk marker for early substance abuse, overt delinquency, and police arrests in the later adolescent years (Coie, Terry, Zakriski, & Lochman, 1995; Lochman & Wayland, 1994).

AGGRESSION AND ANGER

Aggressive behavior in children and adults has been conceptualized as being in part attributable to an inability to regulate emotional responses to anger-producing stimuli (Lochman, Powell, Clanton, & McElroy, 2006; Powell, Lochman, Boxmeyer, Barry, & Young, 2010). Children's aggressive behavior has been related to intense emotional arousal in general (e.g., Cummings, Iannotti, & Zahn-Waxler, 1985) and to high levels of anger in particular (Eisenberg, Fabes, Nyman, Bernzweig, & Pinuelas, 1994).

When individuals perceive themselves as endangered or threatened, they have common physiological responses at two levels (Goleman, 1995) and can have two types of anger (Lochman. Powell, Clanton, et al., 2006). When threat is perceived, the thalamus signals the neocortex, which then processes the perceived causes and possible responses to the threat. The result can be a deliberate, calculated anger response. The action of the amygdala on the adrenocortical branch of the nervous system can create a general background state of action readiness that can last for hours or even for days. This activation can be stimulated by stress of all kinds, and individuals become more prone to serious anger arousal if they are already activated by mild to moderate irritation and frustration. When a person is in this state of readiness, even minor triggers can produce highly intense anger responses. Thus, anger can build on anger (Goleman, 1995). Escalating anger can be the result of a series of perceived provocations, each of which triggers further arousal, which dissipates slowly.

In addition to this first physiological response to perceived threat, the thalamus can also signal the amygdala, and, separate from the collateral cortical processing, the amygdala can directly trigger a surge in heart rate and blood pressure and produce a rage response. This limbic surge can release catecholamines and lead to an energy rush, which may last for a period of only a few minutes. Anger can develop very rapidly because of the initial limbic surge and can be manifest overtly in increased cardiovascular activity. Highly aggressive boys have been found to have lower resting heart rates than nonaggressive boys, but they can display a sharp surge in heart rate following interpersonal provocation (Williams, Lochman, Phillips, & Barry, 2003).

SOCIAL-COGNITIVE MODELS

Angry aggression can be readily conceptualized within a social information-processing model of anger arousal (Crick & Dodge, 1994; Lochman, Powell, Whidby, & FitzGerald, 2006, in press). Many of the most recent interventions for disruptive behavior disorder are based on cognitive-behavioral theories of antisocial and delinquent behavior. The premise behind many of these interventions is that cognitions or thoughts influence the behavior that an individual displays in various situations, thereby altering both the individual's general response (behavioral) patterns and the cognitions that accompany or precede the behaviors. Cognitive-behavioral interventions with aggressive children are thus designed to influence social behavior and related cognitive and emotional processes. These forms of intervention are based on a social-cognitive theoretical model that describes social behavior as a function of children's perceptions of their immediate social environment and of their ideas about how to resolve perceived social conflicts.

The Anger Arousal Model

An early form (the Anger Control Program) of our current cognitive-behavioral intervention program was based on an anger arousal model (Lochman, Nelson, & Sims, 1981) primarily derived from Novaco's (1978) work with aggressive adults. In this conceptualization of anger arousal, which stressed sequential cognitive processing, the child responded to problems such as interpersonal conflicts or frustrations with environmental obstacles (i.e., difficult schoolwork). However, it was not the stimulus event itself that provoked the child's response, but rather the child's cognitive processing of that event. This first stage of cognitive processing was similar to Lazarus's (Smith & Lazarus, 1990) primary appraisal stage and consisted of labeling, attributions, and perceptions of the problem event. The second state of processing, similar to Lazarus's (Smith & Lazarus, 1990) secondary appraisal, consisted of the child's cognitive plan for his or her response to the perceived threat or provocation. This level of cognitive processing was accompanied by anger-related physiological arousal. The anger arousal model indicated that the child's cognitive processing of the problem event and of his or her planned response led to the child's actual behavioral response (ranging from aggression to assertion, passive acceptance, or withdrawal) and to the positive or negative consequences that the child experienced as a result.

The anger arousal model served as the basis for the social-cognitive model in our revised Anger Coping Program (Lochman, FitzGerald, & Whidby, 1999; Lochman, Lampron, et al., 1987; Lochman, Powell, Whidby, et al., 2006; Lochman, White, & Wayland, 1991; Lochman, Whidby, et al., 2000). This social-cognitive model stressed the reciprocal interactive relationships among the initial cognitive appraisal of the problem situation, the cognitive appraisal of the problem solutions, the child's physiological arousal, and the behavioral response. The Anger Coping Program introduced the role that labeling emotions, thought processes, and schematic propositions can have in the child's social-cognitive processes. In this model there is emphasis on the interrelatedness of the different elements of the model in that all processing steps/components have some influence on all other elements. There is also emphasis on the ongoing nature of interpersonal interactions, as children's responses to various social stimuli lead to sets of new social stimuli to be encountered in the future. The level of physiological arousal will depend on the individual's biological predisposition to become aroused and will vary according to the interpretation of the event. The level of arousal further influences the social problem solving, operating either to intensify the fight-or-flight response or to interfere with the generation of solutions. This model helps to explain the chronic nature of aggressive children's difficulties, as there is emphasis on the ongoing and reciprocal nature of interactions. Thus, aggressive children's difficulties may form a circular pattern, and it may be difficult for them to extricate themselves from the aggressive behavior patterns.

The Social Information-Processing Model

As noted in Chapter 1, the social information-processing model developed by Dodge (1993b; Crick & Dodge, 1994; Dodge, Pettit, McClaskey, & Brown, 1986) explicitly expands on substeps in the child's cognitive processing of social problems and serves as an important heuristic for research with aggressive children. In this model there are six sequential steps involved in the processing of social information: (1) encoding relevant social cues, (2) interpreting these cues, (3) identifying social goals, (4) generating possible solutions to the perceived problem, (5) evaluating these solutions, and (6) enacting the chosen response. The first two steps involve cognitive processing of the problem event, and Steps 4 and 5 involve cognitive processing about responses. Aggressive children have been found to have difficulties at each of these stages. They are prone to cognitive distortions when encoding incoming social information (Step 1) and when interpreting social events and others' intentions (Step 2). They also appear to have distinct differences in their social goals (Step 3), cognitive deficiencies in generating alternative adaptive solutions for perceived problems (Step 4) and evaluating the consequences of different solutions (Step 5), and behavioral deficiencies in enacting the solution believed to be most appropriate (Step 6) (Lochman, Whidby, et al., 2000).

Considerable research has indicated that aggressive children do exhibit the distortions and deficiencies suggested here. In terms of the initial stage, the encoding of information, aggressive children have been found to recall fewer relevant cues about events (Lochman & Dodge, 1994), to base interpretations of events on fewer cues (Dodge & Newman, 1981; Dodge et al., 1986), to selectively recall and attend to hostile rather than neutral cues (Gouze, 1987; Milich & Dodge, 1984), and to recall the most recent cues in a sequence, with selective inattention to cues presented earlier (Milich & Dodge, 1984). McKinnon, Lamb, Belsky, and Baum (1990) have suggested that these biases at the encoding phase, which involve selective attention to particular cues in the environment, are a direct result of prior social interactions and are, in fact, a logical outcome of the aggressive child's early affectively toned attachment relationships. Accordingly, the child learns to pay attention to interaction patterns and social cues that are emotionally similar to cues he or she has previously experienced; for instance, if a child has experienced primarily negative or aggressive interactions with a parent, he or she will more likely attend to, and process, aggressively toned cues.

At the next stage, interpretation, aggressive children have been shown to have a hostile attributional bias, as they tend to excessively infer that others are acting toward them in a provocative and hostile manner (Dodge et al., 1986; Katsurada & Sugawara, 1998). This attributional bias can be evident in live interactions as well as in hypothetical vignettes (Steinberg & Dodge, 1983), and both aggressive girls (Feldman & Dodge, 1987) and aggressive boys (Guerra & Slaby, 1989; Lochman & Dodge, 1994; Sancilio, Plumert, & Hartup, 1989; Waas, 1988) have been found to have this attributional bias. In addition, in studies of boys' interpersonal perceptions after actual dyadic interactions, Lochman (1987; Lochman & Dodge, 1998) found that aggressive boys have underperceptions of their own aggressive behavior (i.e., they see themselves as less aggressive than they really are) as well as distorted overperceptions of others' aggression (i.e., they see others as more aggressive than they are). As a result, aggressive boys develop attributions that assign responsibility for conflict to their peers rather than assuming responsibility themselves.

The fourth information-processing stage involves a generative process in which potential solutions for coping with a perceived problem are recalled from memory. At this stage, aggressive children demonstrate deficiencies in both the quality and quantity of their problem-solving solutions (Lochman, Meyer, Rabiner, & White, 1991). These differences are most pronounced in the quality of the solutions offered. For instance, in response to hypothetical conflicts describing interpersonal conflicts, aggressive children offer fewer verbal assertion solutions (Asarnow & Callan, 1985; Joffe, Dobson, Fine, Marriage, & Haley, 1990; Lochman & Lampron, 1986), fewer compromise solutions (Lochman & Dodge, 1994), more direct-action solutions (Lochman & Lampron, 1986), a greater number of help-seeking or adult intervention responses (Asher & Renshaw, 1981; Dodge, Murphy, & Buchsbaum, 1984; Lochman, Lampron, & Rabiner, 1989; Rabiner, Lenhart, & Lochman, 1990), and more physically aggressive responses (Pepler, Craig, & Roberts, 1998; Slaby & Guerra, 1988; Waas, 1988; Waas & French, 1989). In terms of the quantity of solutions, there is little evidence that aggressive children overall offer fewer responses (Bloomquist et al., 1997; Rubin, Bream, & Rose-Krasnor, 1991). However, the most severely aggressive and violent youth do demonstrate a deficiency in the number of solutions they can generate to resolve social problems (Lochman & Dodge, 1994). The nature of the social problem-solving deficits for aggressive children can vary, depending on their diagnostic classification. Boys with conduct disorder diagnoses produce more aggressive/antisocial solutions in vignettes about conflicts with parents and teachers, and fewer verbal/nonaggressive solutions in peer conflicts, as compared with boys with oppositional defiant disorder (Dunn, Lochman, & Colder, 1997). Thus, children with conduct disorder have broader problem-solving deficits in multiple interpersonal contexts, compared to children with oppositional defiant disorder.

The fifth processing step involves a two-step process: first, identifying the consequences for each of the solutions generated, and second, evaluating each solution and the consequences in terms of the individual's desired outcome. In general, aggressive children evaluate aggressive behavior as less negative (Deluty, 1983) and more positive (Crick & Werner, 1998) than children without aggressive behavior difficulties. Children's beliefs about the utility of aggression and about their ability to successfully enact aggressive responses can increase the likelihood of aggression being displayed, as children who hold these beliefs will be more likely to also believe that this type of behavior will help them to achieve their desired goals, which then influences their response decisions (Lochman & Dodge, 1994; Perry, Perry, & Rasmussen, 1986). Research has found that these beliefs about the acceptability of aggressive behavior lead to deviant processing of social cues, which in turn leads to children's aggressive behavior (Zelli, Dodge, Lochman, Laird, & Conduct Problems Prevention Research Group, 1999), indicating that these information-processing steps have reciprocal effects on one another rather than strictly linear ones.

The final processing stage listed by Dodge et al. (1986) involves behavioral enactment, or displaying the response that was chosen in the previous steps. Aggressive children have been found to be less adept at enacting positive or prosocial interpersonal behaviors (Dodge et al., 1986). Improving aggressive children's ability to successfully and effectively enact positive behaviors may enhance their beliefs about their ability to engage in these more prosocial behaviors and thus make them more likely to choose such prosocial solutions.

The Crick and Dodge Reformulated Model

Crick and Dodge's (1994) more recent modification of the original model describes more of the online processing that actually occurs when individuals are engaged in social interactions. This model also contains an explicit reference to the idea that the consequences of one's behavior will feed back into the system and function as the stimulus for the next interaction. In addition, a new step (the third step) was included in the information-processing model. This step involves a clarification of goals that the individual wishes to attain and involves selecting the desired goal from different possible goals (e.g., to avoid punishment, to get even with another individual, to affiliate). It also involves determining which goal predominates during the particular interaction. The goal that the individual chooses to pursue will then affect the responses generated for resolving the conflict, which occurs in the next processing stage. The children's social goals can be conceptualized as being a part of their stable schemas of interpersonal situations, as discussed in a subsequent section. More generally, schemas (or the database) can be accessed at any of the processing stages and can be influenced by stored knowledge derived from experience in a similar situation. Furthermore, each stage will provide information relevant to the ongoing evolution of schemas, which will then have an impact on future interactions.

Social Information Processing among Subtypes of Aggressive Children

Research has begun to examine whether subtypes of children with specific types of aggressive behavior patterns have different patterns of social-cognitive deficiencies. Dodge and Coie (1987) differentiated between proactive aggressive children, who engage in aggressive behavior in a relatively planned, nonemotional way, and reactive aggressive children, who become impulsively aggressive when they are aroused to anger following perceived provocations. Reactive aggressive children have been found to be more likely to have social-cognitive difficulties throughout the full array of information-processing steps. In particular, they are oversensitive to hostile cues and have higher rates of hostile attributional biases. Proactive aggressive children have been primarily characterized by their relatively high expectations that aggressive behavior will work for them (Dodge, Lochman, Harnish, Bates, & Pettit, 1997). Harsh parenting and neighborhood violence appear to be important factors contributing to the development of reactive aggression and to reactive aggressive children's hostile attributional biases (Lochman & Wells, 1999c; Lochman, Wells, & Colder, 1999). Both proactive aggression and reactive aggression predict later substance use, but proactive aggression is the strongest predictor of later delinquency. Different types of peer problems mediate the effects for these two forms of aggression, as proactive aggression leads to later involvement with deviant peers, which in turn leads to adolescent substance use; in contrast, elementary school children with higher levels of reactive aggression are socially rejected by their peers, and their peer rejection leads them to deviant peers and then to greater risk for adolescent substance use (Fite, Colder, Lochman, & Wells, 2007; Fite, Colder, Lochman, & Wells, 2008a, 2008b).

When severely aggressive children and adolescents have been compared with moderately aggressive children, the severely aggressive youth are similarly more likely to display the full array of distortions and deficiencies in their social information processing, and moderately aggressive youth are primarily characterized by having higher expectations that aggression will work and successfully resolve the problem at hand (Lochman & Dodge, 1994). Another method for subtyping aggressive children involves identifying whether they have callous/unemotional or narcissism traits that can be associated with proactive aggression (Barry et al., 2007) and be the predecessor for later psychopathy. Children with a higher level of callous/unemotional traits are more likely to have difficulty in Step 5 of the social information-processing model by having greater expectations that aggression will lead to good outcomes (Pardini, Lochman, & Frick, 2003). These findings suggest that interventionists should be sensitive to variations in the intensity and topography of children's aggressive behavior and that these differences will likely require changes in which certain portions of an intervention will be emphasized more for some children than for others.

The Role of Schemas in Social Information Processing

Although the reviewed research evidence indicates that aggressive children do have certain difficulties in how they process social information, the variations across subtypes of aggressive children suggest that other cognitive and emotional factors within the children contribute to these processing difficulties (Lochman, Magee, & Pardini, 2003). Recent revisions of social-cognitive models have more explicitly examined the role that children's cognitive schemas and beliefs play in their information processing (Crick & Dodge, 1994; Dodge, Laird, Lochman, Zelli, & Conduct Problems Prevention Research Group, 2002; Lochman, Whidby, et al., 2000; Lochman, Wayland, & White, 1993; Lochman, White, et al., 1991). Schemas account for how individuals actively construct their perceptions and experiences rather than merely being passive receivers and processors of social information (Ingram & Kendall, 1986). Schemas have been defined in somewhat different ways by various theoreticians and researchers, but they are commonly regarded as consistent core beliefs and patterns of thinking (Lochman, Holmes, & Wojnaroski, 2008). These underlying cognitive structures form the basis for individuals' specific perceptions of current events (DeRubeis, Tang, & Beck, 2001). Similar to Adler's concept of "style of life" (Freeman & Leaf, 1989), schemas are cognitive blueprints or master plans that construe, organize, and transform peoples' interpretations and predictions about events in their lives (Kelly, 1955; Mischel, 1990).

Schemas have certain basic attributes (Lochman, Holmes, et al., 2008). First, a distinction can be made between *active* schemas, which are often conscious and govern everyday behavior, and *dormant* schemas, of which an individual is typically unaware and that emerge only when the individual is faced with specific events or stressors (Lochman & Lenhart, 1995). Dormant schemas are in a state of "chronic accessibility" (Higgins, King, & Marvin, 1982; Mischel, 1990) or state of potential activation, ready to be primed by minimal cues. Thus, an individual's beliefs and expectations, which emerge when the individual is intensely stressed or aroused, may not be at all apparent when the individual is calm and nonaroused.

Second, existing schemas can be either compelling or noncompelling (Freeman & Leaf, 1989). Noncompelling schemas are not strongly held by a person and can be given up easily. In contrast, compelling schemas are strongly entrenched in the person's way of thinking. They promote more filtering and potential distortions of the person's perceptions of self and others (Fiske & Taylor, 1984). Compelling schemas lead individuals to make more rapid judgments about the presence of schema-related traits in oneself and others, and they often operate outside conscious awareness (Erdley, 1990).

Third, schemas can be more or less permeable. Permeable schemas permit a person to alter his or her interpretation of events through successive approximations, a process labeled by Kelly (1955) as "constructive alternativism." A person with relatively permeable schemas can readily adapt his or her schemas to the specific situations and conditions that person encounters, thereby adding new elements and complexity to the schemas. Schemas are typically more permeable and situational as individuals develop and have experiences in a number of situations (Mischel, 1990; Rotter, Chance, & Phares, 1972). Relatively nonpermeable schemas are preemptive, promote rigid "black-and-white" thinking (Kelly, 1955), and are likely to create strongly held expectations that are not open to change based on new information. The process of altering schemas is essentially conservative (Lochman & Dodge, 1998), as preexisting beliefs are accepted over new ones, and self-centered, because a person's own personal preexisting beliefs are embraced more strongly than new information provided by others (Fiske & Taylor, 1984). Nonpermeable schemas are largely self-maintaining because they lead the individual to seek and recall information that is consistent with his or her conceptions of others and self.

Fourth, schemas permit individuals to predict the outcomes of events (Adler, 1964). Schemas allow people to operate efficiently in their social worlds by providing expectations of how others will react and how they will be able to meet their own goals and needs (Lochman & Dodge, 1998).

Schemas within the Social-Cognitive Model

Schemas have been proposed to have a significant impact on the information-processing steps within the social cognition models underlying cognitive-behavioral interventions with aggressive children (Lochman, Powell, Whidby, et al., 2006; Lochman, White, et al., 1991). Ingram and Kendall (1986; Kendall, 2000) have organized individuals' cognitive processing of events into four categories in their cognitive taxonomic system. *Cognitive products* are the actual cognitions that individuals have in the present when dealing with events (e.g., attributions, decisions, beliefs, thoughts, recognition of stimuli), and *cognitive operations* are the procedures that process information (e.g., attention, encoding, retrieval). Cognitive operations operate on the immediate stimuli and on schemas to produce cognitive products. Schemas have two forms within the cognitive taxonomic system: cognitive structures and cognitive propositions. *Cognitive structures* are the architecture of the cognitions in memory, the structures in which information is organized and stored. These functional psychological mechanisms store information in both short- and long-term memory, placing information in interconnecting categories and nodes. *Cognitive propositions* form the content within the cognitive structures and constitute the information that is actually stored. Cognitive propositions include information both in semantic memory (general knowledge that has been acquired and learned) and in episodic memory (personal information absorbed through one's experiences in the world). In the social-cognitive model, social-cognitive products include elements within the social information-processing steps such as encoded cues, attributions, problem solutions, goals, and anticipated consequences that individuals experience during moment-to-moment processing.

Schematic propositions are those beliefs, ideas, and expectations that can have direct and indirect effects on the social-cognitive products. Schematic propositions include information stored in memory about an individual's beliefs, general social goals, generalized expectations, and understandings about competence and self-worth (Lochman & Lenhart, 1995; Lochman et al., 2003).

Direct Effects of Schemas on Social Information Processing

Schemas can influence the sequential steps of information processing in different ways. Early in the information-processing sequence, when the individual is perceiving and interpreting new social cues, schemas can have a clear direct effect by narrowing the child's attention to certain aspects of the social cue array (e.g., Lochman, Nelson, et al., 1981). A child who believes it is essential to be in control of others and who expects others to try to dominate him or her, often in aversive ways, will attend particularly to verbal and nonverbal signals about someone else's control efforts, easily missing any accompanying signs of the other person's friendliness or attempts to negotiate. Children's schemas about control and aggression will also heavily influence the second stage of processing as the child interprets malevolent meaning and intentions in others' behavior (Lochman, Holmes, et al., 2008).

Schemas can also play a significant role in the fifth stage of information processing as the child anticipates consequences for different problem solutions available to him or her and decides which strategy will be enacted. Social goals (accessed at the third stage of information processing) and outcome expectations are schemas that, from a social learning theory perspective (Mischel, 1990; Rotter et al., 1972), combine to shape children's potential for behaving in specific ways. When the child places a higher value on particular goals or reinforcements, the child will then engage in behaviors that he or she expects have a high probability of meeting such goals. Aggressive adolescent boys have been found to place higher value on the social goals of dominance and revenge and lower value on the social goal of affiliation than do nonaggressive boys (Lochman, Wayland, et al., 1993). In addition, within the aggressive group, very small differences have been found in the values that aggressive boys assign to dominance, revenge, avoidance, and affiliation goals, indicating that aggressive youth are likely to have a "muddy," or conflicted, goal structure. In one study, there was also a clear relationship between social goal choice and problem-solving ability, indicating a direct effect of cognitive schemas on information processing. Aggressive boys proposed fewer bargaining solutions and more aggressive and verbal assertion solutions in comparison with nonaggressive boys, but this problem-solving difference was evident only when the boys' main social goals were taken into account. Thus, children's schemas about social goals and outcome expectations can affect their response decisions in the fifth stage of information processing.

Indirect Effects of Schemas on Social Information Processing

Schemas can also have indirect or mediated effects on information processing through their influence on children's expectations for their own behavior and for other's behavior in specific situations. These indirect effects occur because of the associated affect and arousal when the schemas are activated and because of the schemas' influence on the style and speed of processing (Lochman, Holmes, et al., 2008). In research on socially rejected children, Keane and Parrish (1992) found that knowledge of an antagonist's affect influenced nonrejected children's interpretations of the other person's behavior but that rejected children did not alter their interpretation based on this information. In a related way, schemas about attributes of self and of others, such as aggressiveness or dominance, can produce expectations about the presence or absence of these attributes as individuals prepare to interact with people in specific situations. Lochman and Dodge (1998) assessed aggressive and nonaggressive boys' expectations for their interpersonal behavior before a 4-minute competitive discussion as well as their perceptions immediately after the interaction. Lochman and Dodge (1998) found that aggressive boys' perceptions of their own aggressive behavior, after live dyadic interactions, were primarily affected by their prior expectations, whereas nonaggressive boys relied more on their actual behavior during the interactions to form their perceptions. These results indicate that the schemas of aggressive boys about their aggressive behavior are strong and compelling, leading the aggressive boys to display cognitive rigidity between their expectations and perceptions. The aggressive boys' perceptions of their behavior, driven by their schemas, were relatively impermeable to actual behavior and were instead heavily governed by the boys' preconceptions. Thus, aggressive children in general, like socially rejected children, are more inflexible during the interpretation phase and may not take relevant new information into account (Lochman & Lenhart, 1995).

Schemas are complex blends of cognition and associated emotion, and as schemas are activated during interactions, they can contribute to the intense levels of affect and arousal that a person can experience in response to a provocative event. Thus, although provocative events produce some emotional and physiological arousal in most children, the intense reactive anger and rage of some individuals may be attributable to the activation of schemas about the general hostility of others as well as those relating to the role of others in initiating unjust and unfair conflicts. Emotions have been hypothesized to be the glue between attributions and behavior (Weiner & Graham, 1999) and the adaptational systems that motivate individuals to solve their perceived problems (Smith & Lazarus, 1990). For example, when a child attributes blame for a conflict to another person, the child experiences anger, but when the child perceives him- or herself responsible for the problem, the child experiences guilt (Weiner & Graham, 1999). These attribution–emotion linkages can then produce quite different decisions about behavioral responses (e.g., aggression vs. apology, help seeking, nonconfrontation, or compromise). Schemas about accountability and responsibility, with their implications for who receives blame or credit for events, are closely linked to the experience of anger. Accountability appraisals generate "hot" emotional reactions when a provocative person is perceived to act intentionally, unjustly, and in a controllable manner (Smith & Lazarus, 1990). The arousal and emotional reactions in early stages of interactions then serve to flood the information-processing system (Lochman, 1984) and to maintain the hostile attributions and aggressive response style over time during an interaction. Williams et al. (2003) have found that in a laboratory setting increases in heart rate following a provocation are correlated with increases in hostile attributional biases. This relationship makes it more difficult for the aggressive individual to avoid escalating cycles of aggression and violence. Aggressive children and adolescents are further hampered by schemas and appraisal styles that make them relatively unaware of emotional states associated with vulnerability (e.g., fear, sadness), leading them to mislabel their arousal during frustration or conflict as anger (Lochman & Dodge, 1994).

Aggressive children have an impulsive cognitive style, leading them to spend less time carefully evaluating perceptions and response decisions during interpersonal events. Instead, they rely on reflexive and automatic information processing (Lochman, Nelson, et al., 1981). Schemas can influence aggressive children's overreliance on automatic processing in several ways. Aggressive children can form a belief that it is important to respond quickly to provocative events rather than carefully evaluating their potential solutions to problems. This belief can form because of the real dangers these children have previously faced within their neighborhood or family setting. However, when the belief is strong, compelling, and impermeable, the children may not easily recognize that contextual differences make the belief less legitimate in certain situations (e.g., when at school or with less threatening peers). In addition, because of the internal arousal and the emotions activated by schemas about provocations or threats, aggressive children tend to use rapid automatic processing. Aggressive children's social problem-solving style has been found to become less competent when they are using automatic processing rather than deliberate processing (Lochman, Lampron, & Rabiner, 1989; Rabiner et al., 1990). When using automatic processing, aggressive boys generate more action-oriented solutions, more help-seeking solutions, and fewer verbal assertion solutions. Therefore, children's schemas can have indirect effects on their appraisals of themselves and others and on their problem solving by eliciting excessive automatic processing and short-circuiting the children's more competent deliberate processing.

ANGER COPING: A COGNITIVE-BEHAVIORAL INTERVENTION FOR AGGRESSIVE CHILDREN

Based on this social-cognitive model of the cognitive and emotional distortions and deficiencies that aggressive children display, the Anger Coping Program was developed and refined to address core difficulties with emotional and cognitive self-regulation, including anger management, physiological and emotional awareness, perspective training and attribution retraining, and social problem solving. Following the initial development and evaluation of the Anger Control Program (Lochman, Nelson, et al., 1981), the Anger Coping Program described in this book was developed on the basis of further research on these social-cognitive processes. The Anger Coping Program, created for use in school and clinic settings (Lochman, Lampron, et al., 1987; Lochman, Powell, Whidby, & FitzGerald, 2006), uses an intervention model that is closely linked to the social-cognitive developmental model that accounts, in part, for the initiation and maintenance of aggressive behavior. In subsequent chapters, we describe practical implementation issues involved in the use of this program in school settings.

CHAPTER 3

The Role of Anger Management Training in a Comprehensive School Program of Positive Behavioral Supports

This is a book about helping children manage anger-fueled aggressive and disruptive behavior through the use of small-group or individual cognitive-behavioral skills training. There is a percentage of children in every school building for whom the traditional disciplinary system is, in large measure, ineffective. To the adults in charge, these are students who appear to be aware of the rules of conduct but who are seemingly unable (or, in fewer cases, unwilling) to adhere to them.

- They defy adult compliance requests, sometimes with angry retorts or tantrums.
- They argue, push, and fight on the playground, in the hallways, and in the cafeteria.
- They disrupt classroom cooperative learning groups and are routinely feared and rejected by peers.

As a consequence, these students take up a disproportionate amount of teachers' and administrators' time. They become subjected to a punishment-oriented school disciplinary system that is ill designed to meet their needs (Kaufman, 2005) and that becomes increasingly exclusionary over time (Skiba & Peterson, 2000). The traditional school disciplinary system is typically organized to respond to problem behavior with aversive consequences—a phone call home, a stern lecture by the administrator, after-school detention, in-house suspension, and the like. This system is built on the proposition that most children who engage in problem behavior actually know how to behave appropriately but, through accident or design, have chosen not to and therefore deserve a mild punitive consequence to help remind them in the future.

For the majority of schoolchildren in a normally distributed population, the threat or experience of such unpleasant consequences paired with the naturally occurring reinforcers for appropriate behavior work well. Occasional slippages aside, most students regularly make good behavioral choices. This volume is not about those children.

There is a second, smaller, group of students who come to school each day and who are faced with a succession of problem situations that are beyond their skill levels to resolve with what the school would call "appropriate behavior." Whereas their more behaviorally skilled peers can "ignore," "walk away," "find something else to do," "tell the teacher," or "be assertive, not aggressive," this other group of children seems drawn to conflict. Furthermore, these children seem to be drawn toward conflict with the full knowledge that they are headed for an encounter with the disciplinary policy:

ADULT: What's the rule about hitting?

CHILD: "Keep your hands and feet to yourself."

ADULT: Did you?

CHILD: No.

ADULT: Why not?

CHILD: He started it!

The children whose needs are the subject of this book have not acquired the necessary social and emotional skills to successfully navigate the many behavioral demands of the typical school environment. In our experience, the overwhelming majority of them want to be successful; they just don't know how, and no amount of stern lectures, phone calls home, or detentions will teach them what to do. Behaviorally unskilled children, particularly those with multi-setting anger and aggression problems, are in need of a focused collaborative intervention designed to train them and then generalize the skills needed for success to all of their day-to-day environments.

These skills—including anger regulation, impulse control, and problem solving—can be effectively taught and learned in the context of the daily school routine. Our goal with the remainder of this book is to describe in detail how that may be done.

THE SCHOOL'S CHALLENGE

Educators working in the public schools of the first half of the 21st century are obliged to support the social and emotional needs of an increasingly needy population of students. In 2007, 18% of all children ages 0–17 lived in poverty, representing an increase from 17% in 2006 (Forum on Child and Family Statistics, 2009). Children living in low socioeconomic circumstances have been found to be more likely to exhibit behavioral problems as compared to their peers living in more affluent circumstances (Duncan, Brooks-Gunn, & Klebanov, 1994). In two studies that examined disciplinary referrals to the office from elementary schools in low-SES neighborhoods, researchers found that such offenses as classroom disruption, fighting, inappropriate language, and gross insubordination constituted the majority of referrals (Lo & Cartledge, 2007; Putnam, Luiselli, Handler, & Jefferson, 2003).

African American students from lower socioeconomic circumstances who exhibit school behavior problems are at disproportionate risk for exclusionary discipline procedures, including suspension and expulsion (Fenning & Rose, 2007; Mendez & Knoff, 2003; Rausch & Skiba, 2004), a situation that may contribute to the elevated high school dropout rate, particularly among African American male students. The subsequent unemployment, crime, incarceration, and other individual problems associated with high school dropout are well documented, and the cost to society as a whole is staggering. For example, it has been projected that a mere 1% increase in male high school graduation in the United States would save as much as $1.4 billion in tax dollars, or about $2,100 per additional graduate per year (Moretti, 2007).

Currently approximately 20% of children and youth in the United States have a diagnosable mental health disorder, and of these children only one-fifth are receiving the mental health services that they need and deserve (Hoagwood & Johnson, 2003). Moreover, if the larger percentage of children and youth with only mild to moderate symptoms is included, as many as 70% of children and youth with mental health concerns are not receiving the services that they need (U.S. Department of Health and Human Services, 1999).

Children with evident mental health concerns arrive each day at schoolhouses around the country, seeking equal access to a high-quality education. A small percentage may find appropriate mental health services provided within the context of special education, but the great majority must find necessary academic and social-emotional support within the general education environment. This arrangement places the delivery of mental services squarely in the hands of general education teachers and school-based supportive services personnel. Consequently, it is not surprising to learn that the overwhelming majority of children and youth in the United States who receive any sort of treatment at all for their mental health concerns obtain that treatment *in the school setting* (Rones & Hoagwood, 2000, emphasis added). As Mayer and Van Acker (2009) observe, "Schools have become the de facto mental health system for children and youth in the United States" (p. 85).

THE SCHOOL'S RESPONSE: RESPONSE TO INTERVENTION, POSITIVE BEHAVIORAL SUPPORTS, AND ANGER MANAGEMENT

Although these conditions speak in part to socioeconomic and mental health service delivery problems originating well outside of the public school system, they also highlight the challenges and opportunities faced by the schools. In this chapter, we present a model for addressing the social-emotional needs of all children and describe the critical role of the Anger Coping Program, a research-supported anger management intervention, in this unified effort.

Following reauthorization of the Individuals with Disabilities Education Act (IDEA) in 2004, the academic intervention procedure known as response to intervention (RTI) became a major impetus for intellectual debate, training, and implementation in schools across the country. Over the past 20 years, RTI, with its roots in the problem-solving model, has gathered both adherents and legitimacy. This development has come largely in response to the escalating number of students being placed in special education—in particular, for learning disabilities—and the generally disappointing outcomes in these programs (see Ikeda et al., 2002). The RTI model is designed to replace the traditional refer–test–place model of special education eligibility determination with that of a series of data-driven, evidence-supported general education interventions. The struggling learner is assessed and provided academic support that is then modified and adapted in response to ongoing progress monitoring. Academic support may come in the form of small-group or individualized instruction, with a referral for special education services occurring only after general education options have been exhausted.

It is important to note that RTI is currently implemented in the schools as an *academic* assessment and intervention procedure. Its counterpart in the area of addressing challenging student behavior is positive behavioral supports (PBS). Positive behavioral supports is "a decision making framework that guides selection, integration, and implementation of the best evidence-based academic and behavioral practices for improving important academic and behavior outcomes for all students" (OSEP Technical Assistance Center on Positive Behavioral Interventions and Supports, 2009, "What is SWPBS?" section). PBS focuses on providing a continuum of behavioral supports, from schoolwide policies to individual treatments designed to meet the needs of all students. In similar fashion to RTI, the PBS model takes a preventative approach, systematically matching up a variety of interventions to specific demonstrated needs (Sandomierski, Kincaid, & Algozzine, 2007). Whereas RTI interventions focus chiefly on instructional and curricular modifications, PBS places its emphasis on assessing and manipulating the environment to both teach and encourage appropriate behavior so as to support academic progress. Both RTI and PBS are decision-making frameworks designed to provide students with the most effective but least intrusive prevention/intervention programming.

Small-group skills training procedures, such as the Anger Coping Program, play an integral role in a PBS continuum of behavioral support. This continuum is often conceptualized as a series of three tiers, with each tier providing increasing intensity of support (see Figure 3.1). In Tier 1, the question is "What do *all* of our students need in the way of prevention programming?" For approximately 80–90% of the typical school population, *primary* prevention planning alone is sufficient. Students in this category generally have comparatively higher levels of self-discipline and behavior management skills than some of their less skilled peers. Programs and procedures within a primary prevention focus are referred to as *universal prevention programs.*

Further up the pyramid, in Tier 2, is a smaller subset of the student population consisting of those students who because of personal characteristics or environmental factors are at serious risk for continuing academic and behavioral problems. Behavioral programs designed to meet the needs of these individuals are known as *secondary* prevention, and the procedures used are referred to as *selected* prevention measures. Small-group pull-out programs, such as the Anger Coping Program, are frequently used to address student needs at this level of intervention.

Lastly, at the top of the pyramid in Tier 3 and comprising the smallest group of students, are individuals with the greatest needs for external behavioral/mental health programs and supports. *Tertiary* prevention services are designed to address the needs of these students,

Academic   **Behavioral**

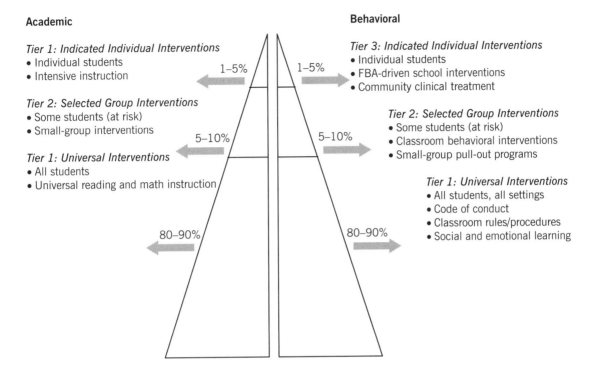

Tier 1: Indicated Individual Interventions
- Individual students
- Intensive instruction

1–5%   1–5%

Tier 3: Indicated Individual Interventions
- Individual students
- FBA-driven school interventions
- Community clinical treatment

Tier 2: Selected Group Interventions
- Some students (at risk)
- Small-group interventions

5–10%   5–10%

Tier 2: Selected Group Interventions
- Some students (at risk)
- Classroom behavioral interventions
- Small-group pull-out programs

Tier 1: Universal Interventions
- All students
- Universal reading and math instruction

80–90%   80–90%

Tier 1: Universal Interventions
- All students, all settings
- Code of conduct
- Classroom rules/procedures
- Social and emotional learning

FIGURE 3.1. Three-tiered model of academic and behavioral prevention in schools.

whose behavior has been unresponsive to universal or selected prevention procedures. These programs are referred to as *indicated* prevention measures. Students who have anger management needs but lack the capacity to function appropriately within a group context may receive individual skills training at this level.

The effectiveness of small-group or individual anger management skills training is predicated upon its appropriate placement within the larger context of schoolwide and classroom-level behavioral supports. Selected (Tier 2) prevention measures are reliant upon the effective implementation of universal (Tier 1) measures in that the two work together to create a continuum of support. What follows is an exemplary model of three tiers of PBS, with particular attention afforded the role of anger management training. Information regarding comprehensive training in the PBS model is available from *www.pbis.org*.

TIER 1: UNIVERSAL PREVENTION PROGRAMS

The majority of students in a typical school building come to school with the requisite skills and dispositions to engage in the curriculum effectively while exhibiting relatively few behavioral problems with the learning experience. In general, these students require only knowledge and understanding of the school or classroom rules and conduct expectations in order to utilize their existing skills and dispositions to adhere to them. Because these students often contrast so starkly with their more problematic peers, adults frequently overlook the fact that these students *also* have deficits or needs in the area of behavioral discipline. The goal of any effective schoolwide disciplinary policy is to nurture the students in this group so that it is as large as possible. These needs are best met through effective school-wide codes of conduct, individual classroom rules, and social-emotional education.

Codes and rules are antecedent-based behavior management programs in that they are designed to prevent the enactment of problem behavior by manipulating the setting events to reinforce predetermined desired behaviors. Well-designed codes of conduct and classroom rules assist students in their efforts to engage in behaviors that will be reinforced and to avoid behaviors that will not. Knowledge of a code principle or a particular classroom rule does not, of itself, necessarily cause students to alter their behavior, but it increases the likelihood that many will. Let us examine these two primary prevention mechanisms.

Codes of Conduct

A code of conduct is a vital aspect of an overall school disciplinary plan in that it helps to establish a norm of expected behavior and serves to justify actions needed to address problem behavior among students (O'Donnell, 2001). Through its official sanction by a governing school board, a code of conduct brings the behavioral expectations of the local community into the schoolhouse. Shannon and McCall (2003), in their review of North American school discipline codes, concluded "that school policies that set reasonable, clearly understood, actively enforced behavioural expectations for students and staff can be effective in protecting the safety of all students as well as in correcting the behaviours of offending students" ("Behavioural Expectations" section, para. 5).

Creating an effective code of conduct is more than merely drawing up a list of undesirable behaviors and connecting them to some form of aversive consequence, however. All too often, codes are devised by the adults in the system and distributed to the students in a manner more akin to a threat than a learning experience. An effective code does not float menacingly above the student body like some dark angel ready to exact retribution upon the transgressor for stepping out of line. Rather, a meaningful code of conduct is organic to the system; it permeates every interaction and helps define the nature of the learning environment. When the code of conduct is essentially indistinguishable from the other learning and social activities within which it is imbedded, then its potential for effectiveness is maximized.

As an example, when emotionally healthy adults come together for a social gathering, there is a "code of conduct" that is embedded in the event that purposefully, even if imperceptibly allows the goals of the event to be met. There is nothing written. No one is handed a card with "dos and don'ts" as he or she arrives. The "code" is just there, rooted in the learned behavior of the participants, emerging into consciousness only in the event of its breach. The likelihood of such a gathering being pleasant and satisfying to the participants is related in large part to the maturity of the participants and the fact that everyone is gathered for pretty much the same purpose.

In contrast, schools are social environments in which multiple individuals with diverse levels of maturity arrive each morning with goals that, in some circumstances, are in direct conflict with the goals of the others.

"I'm here to learn."
"I'm here to have as much fun as I possibly can."

"I'm here to teach."

"I'm here just to avoid a truancy bust."

"I'm here to help my teachers do their jobs."

"I'm here to sell drugs."

"I'm here to protect my pension."

And so on. If it were as simple as "all of the students are here to learn, and all of the teachers are here to teach," then manufacturing a written code to guide behavior would be unnecessary. Alas, that is not the case.

The developmental process and content of useful and effective codes of conduct have been discussed in reviews (e.g., Day, Golench, MacDougall, & Beals-Gonzalez, 1995; Gottfredson, 1997; Redding & Shalf, 2001; Shannon & McCall, 2003) and policy statements (e.g., U.S. Department of Education, 1998). In addition, Redding and Shalf (2001) provided Internet addresses of 11 exemplary codes of conduct from across the United States. Drawing upon these resources, we offer the following elements of an effective code of conduct.

1. **The code should arise naturally out of official school board business.** As Shannon and McCall (2003) noted, codes should have natural legitimacy within the system and reflect the will of the elected representatives of the community who sit on the school board. The impetus for the code and the finalized document itself should be officially recorded in the recognized policymaking procedures of the school board. By these means, the code attains a degree of legal status for disciplinary due process matters in the school.

2. **The code should be developed in a collaborative manner.** Whether a school is rewriting an existing code of conduct or starting from scratch, input and a sense of ownership from all major stakeholders is essential. If the code is to be an integral part of the school's prevention program, then it must be informed by those most closely associated with its implementation. Along with school administrators, representation on the code writing team should include teachers (general and special education), students, supportive services staff (guidance counselors, school psychologists, school social workers), parents, school security officials, and community law enforcement authorities. Each interest group should be asked to address concerns relevant to its area of expertise. For example:

- *Teachers:* What elements in a code are essential to maintaining an environment maximally conducive to teaching and learning in the classroom? How can the code be written so that essentially all students and parents readily understand its meaning and intent? What separate adaptations in wording or form, if any, are needed so that students and parents with special needs are provided an equal opportunity to understand the code? How can the code be reorganized into an easily teachable form or format? What are likely to be the most efficacious and practicable means for teaching the code (i.e., integrate it into classroom content, special modules, special assemblies, or consider other alternatives)?

- *Students:* Which positive behaviors by peers and adults in the school setting should be encouraged by the code? Which negative behaviors should be deterred or punished? What interpersonal problems among students are distinctive to this school and should be addressed in the code (e.g., gang issues, student cliques or societies, racial issues, sexual harassment)? What word usage in the code is out of date or confusing and should be replaced?

  * *Supportive services:* How can the code be constructed to promote optimum mental health for all individuals in the school setting? How does research on the developmental needs and characteristics of adolescents inform the content of the code? How can the code integrate most effectively with the counseling and intervention skills and schedules of the supportive services staff members? What are the prevention needs of the most behaviorally at-risk students that should be addressed in the code?

  * *Law enforcement:* What behaviors designated in the code are also violations of the criminal or juvenile statutes and need to be brought to the attention of law enforcement officials?

3. **The code should reflect the singular setting, mission, and participants of the school.** As far as school codes of conduct go, there is no "one-size-fits-all" solution. Although school officials can learn from the code of another school—and consulting other codes is prudent—ultimately the school's code must reflect the uniqueness of its own students and goals. Attaining this level of individuality comes from a clear vision of the needs of the students and the purposes for which they attend *this* particular school. Frequent mention of the school's name throughout the document (e.g., "Students at Washington School understand that ...") will help both the writers and the readers focus on the issues and the persons most germane to the document. An excellent example of a code uniquely composed for a specific population may be found at the website for the Pegasus Charter School in Dallas, Texas *www.pegasuscharter.org*; this school, located in the central city, serves a population of racially and economically diverse students in grades 7–12.

4. **The code should clearly articulate its role and purpose in the lives of the affected individuals.** The creation of an introductory purpose statement should be one of the first tasks of the code writing team. Initially for the writers and later for the readers, the purpose statement describes the reason why such a code is necessary and defines its relationship to the mission of the school. Creating this guiding statement at the outset assists the writers in maintaining their focus on the agreed-upon function of the code and helps avoid overburdening it with material that arguably belongs elsewhere. At a minimum, the purpose statement should include answers to the following:

  * What is the school's mission, briefly stated?
  * In what ways does this code of conduct assist in accomplishing that mission?
  * Specifically, whose conduct will be guided by this code?

5. **The code should address the conduct of everyone involved in the school, not just that of the students.** The document should be titled "Code of Conduct for _____ School," not "Student Code of Conduct," and should address the rights, responsibilities, and allowable conduct of everyone involved in the educational process. Secondary-level students are much attuned to "fairness," and a document handed down from the adults addressing exclusively what students should and should not do would be less well received than a more globally oriented code. "Student Conduct Codes" conveys an "us against them" tone that is antithetical to the goal establishing appropriate norms of behavior for *everyone* in the build-

ing. Not only is it important for students to see that the adults must comply with accepted norms just as they do, but also codifying educators' and parents' normative expectations can be useful in regularizing new-employee training orientations and in establishing due process proceedings for infractions of the code.

6. **The code should clearly communicate and encourage responsibility and desirable behaviors.** The document should be a teaching tool for success that assists in everyone's decision-making processes. An effective code of conduct goes well beyond the mere enumeration of prohibited behaviors. More than just a statement of rules and disciplinary procedures, an effective code also details the kinds of attitudinal dispositions and behaviors that will lead to success within the school environment. The key question for the code writing team is "What types of behavior and attitudes do we wish to encourage in our students, staff, and parents?" In essence, the code should articulate just what the various members of the school community should be doing when they conduct themselves in ways most conducive to pursuing the mission of the school. These elements should be carefully elaborated in *positive* prose.

7. **The code should clearly articulate student and staff member rights.** A school's code of conduct can never abridge rights guaranteed to students and staff members by federal or state authority. An effective code articulates those rights most relevant to the school setting in developmentally appropriate language and provides examples so that students can readily understand them.

8. **The code should clearly articulate, define, and provide examples of those actions and behaviors that are prohibited.** One of the essential functions of a code of conduct is to place reasonable boundaries on the behavior of persons under its auspices. Clarity and specificity in this section are paramount.

- Identify the behavior in clearly observable terms. Avoid such terms as "disruptive behavior" or "aggressive behavior" without clarifying specifically what is meant and listing the most frequently observed examples.
- Identify the physical locations that are subject to the code. Are the objectionable behaviors also prohibited on the bus? On the walk to and from school? In the community during field trips?
- Identify the time periods (if applicable) when the code is in effect. Under what circumstances are these behaviors prohibited during nonschool hours? (For instance, in an infamous Northbrook, Illinois, powder puff football game hazing incident, the school needed to determine whether its prohibitions against hazing applied during the weekend in a nonsanctioned event.)
- Identify the legal authority behind the prohibition. Is the behavior, class of behaviors, or prohibited action(s) identified in existing school board regulations? Is the behavior identified in the state juvenile, criminal, or civil rights codes?

9. **The code should include distinctions between minor and serious violations.** Prohibited behaviors that the code is designed to deter should be identified on a continuum of severity. The overwhelming majority of code violations are minor infractions (e.g., failure to have supplies, tardiness, swearing, and other acts of nominal misconduct), but their inclu-

sion in the code may be essential from a "quality of educational life" standpoint. These less serious violations are the first level of polish on the floor. Their identification and successful disciplinary response can have an effect upon the frequency of "next-level" violations. For these behaviors, the code should encourage less formal classroom-level responses, increasing from low-intensity, primarily corrective actions to mild punishment. Following this continuum approach, the code should go on to identify increasingly serious categories of behavior and link them to a rationally conceived range of disciplinary responses.

10. **The code should be both preventative and educational and should include procedures to *assist* individuals who violate it.** The code writing team should be highly attentive to the educational mission of public schools and reflect that awareness throughout its drafting. Not only should the code articulate and encourage appropriate behavior, but also it should seek to prevent and remedy inappropriate behavior insofar as possible. It does no good to send a behaviorally unskilled student to either school or home detention and anticipate that he or she will thereby magically acquire the skills needed to avoid subsequent violations. The discipline recommended for each infraction should ideally help each student avoid repeating his or her mistake by learning something new or developmentally helpful. In this way, educators can reduce the likelihood that the student will engage in the proscribed behavior in the future by providing the knowledge or skills necessary for a constructive alternative response.

11. **The code should be taught to all students in a manner consistent with effective instructional practices.** The practice of simply distributing a copy of the code of conduct to each student and then announcing that everyone is now responsible for its observance must be abandoned. Regardless of any stern warnings on the cover sheet (or even an effort to require parents' signatures), information treated in this manner comes with the implied message that it is not a learning priority for the student or a teaching priority for the staff. Complex information distributed only as a reading assignment is poor pedagogy regardless of the subject matter, and that students should subsequently be held responsible for its contents is educationally indefensible. Reading and math are important educational priorities, and this priority is evidenced by the time, effort, and creativity that most often accompany the attendant curricula. Only by helping students to understand the complexities of the code of conduct in a similar manner can educators communicate its importance and increase the likelihood that the code will have its intended effect. Targeting all students by setting aside a few minutes each day at the very beginning of the school year can potentially "pay for itself" through much-reduced disciplinary concerns during the months to come. We recommend the following procedure for familiarizing everyone with the school's code of conduct:

- Render all sections of the code into a series of teaching modules and learner outcomes. Identify what the students should "know and be able to do" at the conclusion of each module, and create appropriate assessment procedures.
- Facilitate the opportunity for master teachers to convert the learner outcomes into effective teacher-friendly pedagogical procedures and activities, with an eye toward minimizing classroom teacher preparation time needed to teach the code.

- Implement the curriculum with all of the students in the first year, and target newly incoming students in subsequent years, with only refresher lessons for older students.
- Consider training a group of students as a "traveling role-play troupe" to visit each classroom and provide live examples of particularly crucial or confusing aspects of the code.

12. **The code should be revisited annually for updates and refinements.** After the school shootings that took place during the late 1990s, many school codes of conduct were changed to reflect what was perceived to be the new reality for heightened security and school safety. In a similar fashion, the increased use of computers in schools over time has created a need for limit setting and guidance in their use. Administrators should include updating the code as a regular annual task at the end of each school year so as to have the latest updated version available at the start of the next school year.

As a further resource, educators Stein, Richin, Banyon, Banyon, and Stein (2000) have written a very valuable and practical book, *Connecting Character to Conduct: Helping Students Do the Right Thing*, in which they expand upon what they see as four critical principles of student conduct, namely, respect, impulse control, compassion, and equity. The authors translated these principles into student behavior standards across multiple school settings and, using the imaginary school district of "Centerville," describe how the principles can be integrated and taught within the existing curriculum.

Classroom Rules

Just as the code of conduct helps to define the nature of the overall learning environment of the school, classroom rules apply similar principles to the idiosyncratic needs of individual curricular environments. Classroom rules are an essential universal prevention measure that enables the code to be individualized to meet specific environmental needs where "the rubber meets the road" in the schooling process.

A teacher friend of ours used to joke that he began each year by showing his students his "Two Simple Rules for Success in My Classroom."

Rule 1: Do what I tell you to do.
Rule 2: See Rule 1.

Joking aside, establishing a short list of rules to guide student behavior in the classroom is one of the most important requirements of a primary prevention program. Classroom rules may be seen as customizing the code of conduct to the unique circumstances of a particular classroom and establishing a norm of behavior for that environment. Rules for the art room, the gymnasium, or the music room will differ qualitatively, but they should all be intended to encourage the kinds of responsible, self-disciplined behaviors that are articulated in the school's code of conduct.

Similar to the broader school code, classroom rules exert their influence at the antecedent, or prevention, level, affecting the choice of behavior *before* it is already enacted.

A student enters a classroom and immediately seeks to engage in behaviors that he or she believes will obtain reinforcement or avoid discomfort. Some students may immediately take their seats and ready themselves for the lesson, others may chat with friends, and still others may engage in horseplay. The students all select behaviors that they believe to be in their best interest, based upon their individual set of knowledge, skills, and experience. In general, their common goals are to (1) continue or begin a reinforcing condition or (2) discontinue or avoid an aversive one.

For example, Jennifer knows that she can continue her conversation with Sara, a reinforcing condition, until the teacher finally shouts at her to sit down. At that time, she knows she can avoid the aversive condition of an office referral by complying. Juan knows that if he readies himself for the class as soon as he gets to the room, he can avoid the aversive condition of trying to play catch-up with the material for the whole class. James knows that if he continues his horseplay behavior, the teacher will send him out, relieving him of the aversive condition of a classroom environment that he does not enjoy. Seek pleasure, avoid pain—it's what we humans do.

In effect, well-written classroom rules provide information as to which behaviors will be reinforced by the teacher in that particular setting. For the large majority of typically unproblematic students, that information is generally sufficient. Provided with such behavioral guidelines, that group is able to select behaviors that will define the expected norms for the classroom. In other words well-written classroom rules help students who want to and are able to engage in academically desirable behaviors to do just that. When that group is demonstrating those behaviors, the students have the potential to be a powerful model for their less skilled or less motivated peers. Absent reasonable and consistently enforced rules, even the least problematic students historically may seek reinforcement from other sources (e.g., peers) or begin to avoid the environment entirely.

Walker, Colvin, and Ramsey (1995) advised that classroom rules should be (1) explicitly stated, (2) functional, (3) established on the first day of class, (4) rehearsed, and (5) practiced. Rules should be clear enough that little or no room is left for interpretation on anyone's part. One should strictly avoid nonexplicit words like *respect*, *inappropriate*, or *unacceptable*, as they lend themselves easily to personal judgment. Instead, phrase the rules in positive functional terms that communicate what the teacher wants the students to do. Walker et al. (1995, p. 157) offered 11 sample rule phrasings, including the following:

- Be on time for class.
- Enter the classroom quietly.
- Go to your assigned areas promptly.
- Listen to the teacher's directions or explanations.
- Raise your hand if you wish to talk or need assistance.

Notice that the rules instruct the students in the desired behaviors and that each is conducive to the maintenance of a positive learning environment. Keeping the list to no more than three to six items will facilitate easier assimilation and accommodation (Striepling, 1997).

The first day of class is the most advantageous time to establish rules in the classroom, avoiding as it does the need for both the teacher and the class to have to possibly unlearn bad habits. Including older students as collaborators in the effort to establish rules is a developmentally important element (Hyman, 1997). Rather than simply announcing the rules, teachers will find that devoting the first 20–30 minutes of Day 1 to working with the students on "our classroom rules" will be beneficial. The teacher should know ahead of time the areas that he or she wants addressed with positive functional rules and guide the classroom discussion accordingly. For example:

> "This classroom is like a workplace environment. Your job is to learn [the curriculum], and my job is to help you do that. In order for each of us to do our jobs effectively and minimize problems, we have to agree on some rules for getting along together. My experience is that rules are best stated in terms of what you are supposed to do rather than what you aren't supposed to do. For instance, a rule in a mechanic's shop might be 'Return tools to their proper place when finished,' rather than 'Don't leave tools lying around.' This way, the workers know exactly what is expected. Let's start by thinking about entering into our classroom from the hallway at the beginning of school or after recess. Let me see raised hands with suggestions about a rule that will help us avoid problems during that transition. How should everyone enter the classroom?"

Exact phrasing of the rules can be left to the teacher for later rendering on a large poster, but the critical feature is that the students see themselves as collaborators in the process, that they feel a genuine sense of ownership. Teachers should remember, however, that the students are collaborating with them, not dictating to them. Never include a rule that runs counter to a safe, orderly learning environment and that cannot be applied fairly and consistently, and never leave out a rule that is personally important.

Once written, the rules must be taught. Five minutes at the beginning of each class for the first week and then a booster lesson or two as needed thereafter is generally sufficient to accomplish this task. Teachers should use a discuss–model–rehearse procedure to clarify the intent of each rule. For instance, when a student has "all necessary supplies," what does that mean? Does "Proceed directly to your desk and be seated" mean a student cannot stop to speak with the teacher? What is the difference between a "low-volume voice" and *not* a "low-volume voice"? Teachers should have students demonstrate adhering and not adhering to the rule for the sake of clarity.

Once the rules are established and taught, an important point to remember is that *when a rule is broken, an aversive consequence must follow each time*. This principle is what distinguishes a "rule" from any other guide or influence on classroom behavior. It is not a suggestion or preference for behavior but, rather, an agreed-upon standard that cannot be breached without entailing a consequence. Fair and consistent application of the rules, right from the start, will help cement the principles in the minds of the students and enable the rules to function as they were intended—that is, to set the norms of acceptable behavior.

Caveat: If an otherwise rule-following student consistently violates a particular rule in spite of having to suffer aversive consequences, the teacher should consider the likelihood that a *skill deficit* rather than *a motivational deficit* exists (i.e., "can't do" rather than "won't do"). While most behaviorally unproblematic students have the ability to regulate their conduct to conform to a rule, some students simply do not have the skill to do so, and these students require additional supports. A problem-solving conference with the student in addition to consultation with school supportive services personnel may be necessary to define and implement needed behavioral supports.

Universal prevention programs address the potential for disruptive student behavior by establishing an environmental norm of nonviolence and predictable civil procedural order. The great majority of students who are characteristically disinclined to engage in disruptive behavior are provided behavioral guideposts and official support for their appropriate behavior. Additionally, the behavior of these students provides positive models and helps to create innumerable setting events around the school that serve to reduce the likelihood of problem behavior among their more aggressive peers.

Social and Emotional Learning

Bierman (2007) identified six developmental skills as essential to social and emotional competency in school-age children, including the abilities to label one's feelings, recognize the feelings of others, inhibit impulsive reactive anger, cope with frustration, communicate to express one's feelings to others, and resolve social problems nonaggressively. Children with chronic anger and aggression problems are frequently lacking in many if not all of these competencies, and they are unlikely to fully acquire them in a timely manner through the course of a traditional school curriculum and disciplinary system. Consequently, it becomes the obligation of school officials to ensure that these competencies are specifically taught and learned. In addition to schoolwide supports through the code of conduct and classroom supports through rule implementation, Tier I may also include research-supported classroom curricula in social and emotional learning.

Social and emotional learning (SEL) is the "capacity to recognize and manage emotions, solve problems effectively, and establish positive relationships with others" (Zins & Elias, 2006, p. 1). At the Tier 1 level, this category of learning entails specific classroom instruction in such areas as self-awareness, social awareness, responsible decision making, self-management, and relationship skills (Zins & Elias, 2006). The Collaborative for Academic, Social, and Emotional Learning (CASEL; see *www. casel.org*) has identified guidelines for program development and implementation as well as numerous evidence-based commercially available curricula. A recent meta-analysis of more than 700 positive youth development, SEL, character education, and prevention interventions indicated that SEL programs

- Are effective in both school and after-school settings.
- Are effective for racially and ethnically diverse students from urban, rural, and suburban settings across the K–12 grade range.
- Improve students' social-emotional skills, attitudes about self and others, connection to school, and positive social behavior.
- Improve students' achievement test scores by 11 to 17 percentile points. (CASEL, "Benefits/Meta-Analysis" section)

At the Tier 1 level the use of rationally conceived schoolwide and classroom-level policies to support positive behavior along with the implementation of evidence-based social and emotional curricula serve to increase the proportion of behaviorally competent students. These universal prevention procedures are necessary but not sufficient to address the requirements of a smaller population of students whose need for social and emotional learning and skill development exceeds that available in Tier 1.

TIER 2: SELECTED PREVENTION PROCEDURES AND THE ROLE OF ANGER COPING

While universal prevention programs are essential components, they are by themselves insufficient to create a schoolwide environment free from interpersonal aggression and disruptive behavior. School officials must also take steps to address the needs of that subset of students that lacks either the skills or personal dispositions to respond to these prevention measures. Students with chronic patterns of disruptive, aggressive behavior need more highly individualized support and more focused opportunities to acquire the skills for behavioral success in school (Walker, Ramsey, & Gresham, 2004). These students are consequently *selected* for additional attention. When school personnel fail to provide adequate behavioral support and skills training and instead direct only punitive sanctions and their own frustration at the misbehaving students, both parties stand to lose.

Which Interventions and Which Students?

In a positive behavioral supports context, Tier 2 prevention strategies involve focusing additional strategies and resources on students at risk for school dropout, serious aggressive behavior, drug and alcohol abuse, and other negative psychosocial outcomes. These *selected prevention measures* may take the form of behavioral skills training, academic support, adjusted school day, behavioral contracting, mentoring, or other research-supported interventions (Walker et al., 1996). The kinds of support will vary with the nature of the presenting problem, but they should always start with the least intrusive procedure that directly addresses the concern. For instance, a classroom reinforcement program or an individual behavioral contract is less disruptive to the normal functioning of the student's day than is a pull-out skills training program such as the Anger Coping Program.

If the universal prevention procedures are well established, the identification of students needing additional support is made less complicated. Such naturally occurring indicators as multiple office referrals can signal the existence of a problem that is not responsive to Tier 1 supports. Once a red flag is raised, one must select procedures that enable one to acquire valid assessment data linking the intervention to the individual needs of the student exhibiting problem behavior.

Effective classroom interventions for behaviorally high-risk students must be informed by individual assessments that usefully define the behavior in terms of its function and the contextual environmental contingencies that encourage and maintain it. Functional behavioral assessment (FBA) is a procedure used to gather the information needed to design positive behavioral supports. When undertaking this process, the term *function* refers to "the purposes the behavior may serve in the environment" (Kazden, 2001, p. 102). The individual conducting the FBA on a student exhibiting angry, aggressive behavior seeks information that will enable hypotheses to be generated about the purpose(s) such aggression serves for the student. Does it serve the function of allowing the youth to escape from aversive interpersonal circumstances? Does it provide anger release? Does it bring peer approval? In addition, an FBA seeks to better define the environmental elements that both increase the likelihood and serve as predictors of the behavior.

O'Neill et al. (1997, p. 3; emphasis in original) defined the five primary outcomes of an FBA:

1. A clear *description of the problem behaviors.*
2. Identification of the events, times and situations that *predict* when the problem behavior *will* and *will not* occur across the full range of typical daily routines.
3. Identification of the *consequences that maintain the problem behaviors* (i.e., what functions the behaviors appear to serve for the person).
4. Development of one or more *summary statements* or hypotheses that describe specific behaviors, a specific type of situation in which they occur, and the outcome reinforcers maintaining them in that situation.
5. Collection of *direct observation data* that support the summary statements that have been developed.

This information may be gathered directly through observation or indirectly through interview or behavioral checklists. The full procedures for conducting an effective FBA are not complex, but they do require a degree of study and preparation and are beyond the scope of this text. Interested individuals are referred to O'Neill et al. (1997) and Watson and Steege (2009). Information derived from the FBA is then used to inform the development of a classroom intervention designed to reinforce an alternative to the problem behavior that will serve a similar function for the student.

Classroom-level behavioral supports are most effective when used to encourage replacement behaviors that already exist within students' repertoires; that is, the students know how to carry out the desirable behaviors but have just not chosen to do so yet. This is what educators refer to as a "won't do versus can't do" situation. Environmental supports are aimed at increasing the probability of the more desirable alternative behavior and reducing that of the problem behavior.

Difficulties arise, however, when the problem behavior originates in a *skill* deficit rather than a *motivational* deficit. In this case, the student may want to enact the replacement behavior but lacks the requisite skills to do so. For instance, if the desired behavior is to ignore teasing by other children rather than explode in anger, the capacity to do so requires more than just motivation—it requires a complex set of social-cognitive skills. In those instances in which classroom-level behavioral supports prove to be insufficient as a response to problematic anger and aggressive behavior, a more intensive level of intervention is required.

The Anger Coping Program

As a Tier 2 behavioral support, the Anger Coping Program is designed to address the needs of students in elementary and early middle school whose angry, aggressive behavior arises in major part from social-cognitive distortions and deficiencies. These students will typically be relatively unresponsive to both the Tier 1 disciplinary structure as well as Tier 2 classroom-level behavioral supports. A huge mistake is made when educators, perhaps frustrated with attempts to reduce angry, aggressive behavior through environmental interventions and supports, turn prematurely to suspension and special education as ready resorts. Actions such as these deprive the student of the full range of general education supports and likely contribute to overrepresentation of minorities in both exclusionary discipline (Fenning & Rose, 2007) and classrooms for emotional behavioral disabilities (Losen & Orfield, 2002). Behavioral skills training, either individually or in a group format, is the *sequentially appropriate next step* for students who have not responded sufficiently to less intensive interventions.

To a large degree, schools are ideal environments for the delivery of skills training interventions such as the Anger Coping Program:

- Critical assessment data can be easily gathered through existing school record review, direct observation methods, or FBA techniques.
- Progress monitoring data in the form of teacher reports, truancy reports, disciplinary referrals, and other naturally occurring data sources can be easily obtained.
- Schoolwide and classroom environmental factors, such as positive behavioral supports and effective mild aversive consequences, can be influenced and manipulated to augment other forms of treatment.
- Classrooms and other social-academic settings in the school provide abundant opportunities for student clients to observe prosocial models and engage in useful behavioral rehearsal strategies.
- The presence of a large cadre of other education professionals in the building affords opportunities for consultation, collaboration, and, when needed, care provider support. (Larson, 2005)

The Anger Coping Program is a pull-out small-group skills training intervention divided into 18 sessions, fully outlined in session-by-session detail in Chapter 8. The program has a strong research base, described in Chapter 2, and can be flexibly adapted to the needs of students from third through seventh grades. Although the skills training portion of this program takes place outside of the classroom, the teacher's role is that of a full collaborator with critical responsibilities for generalization and continued behavioral support. Parents, too, are enlisted in the effort through regular communication initiatives. A well-designed, valid, and reliable screening and identification process is a critical component of selected prevention efforts at the elementary level and is discussed at length in Chapter 4.

TIER 3: INDICATED SUPPORTS

Comparatively uncomplicated and only mildly invasive supports of the kind provided by the Anger Coping Program can be designed to meet the needs of most students at risk for aggressive behavior in the school setting. As noted, however, there is a third, much smaller, subset of students who display chronic and severe emotional and behavioral problems in the school and who require a much more comprehensive support structure. In the three-tiered model, students in this category receive *indicated prevention* programs and procedures.

In some instances, these students receive curricular and behavioral programming through special education in programs for students with emotional and behavioral disabilities (EBD). However, programming through EBD, in and of itself, is hardly a guarantee of adequate behavioral supports. Compared to students in general and other special education programs, youth with EBD "have disproportionately higher rates of dropout and academic failure, and they are more likely to be arrested, poor, unemployed, involved with illicit drugs, and teen parents (Eber, Sugai, Smith, & Scott, 2002, p. 137).

When a student with EBD is also exhibiting chronic patterns of interpersonal aggression in the school setting, providing effective behavioral supports can be a daunting and, indeed, at times precarious undertaking. In similar fashion to students in general education receiving selected-level supports, effective behavioral supports for students with extraordinary behavioral challenges starts with a comprehensive assessment of the environmental and within-student elements that occasion the aggression. These data should drive the design and implementation of the individualized education plan (IEP), a document that should be better known for its fluidity in changing circumstances than its often more typical rigidity. Mandated behavioral goals and benchmarks should be linked to research-supported interventions derived from well-constructed FBAs. When a student with EBD engages in an aggressive act in the school setting, the circumstances of the incident should serve to usefully inform the IEP team by providing its members with useful data to make modifications.

Students receiving Tier 3 indicated-level prevention often require the support of every resource that the school can garner. At this tier the goals of providing knowledge and skills to prevent the onset of seriously disabling emotional problems and behavioral patterns are much more limited than at the other two levels, the major focus instead being on providing support to retard worsening of the problem. Recent investigations by Eber and her colleagues (see Eber et al., 2002, for a review and useful discussion) have examined the use of "wraparound" services for students with EBD:

> Wraparound incorporates a family-centered and strength-based philosophy of care to guide service planning for students with EBD and their families. It involves all services and strategies necessary to meet the individual needs of students and their families. The child, family members, and their team of natural support and professional providers define the needs and collectively shape and create the supports, services, and interventions linked to agreed upon outcomes (Eber et al., 2002, p. 139)

Indicated prevention measures such as these figuratively "wrap" supports around the student, in and out of school, with a highly structured and individualized program (Larson, Smith, & Furlong, 2002). Ideally, a team consisting of school, family, and community support individuals (e.g., the family mental health professional, probation officer, social welfare worker) meet to identify student and family strengths, prioritize needs, and develop a plan of action. Support is mobilized for the school, home, and community settings. Such wraparound plans may include (1) modification of schedules, routines, and supervision; (2) skills training; (3) enhancement of existing strengths; (4) improvement of access to resources; (5) supports for caregivers; and (6) function-based behavioral supports (Eber et al., 2002). In this manner, a student with what may be serious life-course and persistent emotional and behavioral needs is provided with every available opportunity to function effectively in the traditional school environment.

Anger Management Training

Within this context of educational wraparound services, appropriate support may include providing anger management training delivered on an individual basis (see Chapter 10).

SUMMARY

Students with problematic levels of anger and aggressive behavior who disrupt the safety of the learning environment are present in all communities, both rural and urban. It is true that the pernicious effects of poverty and its associated risk factors weigh much more heavily on some communities than others—catastrophically so in some cases—and this contributing factor causes the percentage of students with needs in this area to vary markedly from school to school. However, around the country students in every building in every school district can be assigned a place *somewhere* on the three-tiered prevention pyramid discussed in this chapter. It is the percentage of the whole occupied by each tier that will represent the between-community, between-school differences, and it is those differences that will help define the prevention mission faced by school officials.

The needs of schoolchildren have changed faster than the abilities of educational professionals to adequately address them. It was not so long ago that schools did not even have to accept the challenge of educating students with diverse learning and behavioral needs; students either fit the existing structure or (directly or indirectly) were pushed out of the system. Thankfully, that is no longer the case.

As a consequence, however, university research into meeting the learning and behavioral needs of an increasingly diverse student body has had to play catch-up, and there is still very much to learn. Which programs are best for which students and what combination of programs is best for which schools are questions that have yet to be answered by the empirical research literature. As this research progresses, what is currently available for concerned school personnel are emerging "best-practices" recommendations. The three-tiered pyramid model discussed in this chapter provides a structure within which school personnel may implement a variety of empirically supported prevention measures and then evaluate their effectiveness in the context of their individual situations.

CHAPTER 4

Getting Started with the Anger Coping Program

Group Leaders, Screening, and Identification

James ripped a poster off the wall on the way down to the group room, and then Terry tripped Michael so that he cut his lip on a table. While the co-leader took a bleeding and crying Michael to the nurse, James and Anthony got into a shoving match over some smuggled candy and James ripped Anthony's shirt. The group hadn't even started the session yet.

Too frequently, hard-working group leaders are so understandably concerned about what is or is not happening in the group room that matters of generalization become a "hope for the best" affair. Moving children with aggressive externalizing behavior problems out of their respective classrooms and down the hall to the group room; then, getting them settled, attentive, and participating; and, finally, moving them back to the classroom—all without a major catastrophe—is a success in itself. Additional concerns associated with training for generalization often become lost.

Yet, what is the purpose of all that effort if not to have a positive effect on behavior out of the group room? A young fourth-grade student in a group run by one of the authors once remarked, "I wish this was my classroom, because I do good in here and don't get in no trouble." That child was expressing a critically important training need, namely, "Help me to transfer the lessons I've learned in this therapy room to the day-to-day environment of my classroom." As everyone knows, children are referred to school psychologists and counselors because of their behavior in settings *other than* the group room.

Unquestionably, obtaining insight and skills in the therapy setting is a critical first step—but only a first step. For direct intervention to be useful to the child, a bridge to the daily real-world setting must be constructed. It is the quality of the collaboration between the group leader and the classroom teacher that will define the durability of that bridge. Both of these professionals have critical roles to play in implementing meaningful interventions, and neither can ignore or undervalue the contributions of the other. It is for that reason we dedicate this chapter to a discussion of the interdependent roles of group leaders and teachers in both developing and successfully implementing anger control counseling groups.

QUALIFICATIONS AND QUALITIES OF GROUP LEADERS

The program we will discuss was designed as a school-based intervention for use by a trained co-leader team consisting (ideally) of a counselor and a school psychologist. Involving a community mental health professional as a co-leader is also a highly appropriate option (Lochman & Wells, 1996). Although busy schedules and tight resources may demand that only a single group leader manage the intervention, a co-leader situation is most advantageous for several reasons.

1. Two adults in the group room provide a greater sense of personal security for the children and may reduce any anxiety they have concerning their own safety and well-being. It is not unusual for the children to initially "test" the group environment to determine whether it is one that will be characterized by control or lack of control. The visible presence of two adults can help to reduce or alleviate some of these concerns.

2. Co-leaders can divide the group leaders' chores, with one addressing the training and the other concentrating on behavior management concerns. This issue is discussed in a later section.

3. The addition of a second adult allows the leaders to plan and execute behavioral modeling of the activities or skills for the children to observe. The Anger Coping Program is a skills-based intervention and, as such, draws procedures from effective teaching as well as counseling. Skills are generally inculcated through use of what might be termed a "discuss, observe, rehearse, apply" model. Thus, enabling the group members to watch the leaders role-play the designated skill is a critical feature.

4. The co-leaders can debrief each other following each session to gain additional insight into the progress and direction of the group. Using immediate postsession time to share observations, make instructional adjustments, and plan strategies is very important in helping assure the ultimate effectiveness of the intervention.

It is highly desirable for at least one of the co-leaders to have had previous supervised experience with school-based therapy/counseling groups. Disruptive, noncompliant, and highly externalizing young children are not the ideal subjects with whom to begin learning group counseling techniques without supervision! Although a well-designed and manualized cognitive-behavioral intervention is comparatively structured and clear with regard to session-to-session activities, there is no substitute for the skills and confidence gained through previous experience in managing a counseling group.

Because the most effective anger control programs are based on a cognitive-behavioral framework that draws heavily on a social-cognitive model of anger arousal (see Lochman

& Wells, 1996), it is essential that the group leaders have a strong working foundation in the theoretical underpinnings of the program prior to its implementation. In general, the graduate-level training of school psychologists and school counselors is excellent preparation for the group leader's role. Indeed, their individual disciplines and expertise combine well in addressing both selection assessment concerns and the group counseling requirements. However, not all preparation programs place an emphasis on working with aggressive children. In lieu of specific graduate coursework in cognitive-behavioral theory and intervention techniques, intensive study of the first two chapters of this volume, along with selections from "Recommended Further Reading" (located immediately before the References), is highly recommended. Requesting that the local university provide a continuing education option related to work with angry, aggressive children can also be very beneficial.

Broadly defined, the primary responsibilities of the group leader in an anger control counseling group are to:

1. Initiate, design, and cooperate with the classroom teacher, parents, and relevant others in the process of screening and selecting group members.
2. Establish a collaborative relationship with the classroom teacher and assist that individual in learning his or her responsibilities and ensuring classroom support of the intervention.
3. Collaborate with the classroom teacher on determining the behavioral goals of the group members.
4. Obtain informed parental consent and determine and assure the appropriate level of parental involvement in the intervention.
5. Inform and involve the administrator in understanding and enacting his or her role in the intervention.
6. Develop a behavioral management plan for the group setting, including procedures for moving the students in and out of the space.
7. Secure the appropriate physical setting and necessary supplies for implementing the program.
8. Design appropriate progress monitoring and outcome efficacy assessments.
9. Conduct the intervention training in accordance with the prescribed procedures.
10. Arrange and conduct booster sessions with the group members following completion of the intervention.

Let us address in some detail the first three responsibilities enumerated above, as they effectively set the stage for the others, involving—as they do—the classroom teacher to a significant extent. The teacher has three key responsibilities in an anger control intervention, namely, (1) participating in screening and selection, (2) collaborating on treatment generalization in the classroom, and (3) evaluating classroom behavioral goal attainment efforts. In this chapter, we examine how the group leader and teacher work together in identifying children for the group. In subsequent chapters, we deal in greater detail with the remaining responsibilities they hold in common.

SCREENING AND SELECTION OF STUDENTS

Some years ago, a school psychologist was settling his anger control group in for their first meeting when one of the children suddenly asked how it came to be that he had been selected for the group. Before the group leader could answer, another boy piped up, "He just asked the teacher who the baddest kids were—and here we are!" That answer, albeit reduced to its most oversimplified and colloquial aspects, was actually not far off the mark. However, not every aggressive child needs anger control group skills training, and for some it may even be contraindicated. Although the students may see the selection process as simply identifying the "baddest" pupils, the real process is considerably more complex than that.

It is important to recall that the Anger Coping Program is a Tier 2 prevention strategy, meaning it becomes a consideration only when the universal classroom supports at Tier 1 prove insufficient. Moreover, a pull-out treatment intervention such as Anger Coping should be considered only after less invasive additional supports have also shown themselves to be inadequate to the task. When one removes a child from the classroom into a group treatment setting—even for only an hour or less each week—that option should be implemented only after serious consideration or application of less invasive options. Some of the questions that should be answered include:

- Are the schoolwide and classroom-level universal supports already in place being implemented with integrity?
- Are there any additional universal supports (e.g., new classroom management strategies) that can be implemented first?
- Have school behavior specialists been consulted, and have FBA-driven classroom or schoolwide behavioral interventions been considered and/or previously implemented with integrity?
- Is it clear that the child has a skill deficit ("can't do") rather than a motivational deficit ("won't do")?
- Is it clear that the problem behavior is not secondary to poorly managed attention-deficit/hyperactivity disorder (ADHD) or other mental health concerns that should be addressed first?

Children for whom the Anger Coping Program is an appropriate response often engage in disruptive behavior in the classroom, but such occasions arise at least in part from personal anger regulation problems. Moreover, the problem behavior will be evidenced elsewhere in the larger school environment and frequently in the home and community as well. However, children with disruptive behavior problems that are *limited to the classroom setting only* may be best served by an *in-class* behavioral intervention, at least as a first-choice response.

Careful screening and identification of students for the Anger Coping Program will help to make certain that the intervention truly fits the need. In the remainder of this chapter, we present the elements of a multiple-gating process that will assist professionals in this effort. Careful attention to this process will undoubtedly pay off in professional satisfaction that the children in the group are really the children who *need* most to be there.

Multiple-Gate Screening and Identification

The classroom teacher's active participation in both identifying and treating students in the anger control group is fundamental to any realistic hope of successful outcomes. Identifying the students who are most likely to benefit from a small-group skills training is the first phase of what will be a collaborative effort between the teacher and the group leaders over the course of many weeks to come. The school psychologist or counselor who perceives that a direct intervention group may be the treatment of choice for some problematic students needs to begin the process in a systematic and thoughtful fashion. The teacher may be ready to merely point out "the baddest kids" and leave the rest of reform to the group leaders, but his or her role must invariably go much beyond that.

An effective anger control program is designed to provide angry, aggressive children with important anger management and problem-solving skills and to prevent progressively more serious conduct problems in later years. Consequently, finding and selecting the children most likely to benefit is paramount. The goal of an effective identification process is the early and reliable identification of children most at risk of later serious antisocial behaviors (Charlebois, LeBlanc, Gagnon, & Larivee, 1994). The term *reliable* is key here. The limits on the time and resources of school personnel make it essential that the process identify children who are at "true risk" rather than those with adequate skills and other protective factors who are merely going through a difficult but short-lived period of adjustment.

In addition, the screening and identification process itself must be time- and cost-effective. Procedures that place excessive demands on educators' time and school budgets stand little chance of being absorbed into the regular fabric of the education program. Although providing each child at the grade level with a complete psychological evaluation would likely yield adequate data for reliable selection, few if any school psychologists have sufficient time to make such an assessment. However, some criteria beyond merely having teachers rattle off the names of their most disruptive children should be adopted. Because of his or her expertise in assessment, the school psychologist should definitely be consulted at each step in the screening process, even if he or she is not a part of the treatment team.

The preferred use of *multiple-gating procedures* for the identification of children at high risk for later conduct problems has been advocated by a number of authors (e.g., Loeber & Dishion, 1983; Loeber, Dishion, & Patterson, 1984). These methods normally use relatively inexpensive ratings as a first "gate" and more sophisticated identification procedures for later gates. This "ever narrowing gate" process is an effort to both identify those children who are at true risk and to reduce the number of those who may be false "positives." A number of models have been examined, including those that utilize teacher-driven ratings (e.g., Sinclair, Del'Homme, & Gonzalez, 1993; Walker et al., 1988), peer and teacher ratings (e.g., Roff, 1986), and parent and teacher ratings (e.g., Whebby et al., 1993). Jones, Sheridan, and Binns (1993) used developmental deficits in early social skills as identifying variables for high-risk children.

A large body of research suggests that economic disadvantage, inadequate parental discipline practices, and early oppositional behavior are among the major risk factors related to later conduct disorders (see Dodge & Pettit, 2003, for a review). Specific research on the Anger Coping Program indicates that children with the highest initial level of disruptive or aggressive off-task classroom behavior and with the poorest problem-solving skills have been shown to make the strongest gains (Lochman, Lampron, Burch, & Curry, 1985). An effective multiple-gating process must fully take into account these risk factors and marker behaviors, with the ultimate aim of targeting the children at highest risk of subsequent violence. The multiple-gate screening and selection process described here makes significant use of both teachers and parents' observations and ratings of behavior (see Figure 4.1).

Gate 1: Lowest Socioeconomic Group

Because of the strong relationship between low socioeconomic status and a host of later risks (e.g., Attar, Guerra, & Tolan, 1994; Yung & Hammond, 1998), economically disadvantaged districts or school attendance areas within larger districts with higher proportions of economically disadvantaged families should be targeted as the first gate. This is not to say that comparatively well-off school districts do not have children at risk for aggressive behavior; clearly, they do. However, poverty has the capacity to potentiate other risk factors to such a great extent that its role in the selection process cannot be ignored. If there are no observable variations in the socioeconomic status of the school's students, then the process should immediately proceed to Gate 2.

Gate 1: Lowest Socioeconomic Group

Because of the pernicious effects of poverty on children and families, this demographic is most likely to contain the largest pool of children with the highest proportion of risk factors and the least number of protective factors. Cross-check any tentative beginning list against the school's list of those qualifying for free or reduced-price lunches.

Gate 2: Teacher Nominations

The Teacher Nomination Form provided in Appendix A is the recommended form we use in implementing the Anger Coping Program. See Chapter 9 for adaptations when screening for groups of girls (each group should be gender specific).

Gate 3: Teacher Screening Scale

A copy of the Teacher Screening Scale is available in Appendix B. Parental consent is required at this gate.

Gate 4: Broadband Assessment

Identified students should be further screened with a comprehensive teacher/parent checklist instrument. Priority in enrollment should be given to children with multisetting problem behavior. If necessary, employ additional assessment measures to further delineate any suspected co-occurring disorders or to allay concerns.

FIGURE 4.1. Multiple-gate screening process.

Gate 2: Teacher Nominations

At the identified grade level, teacher nominations of pupils who demonstrate at least three of the following four criteria should be solicited: (1) marked difficulties with interpersonal problem solving and anger management (including interpersonally aggressive and nonaggressive responses); (2) oppositional and disruptive responses to teacher directives; (3) rejection from the more adaptive peer culture; and (4) academic failure or underachievement. A sample Teacher Nomination Form is provided in Appendix A. A more focused discussion of how to screen and identify physically aggressive girls can be found in Chapter 9.

Our experience has been that some teachers are afraid that nominating a child for consideration will "label" him or her unfairly. Group leaders should provide assurance that the teacher is only suggesting names of students who will go on to be carefully screened later. There is no danger that a child will receive services based only on the ratings at this second gate. To that end, teachers should be advised to err on the side of possible overidentification at this stage. Several other factors are considered in the nominations, such as:

1. Children whose aggression provides them with high peer status and who do not express any motivation to change should be *left out* of the nomination process. Often these children are seen as the school bullies, and they may use their aggressive behavior proactively to intimidate, harass, and physically assault other students. These children are a significant source of concern, and their needs—along with those of their victims—should also be addressed by school personnel. Helpful work by Jimerson, Swearer, and Espelage (2010) and Olweus (1993) may provide guidance for such intervention efforts by supportive services personnel.

2. Avoid including children who are substantially different from the proposed pool of nominees. For instance, children who are in the same classroom grade but 2 or more years older, as a result of multiple retentions or for other reasons, may be inappropriate because of differing developmental issues. Similarly, aggressive children who are typically withdrawn or who have very fragile self-concepts may be inappropriate for this intervention, as their impulses may become excessively aroused during the role-playing activities (Lochman, Lampron, et al., 1987). In addition, children who are exhibiting trauma-related behavioral concerns, including aggression, may benefit from an intervention more aligned with their social and emotional needs (see the "Additional Resources" section at the end of Chapter 9).

3. Aggressive children who are currently being served in special education programs for those with emotional disabilities should be included so long as their co-occurring disorders do not (1) provide excessively high stimulation likely to attract verbal or physical abuse from more aggressive peers or (2) represent extraordinary behavior management issues for the group leader.

4. Because of their need to understand the social-cognitive processes involved in the training, participants in the anger control program should be able to function at minimally a low average intellectual level.

Gate 3: Teacher Screening Scale

Following informed parental consent, group leaders should assist each classroom teacher in completing the Teacher Screening Scale (adapted from Dodge & Coie, 1987) for all children included following Gate 2 exclusions. This scale is provided in Appendix B. (Parental consent prior to this step is necessary and proper because a subset of individuals, rather than the entire class, is being assessed.) This scale was selected because of its promising support in research trials and its simplicity and ease of use for larger-scale screenings. However, professionals who trust and have experience with other similar scales should feel free to substitute them. The goal of this stage of the selection process is to establish a hierarchy of need and risk among those children first identified by the teacher.

The Teacher Screening Scale has demonstrated modest promise in its capacity to differentiate between reactive and proactive aggression patterns. Note that the first three items (denoted with single asterisks) are representative of reactive aggression, while the final three items (double asterisks) evidence proactive patterns. Although the data indicate that teachers typically view aggressive behavior patterns in children as unidimensional (Dodge & Coie, 1987), the two-factor nature of this instrument can prove useful in those cases in which the teacher reports strong ratings in one direction or the other. For example, if a child scores very high on items 10, 11, and 12 (see Appendix B) and very low on items 1, 2, and 3, the treatment team may want to further assess whether the child's needs would be better served through a bullying intervention rather than an anger control program. Caution is advised against overinterpreting the Teacher Screening Scale, however. The lack of adequate research support empirically argues for a conservative approach. Look for broad, sweeping differences in scores rather than minor variations. The school psychologist's expertise in psychometrics will be especially valuable in conducting this analysis.

Comparison of the global ratings on this instrument will give group leaders and teachers a rough ranking of the children considered to be in need of anger and aggression management training. Reviewing the Gate 2 nomination list in the light of the new data may enable the educators to move selected children from the prospective anger control group to less intensive classroom-level interventions as a result of Gate 3 screening procedures.

Gate 4: Broadband Assessment

The teacher and the parents of each Gate 3 identified child should be asked to complete a broadband behavior checklist. Such well-standardized assessment tools as the Child Behavior Checklist (Achenbach & Rescorla, 2001), the Behavior Assessment System for Children, Second Edition (Reynolds & Kamphaus, 2005), or similar multidimensional parent or teacher rating instruments should be utilized. The use of multidimensional scales enables one to consider possible co-occurring symptoms that may lead to additional recommendations for treatment. For instance, the high incidence of aggression and oppositional behavior among children diagnosed with ADHD (Barkley, 1998) requires that one actively consider the presence of this particular disability. In this instance, employing a broadband instrument at this juncture enables the treatment team to look for significant elevations on hyperactivity and attention deficit indices. In addition, studies of children who have conduct problems have reported rates of comorbidity with internalizing difficulties as high as 52% (McConaughy & Skiba, 1993). These findings indicate that one must examine the protocols carefully for the existence of all co-occurring problems that may require additional or alternative interventions.

Parents should subsequently be contacted and interviewed in order to clarify their responses and gather specific behavioral information. This juncture is an opportune time to begin to understand the family's strengths and the willingness of the parents to participate in the intervention. At this gate, the treatment team is most interested in determining whether the child is displaying behaviors at home similar to those seen in the school. Issues relating to setting demand levels (i.e., differing demands and behavioral expectations between the home and school settings) should be fully explored. For instance, it is common for parents who place few compliance demands on their children at home to be completely unaware of the noncompliant or oppositional behavior demonstrated at school.

Those children observed by parents and teachers to have significant externalizing behavior problems in both the home and school environments should be identified and considered the first priority for intervention. Children who have been reliably identified as problematic in the school setting but not in the home setting should be included in the second tier of candidates.

Preintervention Individual Assessment

Once the pool of pupils has been winnowed down through the multiple-gating process, the treatment team needs to further evaluate the subjects' individual characteristics. How much does anger play a part in these pupils' difficulties? What are their current problem-solving competencies? What is the function of their aggressive behavior? For instance, children with highly affective reactive aggression will have intervention needs that are, in many ways, very different from those of children with lower-affect, proactive aggression levels (Dodge & Coie, 1987). In addition, children with primarily proactive aggression patterns and adequate peer social acceptance tend to view their behavior as less problematic than their more reactive peers and, consequently, may be less motivated to participate in treatment (Lochman, White, et al., 1991). This individual assessment will allow the group leaders (1) to better understand the functional antecedent and consequent events associated with the problematic behavior, (2) to individualize the intervention emphases to meet the particular needs of the group, and (3) to select out, or drop from the group, those pupils for whom the intervention may be contraindicated because of their characteristic anger or aggressiveness.

The choice of the assessment instrument or procedure will naturally be guided by the nature of the assessment question. Although an exhaustive description of individual assessment procedures and instruments is beyond the scope of this chapter, a number of excellent resources are available. Lochman, White, et al. (1991) have provided a comprehensive discussion of the assessment options available for use with aggressive children. These authors suggest procedures and instruments for the evaluation of social problem-solving strategies, peer group status, familial/parental functioning, cognitive/academic deficits, and self-concept. Furlong and Smith (1994) review an extensive selection of psychometric measures intended to assess anger, aggression, and/or hostility in children and youth. McMahon and colleagues (McMahon & Estes, 1997; McMahon & Wells, 1998) provide a model of assessment that stresses not only the assessment of the child's behavior per se but also behavior in such interactional contexts as the school and home environments. In addition, three scales for the measurement of anger—the Children's Anger Response Checklist (Feindler, Adler, Brooks, & Bhumitra, 1993), the Anger Response Inventory for Children (Tangney, Wagner, Hansbarger, & Gramzow, 1991), and the Children's Inventory of Anger (Nelson & Finch, 2000)—provide useful assessments of anger-related problems and affect.

Pretreatment Authentic Data and the Classroom Progress Monitoring Report

In addition to compiling whatever psychometric data are available, group leaders at this time should obtain "authentic" or school record data on the selected group members. These data may include (1) accumulated discipline reports, such as office referrals, detentions, and suspensions, (2) tardy or absentee reports, and (3) academically related data, such as homework return rate information or other teacher-suggested measures of adaptive classroom skills, resulting in some permanent assessment product for each student. This information will serve the dual purpose of helping group leaders to better understand the actual problems the children are having in school and providing a comparison baseline for posttreatment evaluation.

A useful addition to the existing permanent product data is the Classroom Progress Monitoring Report (CPMR; provided in Appendix M). The CPMR is an easily completed teacher checklist that monitors the following five classroom behaviors:

1. Adherence to classroom rules and routines
2. Self-control of vocal disruptive behavior
3. Self-control of anger
4. Homework returned
5. In-class assignment effort

This instrument can be quickly completed by the classroom teacher on a weekly or every other week during the regularly scheduled consultation time and provides an ongoing data source for progress monitoring. Group leaders should gather a minimum of three pre-intervention CPMRs to establish a baseline. Subsequent data can be graphed and analyzed by following the procedures outlined in Chapter 13.

Regular meetings with the classroom teacher to complete the CPMR allow the collaboration to evolve and information to be shared. Group leaders can use these meetings to learn more about the child's most recent classroom behavior and use the opportunity to nurture the teacher's generalization efforts.

Having a useful data-based estimate of the relative effectiveness of the intervention is essential to good counseling practice. The preintervention data, both psychometric and school-based records, can contribute to that assessment effort. (See Chapter 13 for step-by-step instructions for implementing uncomplicated progress monitoring and program evaluation procedures suitable for classroom settings.)

Child Interview

One of the singular features about doing anger management training in school settings is the comparative intimacy of the environment. In all but the largest schools, by the time a child is typically referred for pull-out treatment of problem behavior, he or she is likely to be known (usually very well known) by the school-based treatment professionals. At this stage of the screening and identification process comes the time to interview and (one hopes) enlist the cooperation of the identified child, a time in which initial positive impressions can definitely pay off. This first meeting may be the group leader's best opportunity to begin to foster the child's all-important sense of being understood and respected. An atmosphere of nonconfrontational acceptance should prevail, even in the face of obvious mistruths and prevarications on the part of the child. The group leader's chief objectives should be to:

1. **Acquire an understanding of the child's conceptualization of the problem.** When and where do most of the problems occur? Who is usually there? What do they do? What do you do? What finally happens when it's over? Who is usually to blame? As was noted in Chapter 2, children with reactive aggressive behavior problems may experience cognitive distortions, particularly in regard to their own attributions of others' intentions. This proclivity may manifest itself in the child's denying problem ownership and considerable finger-pointing at others. Although deflecting blame is common among almost everyone, interviewers should probe for the child's level of commitment to his or her attributional bias, as this understanding will have implications for later training. Dogged denial of responsibility in the face of clear evidence to the contrary may be an indicator of distorted processing. Then again, it may also just be a defensive strategy that has paid off in the past.

2. **Acquire an understanding of the child's problem-solving skills.** "Can you tell when trouble is coming? What kinds of things do you do to avoid trouble? Do you ever get *really* angry? What do you do when you are really angry? What do you do to calm yourself when you are really angry?" Interviewers should try to get a sense of the child's current skills and strategies for anger regulation and problem solving, however poorly conceptualized they might be at this time. Make note of expressed strategies that can be referred to later, even if they do not reflect the child's currently observed behaviors (e.g., "I just walk away," or "I just ignore them").

3. **Describe the Anger Coping Program and obtain the child's assent to it.** In our experience, only very rarely will a child resist or turn down the opportunity to leave the classroom to participate in counseling; most jump at the chance. Make every effort to counter any belief that it is a punishment, but rather frame the group time together as an opportunity to learn new ways of avoiding trouble with others. Discuss meeting times and duration and describe some of the training activities. Make every effort to close the interview on a note of positive anticipation and genuine satisfaction with the child's participation. Appendix D details the Anger Coping Agreement that can serve as a formalization of the child's assent to be included.

Once the group's members have been officially identified, it is now time to assist the teacher in further understanding and refining his or her collaborative role in the intervention.

CHAPTER 5

Generalization and the Role of the Classroom Teacher

Treatment is not only about change but also about *generalization* of that change, that is, successfully transferring it to other settings. It is one thing to demonstrate anger management skills at an appointed time in the group room, but it is quite another to do so in the day-to-day activities of the classroom. Most experienced group leaders working with children who exhibit angry, aggressive externalizing behavior have anecdotes about the failure to transfer or generalize what was seemingly learned in the therapy room. The experience of a group leader believing a student client may now have finally acquired alternatives-to-aggression skills, only to find that student fighting before the morning is out, is not an unusual one. Working hard in the treatment room but leaving generalization to chance often yields predictably disappointing results:

> GROUP LEADER: He teased you and you hit him?
>
> STUDENT: Yeah.
>
> GROUP LEADER: But didn't we just work on that in the group?
>
> STUDENT: Yeah.
>
> GROUP LEADER: And what is the thing to do?
>
> STUDENT: Just walk away or use my self-talk to calm down.
>
> GROUP LEADER: Why didn't you do either of those?
>
> STUDENT: I don't know.

A useful example with which readers may identify is a student learning to drive an automobile. The simulators in the driver's education classes provide opportunities to practice many of the behaviors that demonstrate the required skills in the safety of the classroom. It is, however, unimaginable that students would immediately be handed the car keys without considerable effort aimed at getting them to generalize those skills to a "real" situation.

"Learner vehicles" with dual breaking systems and giant, cone-lined driving courses are all a part of that generalization effort.

Elliott and Gresham (1991) identified three types of generalization, namely, setting generalization, behavior generalization, and time generalization. Setting generalization refers to the child's ability to exhibit a behavior outside of the setting in which he or she was originally trained. For example, if a child has been taught to use self-instruction to control angry outbursts in the training group and then subsequently uses this skill successfully in the classroom, setting generalization has occurred. Similarly, if a child has learned a problem-solving procedure in the therapy situation and later utilizes that procedure to nonaggressively resolve a problem on the playground, then setting generalization has again been demonstrated.

Behavior generalization refers to behavior changes that are related to—but were not the focus of—direct training. For example, a child who was trained to replace aggression with verbal assertion in peer interaction may be observed to have also begun using negotiation strategies. Related behaviors in response to the same problem situation are grouped together under the rubric *functional response class*. Students referred for intervention because of aggressive behavior may have numerous verbally and physically aggressive responses available to them. For instance, a student accused of misbehavior by the teacher might throw a book, knock over a desk, or swear at, threaten, or even assault the teacher, particularly if any or all of these actions have led to a reinforcing outcome in the past. All of these behaviors belong to a functional response class. One of the goals of direct intervention, therefore, is to establish and expand the more adaptive functional response class.

Finally, time generalization refers to the ability of the child to maintain the intervention behaviors after the training is discontinued. Behaviors will likely be maintained only to the extent that they continue to be functional and reinforced. Changes that occur during treatment stand a greater chance of being maintained or generalizing over time so long as reinforcement remains largely the same (Kazdin, 1982; Martens & Meller, 1990). This finding suggests that the use of naturally occurring reinforcers such as teacher and peer approval or positive regard are ultimately best for replacing initial artificial reinforcers.

There is, however, absolutely no research suggesting, or reason to believe, that skills learned in the group room will transfer or generalize usefully anywhere else—whether to the classroom, the playground, or the neighborhood—without specific generalization guidelines built into the fabric of the intervention. Pupil insight and skill mastery within the setting of the group room are critical prerequisites, but they are only prerequisites. The most important objective—indeed, the *raison d'être* of the entire effort—is to facilitate the adaptive transfer of the desired skill to the authentic environments of school and home. The mechanism for this to happen cannot be conceived as an afterthought or an add-on; it must be integrated into the structure of the intervention at the outset. Too much is at stake in the lives of these children to rely on the "train and hope" model.

MEICHENBAUM'S PROCEDURAL CHECKLIST

Donald Meichenbaum (2006) proposed a "procedural checklist" (p. 2) for therapists to follow that is designed to increase both favorable treatment outcomes as well as the likelihood of successful generalization. We provide a condensed overview of some of those recommendations and comment on their applicability to treatment with the Anger Coping Program (original text in *italics*). Readers are encouraged to read Meichenbaum's complete text, which is available at *www.melissainstitute.org*.

At the Outset of Training

Establish a good working alliance with the trainee because the quality of this relationship is the single most important factor in producing positive outcomes and it exceeds the proportion of outcome attributed to any other feature of the training. The trainee needs to feel respected, accepted, engaged, and be treated as a collaborator. Hostile, confrontational, fear-engendering interactions are counterproductive and ineffective. If training is being conducted on a group basis, then the level of group cohesion and identity with the group is predictive of outcome. (p. 9)

This all-important element of close collaboration was first introduced during the pre-group child interview (as noted in Chapter 4) and needs to continue throughout the intervention. Children with serious behavior problems all too frequently are surrounded by numerous adults ready to be confrontational and punitive, and this whole dynamic may be readily understandable and even appropriate, given their roles. However, group leaders need to maintain and communicate their respect and understanding of the child as a person distinct from the child's behavior. Ongoing problem behaviors most clearly define the child's instructional needs, and group leaders should approach them as such.

Engage the participants in explicit goal-setting. Highlight that the treatment is not only about changing, but transferring (extending) the newly acquired skills (changes) learned in the training program to new situations/settings. Discuss the challenge to generalize or transfer skills. Lead participants to view generalization as an attitude, rather than just as a set of transferable skills. Participants need to find (search out) opportunities to practice what was learned in a supportive environment. (p. 9)

The Anger Coping Agreement (Appendix D) is the first opportunity to clearly establish the link between what will happen in the group and what is expected in the school environment. Regular reference to this document and careful attention to the weekly Goal Sheet exercises (see Appendix F for a sample Goal Sheet) will help communicate this important generalization element. Continually remind the group members that these goals are something to be worked toward and that difficulties, missteps, and barriers are to be expected. Remind them that the group is a safe opportunity to practice the skills necessary for effective transfer and that the classroom teacher stands ready to help in that setting.

The skills should be taught in a manner that allows the training to build one skill upon another in a sequenced fashion. Name and describe each skill that is being taught. Encourage the trainees to view these skills as "tools" that they can carry with them and draw upon as needed. (p. 10)

The Anger Coping Program is designed to be a carefully constructed sequence linking knowledge to cognitive-behavioral skills, and each new Anger Coping session opens with a review of the preceding meeting's training focus. Generalization is facilitated to the degree that group leaders help the students make connections between previous and current training and see how the lessons have immediate applications in the authentic environment of the classroom and playground. For example, a role-play activity called "puppet taunting," first undertaken in Session 3, provides the students insight into the concept of self-instruction through the proxy of puppets. In Session 4, the skill is further developed by having group members taunt one another directly. Group leaders enhance generalization when they help the children make the connection through questioning along the lines of "How might this skill be useful later today at recess?" or "Think about the problem you had with Eliot this morning. How might this new tool help you when you see him later today?"

> *Tailor instructions to the developmental needs of the participants and be sensitive to gender and cultural differences and train skills that are ecologically valid. Training should build upon the trainees' strengths and abilities. (p. 10)*

Group leaders should have a deep understanding of the developmental levels of each of the group members when designing training tasks for execution in and out of the group setting. For example, younger members will have to rely more on behaviorally concrete "Do it like this" training, whereas some older group members may have the cognitive flexibility to imagine applications in hypothetical situations more effectively. Recognition of the overall cultural context of the school setting is critical so as to avoid in-group training that is disconnected from the real-life circumstances of the larger environment. The implicit recognition of informal but powerful "street codes" is essential to successfully generalizing certain lessons learned.

During the Training Activities

> *Ensure that the training tasks are tailored to the trainees' levels of competence, namely, slightly above the trainees' current ability levels ("teachable window" or work within the "zone of proximal development" or "zone of rehabilitation potential"). Skills to be taught should be broken down into identifiable parts. Trainers should use minimal prompts and fade supports (scaffold instruction), as trainees gain competence. (p. 10)*

Group leaders should be clear in their own minds about the nature and practical value of the skills that they are attempting to train. Discussions among the leaders that explore these issues can assist them in understanding how the training should best be conducted and paced. Group members will exhibit varying levels of readiness to learn, and ongoing progress across the group as a whole will often be uneven. Small-group remediation interventions call for patience and at times "differentiated instruction" to effectively address the needs of all of the students. Including extra time for individual training sessions as needed is also helpful.

Explicitly instruct on how to transfer. Use direct instruction, discovery-oriented instruction and scaffolded assistance (fade supports and reduce prompts as trainees' performances improve). Employ videotape coping modeling films as training material. Have the trainees make a self-modeling video of successfully performing the skills that they can watch. (p. 11)

Simply encouraging group members to apply their newly learned coping tools in the wider school setting is insufficient preparation for immediate success. Moreover, asking group members if they think that they can use a newly introduced skill in the general school environment and then watching them all nod their heads in the affirmative is also insufficient. Just as with learning other complex skills—such as reading or shooting a basketball—cognitive-behavioral anger management skills require insight, modeling, rehearsal, and feedback—and generally lots of it! Here is where one's active collaboration with the classroom teacher comes into play. Creating a self-modeling videotape is a key aspect of the Anger Coping Program, occupying a major portion of the last half of the intervention. In addition, group leaders can obtain a session-by-session modeling videotape created by the authors for use in training (by contacting *larsonj@uww.edu*).

Provide prolonged, in-depth training with repeated practice to the point of proficiency in order to ensure conceptual understanding. Facilitate skill practice and provide constructive feedback. The length of training should be performance-based, rather than time-based. (p. 10)

The Anger Coping Program has 18 sessions, but group leaders should not be bound to that number of meetings if schedules permit more. The idea is not necessarily to "complete" all the sessions but to help young people acquire a "toolbox" of cognitive-behavioral skills that can be flexibly and usefully applied to reduce problem behavior. In deciding when to terminate the training, group leaders should be guided by what they observe both in and out of the group meetings. Monitoring progress by means of such authentic variables as office referrals and classroom behavior data is often a better barometer of treatment efficacy than counting how many meetings have been held. In assessing treatment efficacy, leaders should keep in mind the old saying "Perfection is the enemy of 'good enough'." Group members' postintervention behavior need not be problem-free, but hopefully it will be sufficiently improved that less intensive schoolwide and classroom behavioral supports will be now be sufficient to manage it adequately.

At the Conclusion of Training

Put participants in consulting reflective roles. Following an experiential exercise have participants reflect on the activity (i.e., think about what they just did and what it meant, how can they use these skills in future situations). Have participants teach (demonstrate, coach) and explain verbally or diagrammatically (alone or with others) their acquired skills and transfer strategies. Have participants be in a position of responsibility, giving presentations to and consult with other beginning participants or younger individuals. (p. 12)

As the Anger Coping Program meetings come to a close, it is important that the group members take ownership of the changes they are making. They should be asked to put into their own words the reasons why they have selected new behaviors or new approaches to thinking about other individuals, problems, and school involvements. What positive benefits will come from making these changes? What are the possible barriers to both maintenance and transfer to other settings as time moves on? How will they address these barriers? It can be helpful to construct role plays or videotape a "TV commercial" with individual group members that will allow them to explain how and when they will use their new skills. Group members may also want to use strategically placed artwork or signage (e.g., "Stop and think!") to serve as aids in generalizing their newfound skills.

Have the trainee develop an explicit written relapse prevention plan and "trouble shoot" possible solutions to potential obstacles, barriers and responses to possible lapses. (p. 12)

Written relapse prevention plans help group members to identify high-risk situations and develop practical strategies for avoiding or successfully managing them. For example: "When I feel myself getting angry at recess, I will take a time-out and use my self-talk" or "I will continue to sit far away from Jeffrey at lunch." However, even the best plans are imperfect, and a lapse into old habits is a possibility that requires attention. The group's leaders should help members reflect on what it will mean if and when the problem behavior recurs. It is important that the students be able to see it as a need for more practice and new coping tools rather than evidence of their "badness." Support from the school administrator in charge of discipline, also reflecting this perspective, can be helpful.

Ensure that participants directly experience the benefits ("pay offs") of choosing new (non-aggressive) options. Ensure that trainees receive naturally occurring rewards. (p. 12)

It is a sad fact of school life that "bad" reputations acquired by students are hard to shake. Many of the children in the Anger Coping group will, in all likelihood, continue with some measure of inappropriate behavior even if their aggressiveness or bellicose behavior substantially diminishes during or following treatment. Consequently it is important for group leaders to rally significant adults in the school to the cause of reinforcing the new (if still somewhat flawed) pattern of behavior. For the students, simply "not getting into really serious trouble" often proves to be insufficient reinforcement if teachers and administrators are still constantly angry at them for lesser transgressions. Group leaders should request that teachers and administrators combine any necessary disciplinary measures with encouragement and support for continued improvement and that they actively promote spontaneous verbal reinforcers, positive letters home when warranted, and increased opportunities for participation in school events, even in leadership roles. Additionally, sustaining treatment gains will require that group leaders help their pupils find and connect with prosocial peers and engage in activities supervised by competent adults. The influence of antisocial peers, including gang members and drug abusers, increases significantly as children approach adolescence. Making connections to such organizations as the Boys and Girls Club, scouting, or

4-H Club can help engage group members with both new peers and supervising adults, as can increased involvement with athletic and specialized academic pursuits. Some children may require active and persistent encouragement and support to disengage themselves from familiar antisocial peers and activities, but eventually doing so is absolutely critical to their long-term success.

Use a graduation ceremony, involving significant others and include certificates of completion and appreciation. Provide booster sessions and ongoing follow-up group meetings. Have trainees reenter group training if they fail to handle lapses successfully. (p. 13)

When the training contained in the 18 sessions has been nearly completed, and performance indicators make weekly meetings no longer essential, group leaders should prepare members for the upcoming conclusion of regular meetings. Our experience has been that some sort of a graduation ceremony is highly appreciated by the children. This is a time when they can screen their videotape for assembled teachers, administrators, and parents and receive a certificate of completion from the group leaders. Booster sessions should be immediately scheduled, with the first two at 2-week intervals. Additional sessions in that school year are at the group leaders' discretion, but the newly "graduated" group members should be interviewed at the outset of the next academic year to assure them of ongoing support, relapse prevention advice, and problem-solving counsel.

THE CRITICAL ROLE OF TEACHERS AS COLLABORATORS IN GENERALIZING LESSONS LEARNED TO THE CLASSROOM

Lochman and Wells (1996) observed that children who have a history of objectionable behavior in the classroom typically create expectations on the part of the teacher that the bad behavior will persist over time. This impression creates a self-perpetuating cycle in which the teacher assumes that a particular child is responsible for any unexplained mischief that occurs, and he or she may automatically blame the child even in questionable circumstances. The unfairly blamed child then responds angrily, quickly transforming him- or herself from "victim" to "perpetrator" and thereby reinforcing the teacher's original belief. This common pattern of a vicious cycle makes it absolutely essential that the teacher become an active, full partner in the intervention process.

From a group leader's perspective, the Anger Coping Program brings together both *direct* and *indirect* intervention—the group leader working directly with the children in the treatment room and indirectly through the teacher in the classroom. For this combined approach to result in positive outcomes for the children, the group leader and the teacher must have a strong professional working relationship.

When school psychologists and other supportive services personnel engage in direct intervention efforts, it is not unusual for the child's classroom teacher to be relegated exclusively to the role of a clock-watcher who says to the child once a week, "Time to go to group." Not that this function is unimportant, but it hardly even registers in terms of the upside potential of the classroom teacher to actively participate in the change process. One of the principal factors that makes school-based therapy so viable and efficacious relative to clinic-based therapy is its location in the authentic setting (Coie, Underwood, & Lochman, 1991; Tharinger & Stafford, 1996).

Along with the obvious benefit of ease of access to the population of concern, the potential for generalization offered by conducting treatment in the school is considerable. School is where the children interact with one another and is a major arena for interpersonal aggression. Having ready access to the problematic individuals while they are within the problematic setting provides significant opportunities for creative, collaborative, and potentially generalizable treatment programs.

To upgrade the classroom teacher from "timekeeper" to true collaborator, the group leader must take into consideration two pertinent issues: (1) the skill and willingness of the teacher to become involved in classroom-level interventions and (2) the actual time the teacher has available to participate, given his or her myriad other responsibilities.

Experience has shown that most teachers are willing—sometimes eager—to assist in the treatment of children in their classrooms. However, it is a rare teacher who will spontaneously *volunteer* to work with a group leader unless the two have collaborated similarly in the past. Typically, the group leader—school psychologist or counselor—must initiate the collaboration.

The literature on school-based consultation is rich with discussions and recommendations for consultants attempting to establish effective working relationships with teachers (see, e.g., Brown, Pryzwansky, & Schulte, 1995; Conoley & Conoley, 1992; Marks, 1995). Some related points are addressed here.

Promoting an Egalitarian Relationship

Like the consultation between teachers and supportive services staff members for purely academic problems, the cooperation between teacher and group leader is a collaboration of two professionals, each with his or her own area of expertise. If the group leader attempts to enter this collaboration with the implied message "I'm here to rescue you from these difficult children," a potentially ruinous relationship based on the concept of the "expert therapist" and the "inadequate teacher" may evolve. The tendency for this skewed relationship to become firmly entrenched, particularly with new or less skilled teachers, is a serious concern. When a group leader enters a classroom and hears the teacher say "Well, guess what *your* kids did today!," then the time has come to reexamine the collaboration.

The group leader needs the teacher as an equal working partner in order to achieve success in the intervention. Communicating respect for the expertise that teachers bring to the collaboration is a critical feature leading to that desired partnership. Among other important skills, the classroom teacher has (1) a knowledge of the course and nature of the curriculum, (2) instructional abilities, (3) classroom discipline strategies, (4) an understanding of the interpersonal dynamics in the classroom, and (5) a knowledge of his or her own skill and willingness to participate in the intervention. Also important, the teacher has regular access to the child and influence over the child's behavior. The capacity of the classroom teacher to be an effective agent of change should not be underestimated.

Emphasizing Voluntary, Time-Limited Cooperation

One should assure teachers that their cooperation is voluntary and that the classroom aspect of helping will be limited, naturally, to that allowed by their available time and energy. If at all possible, one should avoid any implication that a "higher authority" (e.g., the principal or a powerful parent) is encouraging or requiring the intervention, as this perception might cause the teacher to view the intervention as just another "duty" that is being observed from above (and few teachers believe they have extra time for more duties). Likewise, a group anger management program should not be presented to the teacher as though it were some benevolent gift that the teacher has no choice but to accept (e.g., "I'm the school psychologist, and I'm here to do you a *really big favor*").

Instead, the most effective collaborations arise logically and systematically from the authentic situation. Because direct intervention is more "invasive" than indirect—in that the children must be *extracted* from the classroom environment for the treatment—it should be among the last interventions attempted. A pyramidal structure of intervention—with a schoolwide discipline plan at the base, working upward toward direct intervention near the top—exemplifies this principle (see Figure 3.1). Natural questions arise, such as: Has the teacher exhausted all the classroom-level interventions? Should this intervention be directed instead at enhancing teacher skills in an area such as classroom discipline or conflict resolution?

The amount of time a teacher must devote to his or her part of the intervention is a major variable in determining its acceptability to the teacher (Conoley & Conoley, 1992; Elliott, Witt, Galvin, & Peterson, 1984). Group leaders who themselves have never had responsibility for the day-to-day education of an entire classroom of elementary schoolchildren may have difficulty understanding a teacher's hesitancy to surrender even small amounts of time. While working as a school psychologist, one of us (Larson) was approached by a teacher who requested that he administer an intelligence and achievement test to all 32 of her second-grade pupils. Because it was September, she reasoned that the data would be a helpful guide in her instruction as the year progressed. This well-meaning teacher was ignorant of the other demands on the school psychologist's time and may not have understood either his initial look of horror or his attempts to gently suggest an alternative strategy.

In a similar way, nonteaching support personnel must respect classroom teachers' ownership of their available time. An honest estimate, based on experience if possible, should be provided so that teachers can realistically assess their availability to participate. For example, the group leader might say the following:

"In my experience, teachers have found that an extra 10 minutes per day is the average time they have devoted to the Anger Coping Program responsibilities, with perhaps a little more on our meeting day."

Or:

"Since the group is just beginning, we are not sure yet what the time commitment will be. Can we see how the first week goes and make any adjustments we feel necessary at our next meeting?"

It is also important to be open to teachers' conclusions about what they can or cannot do. When teachers say "I'll do *this*, but I don't think I have time to do *that*," they almost always mean it. Trying to persuade a reluctant teacher to agree to additional intervention time creates a genuine danger that he or she might assent to an unrealistic commitment. A collaboration in which one partner believes that he or she is working too hard is not a healthy situation for either party.

THE GENERALIZATION LINK: THE GOAL SHEET PROCEDURE

A central feature of the Anger Coping Program involves the development by the individual group members of classroom behavioral goals. It is through this critical aspect of the intervention that a bridge between the group room and the classroom is fostered. In the program manual contained in Chapter 8, the entirety of the second session is devoted exclusively to instruction and practice in developing and writing personal behavioral goals. Each subsequent session opens with an evaluation of how the children are progressing toward these goals. Attained goals are replaced with newer ones.

A goal is defined for the group members as meeting the following two criteria: (1) something you want and are willing to work for and (2) something that is real and possible for you.

The training involves helping group members devise classroom goals that address behaviors that are both currently problematic but within their ability to reshape in a positive direction. Overbroad, ill-defined goals such as "I will not get into any trouble" are rejected in favor of more specific, behaviorally defined goals such as "I will remember to ask permission to get out of my desk during seat work time." The goals are written on individual Goal Sheets and delivered to the classroom teacher at the conclusion of each group session.

The group members' goals are the major training link to generalizing behaviors to the authentic setting. The question of whether a group member has or has not attained his or her goal is the sole domain of the classroom teacher who signs the Goal Sheet (see Appendix F for the form) at the conclusion of each school day. This makes it essential that each goal, as derived and defined by the child, be clearly expressed and pertinent to teacher concerns. A goal devised by a child that the teacher sees as meaningless or too easy among the child's larger constellation of problematic behaviors will work against both generalization and teacher cooperation. For instance, a child may express a goal of "no fighting in the classroom for at least 4 out of 5 days," only to have the teacher confirm later that historically the child's problem has been at recess and never in the classroom.

Identifying Goals through the Teacher Interview

To help ensure that the children will be using the Goal Sheet procedure to address classroom behaviors that their teachers agree are problematic, a pregroup conference between group leaders and the classroom teachers is essential. This conference should occur once the final roster of group members has been solidified and before the first group meeting, and during this meeting the role of the Goal Sheet in the intervention should be thoroughly explained to the teachers:

"If you will recall from our previous discussion of the Anger Coping Program curriculum, the children will be learning how to develop personal behavioral goals at our second meeting. This is a very critical aspect of our effort because it serves as one of the major bridges between what we are doing in the group room and what you are doing in the classroom. To facilitate the children's goal development, it will be helpful for you to give me some guidance regarding the nature of their problems in your classroom. If I understand your concerns, I can more easily help guide the children toward useful, appropriate goals."

Group leaders are urged to familiarize themselves with techniques of behavioral interviewing (e.g., Busse & Beaver, 2000; Kratochwill & Bergan, 1990) and, if necessary, goal development (e.g., Fuchs, 1995; Meichenbaum & Biemiller, 1998). Teachers of children with externalizing behavior problems often have a difficult time expressing their concerns in terms amenable to intervention. "He never does what he is supposed to do, he's always out of his seat, blows up at everything, and he can't keep his hands to himself" expresses the teacher's frustration adequately but provides only minimal guidance for behavioral goal setting. Once teachers have described the problematic behaviors in their own terms, group leaders should encourage them to focus their concerns in a more behaviorally oriented way.

> GROUP LEADER: It certainly sounds like Michael is quite a handful. I am glad we have decided to work together on his problems. You mentioned that he doesn't comply with your directions, hits other children, aggravates the hamster with his pencil, and pushes and shoves in the recess line. Are those the problems of greatest concern to you?
>
> TEACHER: Yes, along with never finishing his seat work in math.
>
> GROUP LEADER: Okay, considering those problem behaviors, when you say that he "doesn't comply with your directions," what do you mean by that? Can you provide me with a typical example?
>
> TEACHER: I guess I mean that he is the slowest one in the class to comply with what I want students to do. I'll say, "Take your social studies book out," and 5 minutes later Michael is still engaged in whatever we were doing previously.

Group leaders should work through the teachers' concerns in such a manner as to acquire a useful behavioral definition of the problem. For example:

> "In unstructured settings such as recess, Michael will strike another child with his fists when upset or frustrated an average of three times a week."
> "Michael will have to be told to keep his hands out of the hamster cage an average of once a day."
> "Michael gets out of his seat without permission an average of four times an hour during seat work periods."

Once these "topographical" descriptions of the behavior are agreed upon, the group leader should determine which of the behaviors the teacher believes to be within the ability of the child to self-monitor and exert some control. *It is important to note that the behaviors need not of necessity be aggressive or anger-induced to be appropriate for the goal-setting activity, particularly at the outset.* Aggressive externalizing children often have a host of disruptive, poorly socialized behaviors that contribute to their overall problematic adjustment in school. The goals may address not only aggression toward peers but also social skills with peers, oppositional and disruptive behavior, and failure to complete various school tasks (Lochman & Wells, 1996). The objective of the goal-setting activity—again, particularly at the beginning of the intervention—is to provide the child with an opportunity to move him- or herself in a positive social direction through his or her own self-control efforts. Because Michael has been referred to the anger control group to *learn* anger and aggression management, it makes little sense to expect it from him early on. If, however, during the initial weeks he succeeds in reducing his out-of-seat behavior during seat work time, this can be viewed by all parties as a positive social and academic gain. As training in the group progresses, those goals should become more directly associated with anger and aggression management. Appendix C (Classroom Goals Interview) provides a useful teacher interview format for determining overall classroom goals for each student enrolled in the intervention.

When at least one primary classroom goal has been agreed upon, that goal may be selected for use as a part of the overall program evaluation through use of the Goal Attainment Scaling Form (Appendix G). This is a simple procedure for monitoring progress on a regular basis that yields data that can be analyzed for effectiveness. Group leaders should begin this process before the start of the group. A discussion of the procedure is found in Chapter 13.

Collaborative Mapping of Responsibilities

Ensuring that teachers have a sense of ownership in the Tier 2 intervention at the outset by involving them systematically in both the student selection process and in goal development is the first important step. The next step is to educate them regarding their specific roles. For teachers to take on these roles as true collaborators, it is necessary for them to know certain specifics about the intervention. Although this comment might seem obvious, it is too frequently the case that psychologists and counselors do not share the specifics of the treatment with classroom teachers. It may well be that some supportive service people prefer to maintain a certain "mystique" about what happens in the treatment room, or, more likely, it may be that they have never perceived the need to be more forthcoming with teachers. The group leader and the classroom teacher, as a collaborative team, need to be as informed as possible about what is happening in each other's environment. Role plays and behavioral rehearsals in the treatment room that are directly related to actual classroom situations are more useful to the child than those that are unrelated. Similarly, in the classroom the teacher is more able to accurately observe and reinforce a newly acquired treatment behavior if the teacher knows what to look for and expect.

For teachers of students in the Anger Coping Program to facilitate generalization to the real-world environment, it is critical to provide them with an adequate understanding of the goals, objectives, and procedures of the intervention. The following approach may best enable group leaders to accomplish this task:

1. Schedule a period of 30 minutes to 1 hour during the week before the sessions begin to gather together all of the teachers who will have students in your Anger Coping Program group. A group meeting is preferable because teachers can share concerns with one another, and it saves time for all.

2. Provide the teachers with a handout that summarizes the objectives of each session and offers suggestions for facilitating the generalization of skills to the classroom (see Appendix E for a partial example). If the *Anger Coping Video* (Larson, Lochman, & McBride, 1996) is available, it can be screened to provide a helpful visual aid for selected sessions.

3. Preview the various sessions in order, discussing the objectives and soliciting ideas for mutual assistance—for example, "How can we best help one another so that the intervention is most effective?" or "How might this skill be transferred to the classroom setting?"

4. Solicit input from the teachers regarding treatment group behavior management strategies with the children identified for the intervention. Their knowledge of the children can prove valuable and may enable initial meetings to proceed more smoothly. Knowing ahead of time, say, that Manuel is instantly angered by Jason's chronic teasing about his father, or that Samantha responds very well to adult praise, can be useful input.

5. Make arrangements to meet with each teacher individually prior to the start of the first group meeting in order to gather behavioral data for the goal-setting aspect of the collaboration.

Once classroom teachers have knowledge of the goals and structure of the Anger Coping treatment and have shared their concerns and ideas, their ability to function collaboratively with the group leader is much improved. Our experience is that some teachers will welcome the new challenge and others will be less enthusiastic. Group leaders must always keep in mind that the subject students were referred initially because their teacher viewed them as problematic, and the remaining enrollees once the selection process is completed are typically the *most* problematic. It takes little imagination to understand why a teacher, besieged with the needs of a classroom full of other children, cannot usually match the group leaders' enthusiasm in addressing the needs of the one or two most disruptive students in his or her classroom.

THE TEACHER AS GROUP CO-LEADER

Implementing the anger control group in a small-population classroom for students with emotional/behavioral disabilities can be an efficient and effective way of addressing some of the children's behavioral problems. In such a scenario, the classroom teacher is an ideal candidate for the role of co-leader in partnership with an experienced school psychologist or counselor.

One of us (Larson) encountered the opportunity to participate in such an arrangement while working as a school psychologist in a large elementary school. Following a presentation to the general faculty on the roles of the school psychologist, including a brief discussion of implementing anger control training, he was contacted by one of the special education teachers. Her nominated class consisted of fourth- and fifth-grade students who had been diagnosed with emotional/behavioral disabilities. She had a resource-type classroom, into which various groups of students came and went during the day, depending on the instructional settings described in their IEPs.

The teacher approached the school psychologist with particular concerns regarding a group of children whom she saw for a 2-hour block daily for math and science instruction. She described the children as generally impulsive, quick to anger, and quick to fight. The teacher was concerned because so much of her time was being diverted to physically restraining students or putting herself between a pair of potential combatants that very little math or science was being taught or learned. These patterns of behavior were also carried over into the general education inclusion classes and onto the playground. She wondered whether she could collaborate on an anger control program with her entire classroom of students.

The school psychologist observed the classroom and reviewed the existing assessment information in the special education folders. Clearly, five of the children were a handful and were everything the teacher described them to be. A sixth boy and a single girl, who completed the classroom population, were much more inhibited and withdrawn than the other five. Parental consent for additional assessment was obtained for the five aggressive children. The teachers of the general education inclusion classroom were asked to complete a broadband classroom rating scale on each child, and parents were asked to complete the home version. The resulting data, although somewhat variable among the children and demonstrating some anticipated differences between settings, was supportive of significant externalizing difficulties in the school setting for each child.

Because the students were in special education, an IEP team had to be convened for each student in order to approve the adjustments in the plan for the Anger Coping Program and to provide an alternative instructional setting for the two children who would not be involved. At those meetings the intervention was explained to the parents, and informed consent was obtained.

The classroom teacher had a solid training foundation in behavior modification techniques but needed to learn the procedures in the Anger Coping Program before the program could begin. Before the start of the school day, the school psychologist helped the classroom teacher to learn the intervention. It was decided that the school psychologist would take the role of the skills trainer while the teacher would take up the role of managing group behavior.

Fortunately, this teacher was a truly outstanding co-leader. Her deep knowledge of the children and the skills she learned and applied as a behavior manager within this setting were a perfect complement to the skills of the school psychologist. Although no "publication-ready" behavioral data were obtained on the effectiveness of this intervention, the teacher was clearly pleased with the effects, and a graphing of discipline reports demonstrated a trend in a positive direction. Anecdotal reports from the general education classroom teachers were also encouraging.

When working with a teacher as a co-leader in "ready-made" groups such as the one described, group leaders should keep the following in mind:

1. For students who are protected under the Individuals with Disabilities Education Act, additional approval procedures are required prior to implementation of any behavioral intervention not already defined in the students' IEPs. This can be a time-consuming task that the teacher may not have anticipated.

2. Be certain that the teacher has cleared his or her schedule for the period of the intervention and knows that it must be maintained for the duration. As busy as most teachers are, it is tempting for them occasionally to double-schedule the time slot for other obligations, knowing that their co-leader will be with the class. Although this may be the innocent move of an overworked educator, it can have a disruptive influence on the group.

3. Help the teacher to avoid problems with his or her dual role as both the students' teacher and the group's co-leader. Being able to "take off the teacher's hat and put on the co-leader's hat"—mentally leaving behind any previous interpersonal classroom problems—can sometimes be a real challenge.

4. Remember that it is ethically irresponsible to involve a child in an intervention for whom an assessment has not indicated a need. Take care *not* to allow *any* students to "sit in" on the group just because they happen to be assigned to a particular classroom at the time scheduled for the anger control program. It may indeed be true for some that "it won't hurt them any," but psychological or counseling services are not properly delivered under those terms. Alternative programming consistent with the IEP or other educational plan should be provided to the stranded students.

5. Our experience is that co-leaders can successfully lead a group of as many as seven students. A single leader is advised to limit his or her group to four or five students.

OBTAINING PARENTAL CONSENT

The need to obtain the informed consent of parents or legal guardians prior to delivering direct therapeutic intervention services to children in the school setting is well established within the profession of school psychology (National Association of School Psychologists, 1984). Although school psychologists tend to routinely obtain consent for intervention services, this may not be the practice of other school-based professionals. Because of the comparatively invasive nature of this intervention—assessment and periodic removal from the academic setting over an extended period of weeks—it is our bias that informed consent prior to implementation of the anger control program is essential. Readers are referred to Jacob-Timm and Hartshorne (2007) for a comprehensive discussion of the numerous legal and ethical issues surrounding the subject of informed consent.

A sample consent form is included in Appendix H. This format will work as a mailed consent letter in the event that the parent is unable to come to the school, or, preferably, it can be used as the final signature sheet following an in-person explanation. Schools should modify this sample to meet their own local needs.

CHAPTER 6

Preparing for the First Meeting

Procedures to Implement and Pitfalls to Avoid

In this chapter we discuss some of the "nuts and bolts" issues involved in making the group function as smoothly as possible. The insights and suggestions in this chapter are drawn not only from our own experiences in conducting the Anger Coping Program and related interventions but also from those of the numerous interns whom we have supervised and from practitioners' feedback at advanced training sessions. Clearly many "wheels" have already been invented, and we hope to spare the reader the task of having to invent them all over again.

THE GROUP ROOM

To say that available space to run counseling groups in school buildings is a prized commodity may be an understatement. Those who have been asked to conduct psychological or counseling services in converted storage closets, book rooms, stage areas, and old basement staff lounges ("What's that smell?") know of what we speak. It often seems that supportive services personnel are at the bottom of the room and space allocation hierarchy in the school building. Even when a decent office exists, the act of trying to stuff a group of children into a space best fitted for individual services invites the kind of trouble so frequently associated with overcrowding—further intensified by the presenting problems of externalizing children. All the desire and know-how needed to conduct therapy groups is useless if there is no place to implement the intervention.

Ideally, the group area should be large enough for four to seven children to be seated, with abundant space between them to discourage physical contact. In addition, the space should provide enough "moving around" area to conduct activities and role plays. School personnel without their own large office space may have to become creative. The following building locations have been used by previous Anger Coping groups and are noted here as suggestions:

- A classroom emptied for a weekly library, art, or physical education period
- The gym or a multipurpose room, with portable dividers used for a corner area
- The stage area
- The cafeteria
- The conference room
- The nurse's office

A good group room setup is thoughtfully designed in much the same way that a good classroom is arranged. The goals in both cases are to minimize antecedent conditions that might help foster disciplinary problems while enhancing those that might help promote personal self-control and wider participation by all group enrollees. Group leaders are urged to approach this matter of the instructional environment seriously and systematically, as it can either pay off handsomely or punish one's efforts in the end. The leaders should carefully examine the prospective space with an eye toward creating a counseling environment well suited to encouraging self-control.

To the greatest extent possible, the room should be a low-stimulus environment. This requirement may mean placing distracting toys, games, and other items out of sight during the period the group is in session. Drapes or blinds should be drawn to minimize the possibility of outside distractions. Portable room dividers can also serve a useful purpose in that regard, providing both a space delimitation and a shield against potentially distracting stimuli. Ambient sounds are more difficult to control within any school building, but meeting times carefully chosen to not conflict with recess and other times characterized by mass student movement can alleviate that problem. One intern who conducted a group in a relatively noisy part of a building played classical music at a low volume within the space. She reported that, while the effect on the children was both modest and unclear, the effect on her was both positive and significant!

Experience has shown that the most advantageous seating arrangement has the chairs placed in a semicircle, with one leader at the opening of the circle and the other seated midway through the circle. Retaining ample space between the chairs is very important, to discourage the impulse for even playful physical contact. Taped lines on the floor to indicate intended chair spacing can be a useful device that gives group members a sense of each having his or her own area.

Some groups may be successfully positioned around a large table, but such an arrangement has distinct drawbacks. Tables in therapy situations have traditionally been seen as offering "psychological protection" for the client that is absent when the chair is in the open. (Note that normally the TV talk show host sits behind a desk while his or her guests typically do not.) Whether or not this latter notion has merit, the table *does* offer abundant unmonitored space beneath it for kicking and other mischief. In addition, tables can too easily turn into headrests, game boards, or drum surfaces, creating potential distractions for everyone. Group leaders who find themselves forced to use a table will have to provide students with additional structure and training to help them avoid attendant problems.

BEHAVIORAL MANAGEMENT STRATEGIES

Group counseling with highly externalizing children provides an opportunity for them to learn how to function adaptively in a controlled, safe, rule-governed environment. They have been assessed and found to have behavior repertoires that are incompatible with many of the stimulus demands of the classroom. The group environment creates a miniworld with stimulus demands that are designed to be more easily learned and assimilated. Along with the anger management and problem-solving skills that are part of the training, the child in the Anger Coping group also learns how to modify and adapt his or her behavior to meet the demands of the setting. In doing so, the child gains experience and practice in the controlled setting that can be used in efforts at generalizing new perceptions to the classroom setting. For all of this to happen, a systematic program of external consequences and self-management strategies must be designed by the group leaders.

A key phrase is "simple but effective." Complex, elegantly conceived behavioral plans may look good on paper, but they often wither under the reality of fast-paced group interactions and competing stimuli for the group leader's attention. Skill training is difficult enough without the additional stress of trying to remember and implement an overcomplicated management strategy that may be more intrusive than effective. Our experience has been that groups work most effectively when the management strategy stays in the background, operating beneath the skills training and not competing with it for the group members' attention. When everything grinds to a halt so that the group leader can engage in a dispute with a child about whether points (or stickers or candy) were or were not earned, then the management strategy has intruded too far into the training.

In the Anger Coping Program, a simple operant reinforcement strategy and a response cost strategy work in tandem. Simply stated, group members are reinforced for targeted behaviors that are to be increased, and they experience mild aversive consequences for targeted behaviors to be decreased. These targeted behaviors are kept relatively few in number and make intuitive sense within the framework of a smoothly running group.

Recall that *positive reinforcement* is the presentation of a consequence immediately following a behavior that increases the likelihood of that behavior being repeated (Kazdin, 2001). If the consequence has no subsequent effect on reproducing the desired behavior, it is not really a reinforcer. For example, a child may be presented with a sticker following a desirable behavior, but if the probability of that behavior's being repeated does not then increase, the sticker is not a reinforcer. Similarly, a child may be presented with a smile or a "high-five" following a desirable behavior, and if the probability of the behavior's recurring increases, then the consequence (whether a smile or high-five) is a reinforcer. It is not unusual to hear inexperienced therapists complain that a child "is not responding to the positive reinforcement." That complaint is a contradiction in terms in that, if there is truly a positive reinforcement, *by definition* it must have a subsequent effect on behavior. The therapist most likely has just not identified a true positive reinforcer.

POINTS AND STRIKES

Points

In the Anger Coping Program, we have found that desirable behavior is best encouraged and strengthened through use of a point-based token system. A token system uses tokens or "points" that serve as conditioned reinforcers exchangeable for more tangible backup reinforcers (Miltenberger, 1997). The basic components of a token system include identifying the following:

1. The tokens that will be used as conditioned reinforcers
2. The desirable target behavior that the group leaders want to strengthen
3. The backup reinforcers or tangibles that will be exchanged for the tokens
4. A reinforcement schedule for delivery of the tokens

Simply acknowledging and recording points in a designated spiral notebook as they are earned is the least obtrusive way to award the tokens (e.g., "I like the way you helped Raymond solve that problem, Hector. That's a point"). Group leaders can pair their verbal praise with a nonverbal signal, such as lightly touching their nose, and eventually fade the verbal praise to the extent desired. Approaches that are more complex—and thus somewhat more open to problems—include using manipulatives such as poker chips, playing cards, or play money as tokens. Our experience with manipulative tokens is that they often give rise to intrusive counting and comparing among the group members. On the other hand, many veteran therapists have skillfully used manipulative tokens effectively in other contexts and can easily adapt the procedure to the Anger Coping Program. We are aware of one group leader who used playing cards presented face down for points and then at the end of the exercise granted a bonus point to the child with the winning poker hand.

Regardless of the procedure, leaders should maintain a visible running total on a poster board or other medium. Group members will always be interested in how many points they have earned. It is recommended that leaders not waste valuable group time entering the figures from prior sessions during current sessions but instead do it themselves ahead of time. (However, one of our interns had the children enter their own totals weekly onto a computer spreadsheet program with reported success.)

There is a final caveat. As with any behavioral intervention, if the procedure works, use it; if it doesn't, change it. Don't adhere doggedly to an ineffective behavior management approach just because it was the one that seemed appropriate at the beginning. Monitor the effects, and make adjustments as necessary.

In the Anger Coping Program, group members typically can earn points for the following:

1. **A smooth transition from the classroom to the group room.** This is an often-overlooked but important element in that it serves the dual purpose of setting the proper behavioral tone for the initiation of the day's work and prevents difficulties with school personnel who might be encountered on the way to the group room. We have found this transition phase important enough to encourage leaders to actually practice the transition with the children prior to the first group meeting.

2. **Cooperation and participation in the group.** This important criterion for awarding points enables group leaders to reinforce targeted group behaviors that they wish to increase. Active participation, cooperating with others, ignoring another's misbehavior, and positive leadership can be immediately reinforced. In Session 1, group members are asked to identify positive behaviors to be encouraged. Providing the opportunity for group members to have a true voice in the establishment of the rules of behavior enables them to assume a level of ownership of group behavioral norms and minimizes future adult–child power struggles (Lochman, Whidby, et al., 2000).

3. **Signed Goal Sheet brought to the group.** Group members need to remember to bring the sheets on which they have written their weekly goals (see Session 2 description in Chapter 8), and this is a task that often requires considerable assistance from adults. Providing a point incentive is a part of this effort.

4. **Excused absence points.** We have found that granting 2 or 3 points gratis if a group member is forced to miss a meeting for an excused reason avoids the unhappiness that comes with falling too far behind the others in point totals.

5. **Smooth transition back into the classroom.** This is always appreciated by teachers, and the points are awarded by the group leader as observed following each session. The criteria for earning transition points to and from the classroom should be should be collaboratively devised with the teacher and fully explained to the group members.

The point system serves the dual purpose of reinforcing desirable behavior and providing an opportunity for the group members to learn to manage delayed gratification. We have found that having a time set aside for exchanging points for tangible backup reinforcers approximately every fifth session maximizes the value of the system. Group leaders should acquire a variety of tangibles such as pencils, pens, notebooks, and other teacher-approved items for "purchase" at these times. Our experience has been that school personnel are often quite willing to donate these items to the cause; as an alternative, large department store chains and fast-food restaurants rarely need little more than a request on school letterhead to provide free-of-charge items or gift certificates. Group leaders are advised to be certain to obtain school approval for all tangible reinforcers, however. A final "grand prize"—such as a pizza party or popcorn and movie—contingent on the cumulative group total as determined by the leaders, is often very well received and encourages positive peer support for points earned. Figure 6.1 lists many ideas for free or low-cost incentives that have been used at times by Anger Coping group leaders in the Chicago public schools.

We wish to make one additional observation regarding points. Group leaders should be alert to variations in individual behavioral baselines among the children. For example, some children are skilled vocal participants, and if "positive verbal participation" is a criterion for awarding points, such children are capable of accruing a disproportionate number of points. Use the point system to help each child grow from his or her own *current* skill level. In other words, avoid overreinforcing those children who already have the requisite skills to earn points while underreinforcing those who have fewer skills. Leaders should keep a flexible "bar" and raise or lower it according to their own clinical judgment in order to bring the group along with as much overall parity as possible among group members.

Tangible Rewards • Music (CD burn) • Tattoos (temporary!) • Pencils/notebooks • Water bottles • Carnival prizes • Jerseys/school spirit items • Snacks	Adult Relationship Rewards • Lunch with a leader • Reading with the principal • Messenger for the teacher • Interview principal • Extra time with teachers • Extra time with leader (preparation/helper/lunch) • Time with volunteer "artists"/local celebrities • Principal/maintenance helper • Time with teacher who shares a common interest (music, art, poetry, etc.) • Coffee clubs/breakfast club or "cocoa and cookies" with leaders/teachers or principal
Experiential Rewards within the Group • Dodgeball game • Door monitor • Longer lunch • Classroom jobs (in group or in classroom) • Help in setting up • Movie, music—special activity in the group • Free time (games/art/creative) • Gym, play game outside	Special School/Group Recognition • "Wall of Fame" (if approved) • Special mention in the school paper • Special acknowledgment from principal • Special mention in announcements • A commendatory letter sent home • Read morning announcements on public address system
"Free Passes" • Free activity ticket for class • Pass for recess • Pass to help younger students • Dress down (no uniform/out of uniform pass) • Computer time • Basketball/football game or school dance passes • Study time	Online • *www.donorschoose.org*—A website that will allow group leaders to post their funding needs online

FIGURE 6.1. Low-cost or free incentives for groups.

Strikes

Working in tandem with the "positive" point system is a "negative" response cost procedure (Kazdin, 2001) known in the Anger Coping Program as "strikes." In assessing response cost, contingent negative behaviors are identified, and the individual loses access to a reinforcing condition upon their presentation. Removing access to a favorite toy in response to misbehavior is a common example of response cost. In the Anger Coping Program, group members are allowed three chances to engage in undesirable behavior at the outset of each meeting (three strikes) before losing the opportunity to stay in the group for the day (the reinforcer). The criteria for losing a strike are decided by the group at the first meeting and are generally some form of a "negative opposite" of the positive points already discussed (e.g., disruptive behavior, aggression, teasing, noncompliance, etc.). Once again, it is important to fully engage group members in the discussion of strikes so that they have the same sense of ownership as they do with the point system.

The group leader is the final and unassailable arbiter of whether a strike is called. Leaders are advised not to engage in a power struggle with a transgressing child. If the child violates the rule, state the violation in a matter-of-fact tone and call the strike. Avoid excessive warnings such as "Jason, I'm telling you for the last time. If you do that again, I will call a strike on you."

Of course, leaders should make an effort to keep their own irritation and anger under control at all times, using the strike as feedback rather than an expression of exasperation. At the outset, in particular, it is important to be consistent, predictable, and clear. Gently but firmly calling strikes as they occur early on in the training can pay huge dividends later. As noted by Lochman, Whidby, et al. (2000), "This early 'detoxification' of corrective feedback helps defuse aggressive children's tendencies to overpersonalize adult feedback and respond with oppositional or challenging behavior" (pp. 66–67).

Using various manipulatives to keep an accurate count of strikes is recommended so that the student is visually assisted in the effort to monitor his or her own behavior. Previous successful methods include:

1. Placing three pencils in a cup in front of each child and pulling one for each strike.
2. Placing three playing cards or three strips of tape on the floor in front of each child and removing one for each strike.
3. Writing each child's name on the chalkboard and placing three checks beside each name, then erasing one check for each strike.

If the child has three strikes called, that child should be escorted back to the classroom. *Under no circumstances should the child be able to negotiate the option of remaining with the group for that day* (although it is our experience that most will try). Leaders should always keep in mind that following through on an aversive consequence for one child presents a social learning opportunity to the others. In other words, they are all watching to see what happens. Occasionally the calling of the third strike will provoke the child to demonstrate anger or obvious upset. In such a case, if the child needs time to calm down before returning to class, he or she should be escorted to a neutral, nonstimulating third location, such as the administrator's office. Of course, never return an upset, angry child to the classroom.

Group leaders should avoid the inclination to comingle points and strikes by, for example, offering a point to those who do not have any strikes called for an entire session. Leaders should provide points only for the observed expression of desirable behavior, not just for the absence of undesirable behavior (see Figure 6.2 for a summary of point and strike possibilities). A child who sits stoically and pouts for an entire session, though not disrupting, surely is not engaging in desirable behavior worthy of reinforcement.

Children earn POINTS for:
- A smooth transition from the classroom to the group room
- Cooperation and participation in the group
- Bringing a signed Goal Sheet to the group session
- An excused absence
- A smooth transition back into the classroom
- Other desirable behavior observed by group leaders

Children earn STRIKES for:
- Verbal or physical aggression or threats
- Teasing or harassing
- Noncompliance with the group leader's request(s)
- Other undesirable behavior as decided by the group or group leaders

FIGURE 6.2. Point and strike possibilities.

CHILDREN WHO NEED EXTRA SUPPORT

Some children with entrenched oppositional or highly volatile behaviors may struggle with the points-and-strikes system and provide the leaders with a genuine behavior management challenge. If the leaders find that after two or three sessions a particular child has been an extraordinary management problem and persistently disruptive to the group process, action must be taken. Ranging from the least to the most serious, the following options should be considered:

1. Confer with the child individually to determine whether there are some minor changes that can be made to accommodate him or her. Sometimes such ecological issues as the placement of chairs, the fear of another member, or reluctance to be called on can stimulate misbehavior. Occasionally some children are so frightened of being called on to speak that they will deliberately misbehave to keep that possibility at bay. Assuring the child that he or she will not be pressured into participating unwillingly can often address this problem successfully. Consider the function of the misbehavior. Is the child trying to avoid or acquire something? Is the child misbehaving so that he or she will be returned to a preferred setting? Is the attention that comes with misbehaving reinforcing to the child?

2. Bring influential others into the problem, such as parents, teachers, an administrator, or another favored adult. Encourage their vocal and enthusiastic support of the child's appropriate behavior in the group setting. Consider a weekly "report card" to a favored adult.

3. Draw up an individual behavioral contract (e.g., Kazdin, 2001) that identifies the specific behaviors to be increased or eliminated and the consequences that will follow. For some children, more frequent and more powerful reinforcers that go beyond those available to other group members may be necessary. Any concerns by the other group members about perceived unfairness should be addressed in the context of understanding individual differences.

4. Remove the child from the group altogether. Some children are simply not emotionally, developmentally, or behaviorally ready for a highly stimulating interactive group therapy experience. Indeed, such an experience may be contraindicated, as it may contribute to the child's problem behavior rather than diminishing it. Once other efforts have been exhausted, do not hesitate to remove the child and seek an alternative intervention. This course of action, although unfortunate, is certainly preferable to (as one inexperienced therapist put it) "hoping each group day that the kid will be absent from school."

USE OF VIDEO: PLANNING AND LEGAL ISSUES

A major portion of the Anger Coping Program is given over to addressing deficient problem-solving skills among the group members. This task is accomplished by teaching a stepwise model of problem identification, solution generation, and consequence prediction. During the latter sessions of the program, the major vehicle for this learning process is the production of videotaped scenarios for which the group members write, rehearse, and videotape their own conflict situations for later viewing and analysis. Well before these sessions, it is recommended that the group leaders take time to secure a camera, as they are often in great demand in some schools. In addition, those who may be unfamiliar with the mechanics of video recording are advised to take time to become comfortable with the technology. A headache prevented is one more that does not have be suffered.

Importantly, group leaders should be certain that they have the necessary consents to videotape the students in their group. This requirement can be a thorny issue in the new age of easy online uploads of digital media, and parents may be rightly concerned. Our suggestions are as follows:

- It is recommended that a separate parent/guardian consent form be used for videotaping consent, one that is distinct from the general intervention consent. This precaution will increase certainty that the parent or guardian's signature is truly informed.

- The consent form should describe the purpose of the videotape as a means of helping the children learn, practice, and demonstrate their new skills. Include who will see the finished video, and provide information about future viewing opportunities for parents or guardians.

- Inform the parents/guardians that personal copies will not be made and the original will be destroyed.

- Have the form reviewed by system legal counsel and clarify whether, for your district, the completed video will be considered "school records" covered under the Family Educational Rights and Privacy Act (FERPA). This may have implications for parental rights to a copy of the video.

- Refuse to make copies for anyone, whether children or parents/guardians. Unless there is a legal need to retain it, destroy the original, and delete all traces from the camera's memory.

- Never use a finished videotape as a promotional tool for future groups. The *Anger Coping Video* available from the authors can be used for this purpose. (See the end of Chapter 12 for information on how to obtain this video.)

The next chapter acquaints the reader with relevant outcome research for the Anger Coping Program and its sister intervention, the Coping Power Program.

CHAPTER 7

Outcome Research Results for the Anger Coping Program and the Coping Power Program

There have recently been efforts to identify empirically supported treatments and prevention programs for a variety of types of developmental psychopathology, including externalizing conduct problems in children. Kazdin and Weisz (1998) have identified three groups of promising treatments for children with externalizing behavior problems. In addition to parent training (Patterson et al., 1992) and multisystemic therapy (Henggeler, Melton, & Smith, 1992), cognitive problem-solving skills training has been found to produce significant reductions in aggressive and antisocial behavior. As part of task forces on effective psychosocial interventions, Brestan and Eyberg (1998) and Eyberg, Nelson, and Boggs (2008) reviewed the intervention research on children with conduct problems and concluded that the Anger Coping Program was a promising cognitive-behavioral intervention for children with aggressive behavior problems. Similarly, Smith, Larson, DeBaryshe, and Salzman (2000) conducted a meta-analysis of anger management programs for children and youth and concluded that the Anger Coping Program was among the few with both strong design and research support. In this chapter we review the empirical evidence supporting the effectiveness of the Anger Coping Program and describe the Coping Power Program, which is currently being examined in several outcome research studies.

ANGER COPING OUTCOME RESEARCH

Empirical Evidence for the Anger Coping Program

A preliminary uncontrolled study of a school-based Anger Control Program for 12 aggressive children in the second and third grades showed significant posttreatment reductions in teacher-reported aggressive behavior and trends indicating reduced teacher checklist ratings of acting-out behavior (Lochman, Nelson, et al., 1981). These improvements in children's aggressive behavior were accompanied by increased teachers' daily ratings of children's on-task behavior in the classroom. All of the children were African American and lived in single-family homes in a low-income urban neighborhood. The children met with a graduate student therapist twice a week for 12 sessions. These findings spurred a programmatic series of subsequent studies comparing the further refined Anger Coping Program with alternative interventions as well as untreated control conditions (Lochman, 1990).

In a subsequent study, 76 aggressive boys from eight elementary schools were randomly assigned to anger coping (AC), goal setting (GS), anger coping plus goal setting (AC + GS), or untreated control (UC) groups (Lochman, Burch, Curry, & Lampron, 1984). The boys were identified as aggressive based on teacher checklist ratings. The boys were in the fourth through the sixth grades; 53% were African American and 47% white. They participated in a 12-week Anger Coping group program based on the earlier Anger Control Program. The boys met in weekly group sessions, lasting 45–60 minutes, in their elementary schools. Groups were co-led by university-based project staff (psychologists, social workers, psychology interns) and school counselors based at each school. Goal setting was conceptualized as a minimal-treatment condition and included eight group sessions in which the boys set weekly goals for classroom behaviors and received contingent reinforcements for goal attainment. In comparison with the UC and GS conditions, aggressive boys in the anger coping cells (AC, AC + GS) displayed less parent-reported aggressive behavior, had lower rates in independent observers' time-sampled ratings of the boys' disruptive classroom behavior, and tended to have higher levels of self-esteem at posttreatment. The addition of a goal-setting component, in the AC + GS group tended to enhance the treatment effects of the program (Lochman, Burch, et al., 1984), indicating that behavioral goal setting can increase the generalization of cognitive-behavioral intervention effects. Boys in the AC group who had the greatest reductions in parent-rated aggression were those who initially had higher levels of peer rejection, more comorbid internalizing symptoms, and the poorest problem-solving skills (Lochman, Lampron, Burch, & Curry, 1985). The last-mentioned variable was a particularly important predictor of treatment effectiveness because boys with the poorest social problem-solving skills in the UC condition were likely to have increasingly higher levels of aggressive behavior by the end of the school year.

The effects of the Anger Coping Program have been found to be augmented by the use of an 18-session version of the program, in comparison with the earlier 12-session version (Lochman, 1985). In this quasi-experimental study, 22 teacher-identified aggressive children were included in an 18-session version of the Anger Coping Program (with more emphasis on perspective taking, role playing, and more problem solving about anger-provoking situations) and were compared with the boys who had been in the 12-session program in the Lochman, Burch, et al. (1984) study. With the longer 18-session program, aggressive boys displayed significantly greater improvement in on-task behavior and greater reduction in passive off-task behavior, illustrating the need for longer intervention periods for children with chronic acting-out behavior problems.

However, in two other studies of the effects of variations in delivery of the Anger Coping Program, the addition of a five-session teacher consultation component (Lochman, Lampron, Gemmer, Harris, & Wyckoff, 1989) and a self-instruction training component focusing on academic tasks (Lochman & Curry, 1986) did not enhance intervention effects. Lochman, Lampron, Gemmer, et al. (1989) had randomly assigned 32 children (average age = 11 years) to anger coping, anger coping plus teacher consultation, or an untreated control condition. Lochman and Curry (1986) assigned 20 teacher-identified aggressive boys (average age = 10 years, 3 months) either to anger coping or to anger coping plus self-instruction training. In both studies, the school-based groups lasted for 18 weekly sessions, and the boys in the anger coping conditions displayed reductions in parent-rated aggression (Lochman & Curry, 1986), reductions in teacher-rated aggression (Lochman, Lampron, Gemmer, et al., 1989), improvements in perceived social competence and in self-esteem (Lochman & Curry, 1986; Lochman, Lampron, Gemmer, et al., 1989), and reductions in off-task classroom behavior (Lochman & Curry, 1986; Lochman, Lampron, Gemmer, et al., 1989). The Lochman, Lampron, Gemmer, et al. (1989) findings, in comparison with an untreated control condition, replicated the earlier positive effects for the Anger Coping Program evident in the Lochman, Burch, et al. (1984) study.

In another study of child characteristics that predict intervention outcomes, Lochman, Coie, Underwood, and Terry (1993) found that a social relations program that included anger coping and social skills training components had a significant impact at postintervention and at a 1-year follow-up with aggressive rejected fourth-grade children but not with rejected-only children. Relative to control conditions, the intervention outcomes with aggressive rejected children were reductions in peer-rated and teacher-rated aggressive behavior. This study involved an African American sample from an inner-city area. The result indicated that the intervention was successful because it appeared to influence the mediator variables associated with children's aggressive behavior but did not influence mediator variables associated with nonaggressive peer rejection.

In addition to the consistent findings from this series of studies indicating that the Anger Coping Program can produce reductions in children's aggression in the home and school settings at the end of intervention, and the Lochman, Coie, et al. (1993) finding that an Anger Coping Program with social skill training components can lead to sustained improvement at a 1-year follow-up, two other studies have examined the follow-up effects of the Anger Coping Program. Lochman and Lampron (1988) conducted a partial follow-up of the Lochman, Burch, et al. (1984) sample in four of the eight schools. In the follow-up sample 21 boys had been included in the Anger Coping Program, and 10 had been in the untreated control condition. When children's classroom behavior was examined at a 7-month follow-up, the boys in the Anger Coping Program had significantly improved levels of independently observed on-task classroom behavior and significant reductions in passive off-task behavior.

At a 3-year follow-up when the boys were 15 years old on average, those who had received the Anger Coping Program training ($N = 31$) exhibited lower levels of marijuana and drug involvement, lower rates of alcohol use, and had maintained their increases in self-esteem and problem-solving skills (Lochman, 1992) in comparison with those in an untreated control condition ($N = 52$). Boys who were followed up were highly similar in baseline measures of peer aggression nominations and social status ratings to boys who were not available for follow-up. These results indicate that the Anger Coping Program produced long-term maintenance of social-cognitive gains and important prevention effects on adolescent substance use. Boys in the Anger Coping Program functioning in these domains were within the range of a nonaggressive comparison group ($N = 62$), indicating the clinical significance of these positive effects. However, boys in the Anger Coping Program did not have significant reductions in delinquent behavior at follow-up, and their reductions in independently observed off-task behavior and parent-rated aggression were maintained only for a subset of boys who had received a brief six-session booster intervention for themselves and their parents in the school year following their initial anger coping group. Thus, across multiple controlled intervention studies, this child-centered cognitive-behavioral intervention reduced children's disruptive behaviors immediately after treatment and provided important preventive effects on adolescent substance use. Booster interventions in subsequent years may lead to less dissipation of treatment effects on children's overtly aggressive or disruptive behavior.

Effects of the Dissemination of the Anger Coping Program

The next stage of intervention research with the Anger Coping Program assesses the program's impact when it is conducted in the field by trained school personnel rather than the program developer's trained staff. In this dissemination phase, program developers provide training to school staff and assist with the evaluation, but the program is completely implemented by school staff. As part of a Safe Schools grant, the Wake County (North Carolina) public school system provided anger coping training to all of the school psychologists and school counselors in the system (Lochman, Rahmani, 1998). The training consisted of three full-day workshop training sessions in the spring and summer prior to implementation of the program, monthly 2-hour large-group consultation sessions during implementation of the program, and two telephone "hotline" hours per week during implementation of the program. The ongoing consultation and hotline hours were believed to be essential in assisting staff in successfully handling both routine and unexpected problems encountered by school staff during the implementation of the program. Each group was co-led by a school counselor and a school psychologist, and four to six children were typically assigned to each group. Groups began in the fall of the school year and continued through the spring.

Children were identified for inclusion in the Anger Coping Program on the basis of referral from regular education teachers, who selected them based on high rates of physically and verbally aggressive behavior and disruptive classroom behavior. Children in self-contained special education classes were not included in the groups, but mainstreamed special education students were eligible. Forty-one anger coping groups were begun at 40 elementary schools, providing service to 200 aggressive children. Pre- and postintervention self-report data were obtained from 161 students. Postintervention data were not obtained from students who moved from their schools ($N = 11$) or from students who could not be assessed by the end of the school year ($N = 28$). Because of the limited resources available to pursue nonreturned measures, the rates of completion of pre- and postintervention teacher data ($N = 119$) and of parent data ($N = 51$) were lower.

The 161 students with at least partial post-data had an average age of 9.8 years, ranging in age from 8 to 12 years. Some 150 of these children were male, and 11 were female.

Eighty-one were of minority racial status (primarily African American). Some 46% of these children received free or reduced-cost lunches, indicating a relatively high rate of low-income children. Some 41% were receiving special education services (35 had a learning disability, 7 had a behavioral or emotional handicap, 13 were academically gifted, and 11 had other, health-related, problems).

The design of this evaluation consisted of pre–post assessment of children selected for intervention without a control group. However, multiple sources of information about the children's behavior and social competency were obtained to "triangulate" the effects and reduce the likelihood that changes would be simply due to a single-source bias or to artifacts of measuring. A 1-year follow-up of children's academic progress was also performed.

The pre–post analyses indicated that the Anger Coping Program had effects on the relevant mediating variables that should have been affected by the program (Lochman, Rahmani, et al., 1998). Children in the anger coping groups displayed significant improvements in their ability to generate competent solutions to social problems on a measure involving vignettes of hypothetical social problems with peers, teachers, and parents. By postintervention, they evidenced a higher rate of verbal assertion, compromise, and bargaining strategies. They also showed a reduction in their rate of irrelevant problem solutions, indicating that they had improved their cause–effect reasoning in social situations. This reduction in irrelevant problem solutions parallels one of the problem-solving outcomes found in the earlier 3-year follow-up study of anger coping outcomes (Lochman, 1992) and indicates that the problem-solving training in the Anger Coping Program appears to be producing an anticipated effect.

Children in the anger coping groups also showed significant improvements in self-reports and teacher reports of their social competence. Teachers rated the children as being better able to calm down when upset, to recognize their feelings, to handle conflict in more adaptive ways, to cooperate with peers, and to interact in fair ways with peers. The children themselves, on a measure of perceived competence, perceived that they had become more competent in their interactions with peers and more accepted by their peers.

These changes in the children's social competence and social-cognitive skills were accompanied by positive improvements in the children's behavior. Parents reported that the children's externalizing problem behaviors had declined by postintervention, and teachers' ratings indicated that the children's social problems and attention problems had decreased. Teachers reported that 85% of the children displayed at least some reduction in aggressive and disruptive behaviors. Because parents also rated the children as having significant reductions in attention problems, the Anger Coping Program appears to assist children in better focusing their attention in appropriate ways at home and at school. These changes in attentional control may have partially mediated the reductions in externalizing behavior problems, as indicated by the significant correlation between these change scores.

The children's academic achievement was assessed by a state-created achievement measure. The children included in the Anger Coping Program had a 12% improvement at the 1-year follow-up in their rates of grade-level achievement in mathematics and reading, and this improvement was significantly higher than the systemwide improvement rate over the same time period. These children were also found to have a significantly lower rate of increase in school suspensions than was evident for other children their age in this school system. The academic gains at the 1-year follow-up suggest that the children's improved behaviors by the end of the intervention may have contributed to their improved attention and motivation in their class work, which may in turn have led to increased academic achievement. The relative improvement in their school suspension rate suggests that the children's behavioral improvements had generalized over time.

COPING POWER PROGRAM AND OUTCOMES

Coping Power Child and Parent Components

The Coping Power Program (Lochman, 2003; Lochman & Wells, 1996) is a lengthier multicomponent version of the Anger Coping Program designed to enhance outcome effects and to provide for stronger maintenance of gains over time. Session-by-session treatment manuals and workbooks are available for both the child and parent components (Lochman, Wells, & Lenhart, 2008a, 2008b; Wells, Lochman, & Lenhart, 2008a, 2008b). Two case studies have indicated how the program has been delivered to individual children (Boxmeyer, Lochman, Powell, Yaros, & Wojnaroski, 2007); Lochman, Boxmeyer, Powell, Wojnaroski, & Yaros, 2007). The Coping Power Program has added sessions to the basic Anger Coping Program framework to create a Coping Power Program Child Component (for a total of 33 group sessions), addressing additional substantive areas such as emotional awareness, relaxation training, social skills enhancement, positive social and personal goals, and peer pressure. The Child Component addresses the social-cognitive deficits identified in prior studies. It focuses on (1) establishing group rules and contingent reinforcement; (2) using self-statements, relaxation, and distraction techniques to cope with anger arousal; (3) identifying problems and social perspective taking with pictured and actual social problem situations; (4) generating alternative solutions and considering the consequences of alternative solutions to social problems; (5) viewing modeling videotapes of children becoming aware of physiological arousal when angry, using self-statements ("Stop! Think! What should I do?"), and the complete set of problem-solving skills with social problems; (6) the children planning and making their own videotape of inhibitory self-talk statements and social problem solving with problems of their own choice; (7) enhancing social skills, involving methods of entering new peer groups and using positive peer networks (with a focus on negotiations and cooperation in structured and unstructured interactions with peers); and (8) coping with peer pressure.

Other elements of the Coping Power Program Child Component include regular individual sessions taking place monthly between a child and one of the group leaders that are designed to increase individualized generalization of the program content to the children's social situations. The individual sessions are used primarily for monitoring and reinforcing children's attainment of classroom and social behavior goals (e.g., avoiding fights with peers, resisting peer pressure) and for coping with specific attributional biases and social problem-solving deficiencies the children have had in recent social conflicts with peers, teachers, or parents. The individual sessions can also be important in helping to create productive, positive working relationships between each of the children and the group leaders, thus enhancing the positive reinforcement value of the adult group leader. Periodic case-centered consultation is also provided to the teachers of children who are making some progress in group sessions but who are still having recurrent behavior problems in school.

The Coping Power Program also has a Parent Component that is designed to be integrated with the Child Component and to cover the same 15- to 18-month period of time. The Parent Component consists of 16 parent group sessions. Parents meet with the two co-leaders either in groups of 10 to 12 or in parent pairs. Repeated attempts are made to include fathers as well as mothers in parent groups. For some sessions, the school counselor may also be able to join the leaders in presenting material relevant to greater parental involvement in the school.

The content of the Coping Power Program Parent Component is derived from social learning theory-based parent training programs developed and evaluated by prominent clinician-researchers in the field of child aggression (Forehand & McMahon, 1981; Patterson et al., 1975). Over the course of the 16 sessions, parents learn skills for (1) identifying prosocial and disruptive behavioral targets in their children, using specific operational terms; (2) rewarding appropriate child behaviors; (3) giving effective instructions and establishing age-appropriate rules and expectations for their children in the home; (4) applying effective consequences to negative child behaviors; (5) managing child behavior outside the home; and (6) establishing ongoing family communication structures in the home (such as weekly family meetings).

In addition to these "standard" parenting skills, parents in this project also learn skills that support the social-cognitive and problem-solving skills that the children learn in the Coping Power Program Child Component. These parent skills are introduced at the same time that the respective child skills are introduced so that parents and children can work together at home on what they are learning. For example, parents learn to set up homework support structures and to reinforce organizational skills around homework completion just as children are learning organizational skills within the Child Component. Parents also learn techniques for managing sibling conflict in the home as children begin addressing peer and sibling conflict resolution skills in the group. Finally, parents learn to apply the problem-solving model to the family's situation so that the skills learned by children in the group will be promoted and reinforced within the family context. Children enrolled in the school group who (for lack of an available baby-sitter at home) also attend the parent group on family problem solving have usually already learned the problem-solving model approximately halfway through their schooltime sessions. These children and their parents are able to role-play the problem-solving skills in the parent group, getting excellent practice themselves and modeling them for the other parents.

A final section of the Coping Power Program Parent Component includes sessions on stress management for parents. Part of the rationale for this subject matter is to help parents learn to remain calm and in control during stressful or irritating disciplinary interactions with their children. Parents also receive small stipends for attending parent group meetings. Thus, the Parent Component addresses the mediating factors of parental engagement and children's social-cognitive processes.

Parents are informed of the skills their children are working on in the school sessions and are encouraged to facilitate and reinforce the children's use of these new skills. The Coping Power Program Parent Component also includes periodic individual contacts with the parents through home visits and telephone calls to promote generalization of the skills learned.

Empirical Evidence for the Coping Power Program

Efficacy Study

In an initial efficacy study of the Coping Power Program, Lochman and Wells (2002a, 2004) randomly assigned 183 aggressive boys (60% African American, 40% white non-Hispanic) to one of three conditions: a cognitive-behavioral Coping Power Program Child Component, Combined Coping Power Program Child and Behavioral Parent Training Components, and an untreated component. The two intervention conditions took place during the fourth and fifth grades or the fifth and sixth grades, the intervention lasting for 1.5 school years. Screening of risk status took place in 11 elementary schools and was based on a multiple-gating approach using teacher and parent ratings of children's aggressive behavior. The at-risk boys were in the top 20% of all the students in the classroom according to teacher ratings of the aggressive behavior of their students.

Analyses of outcomes at the time of the 1-year follow-up indicated that the intervention cells (Child Component only; Child plus Parent Components) have produced reductions in children's self-reported delinquent behavior, and parent-reported alcohol and marijuana use by the child, as well as improvements in their teacher-rated functioning at school during the follow-up year, in comparison to the high-risk control condition (Lochman & Wells, 2004). Results indicated that the Coping Power Program intervention effects on lower rates of parent-rated substance use and of delinquent behavior at the 1-year follow-up, in comparison to the control cell, were most apparent for the children and parents who received the full Coping Power Program with child and parent components. In contrast, boys' teacher-rated behavioral improvements in school during the follow-up year appeared to be primarily influenced by the Coping Power Program Child Component. Mediation analyses, using path analytic techniques, indicate that the intervention effect for both of the intervention cells on the delinquency, parent-reported substance use, and teacher-rated improvement outcomes at the 1-year follow-up were mediated by intervention–produced improvements in children's internal locus of control, their perceptions of their parents' consistency, children's attributional biases, children's person perception skills, and children's expectations that aggression would not work for them (Lochman & Wells, 2002a).

Effectiveness Studies

Given these positive findings from the prior efficacy study, the next research questions examined whether the Coping Power Program has similar positive effects in other settings and with personnel who are more equivalent to typical school and agency staff. Several types of effectiveness and dissemination studies have been conducted with the Coping Power Program, indicating intervention effects on children's aggressive behavior and problem-solving skills among aggressive deaf children in a residential setting (Lochman, FitzGerald, et al., 2001), as well as on the overt aggression of children with oppositional defiant disorder or conduct disorder in Dutch outpatient clinics in comparison to care-as-usual children (van de Wiel et al., 2007). Long-term follow-up analyses of this sample 4 years after the end of the intervention indicated that the Dutch version of the Coping Power Program (Utrecht Coping Power Program [UCPP]) had preventative effects, reducing as it did adolescent marijuana and cigarette use by Coping Power children in comparison to the care-as-usual children, although long-term effects were not found on alcohol use. These rates of substance use by the UCPP children were within the range of typically developing Dutch adolescents (Zonneyville-Bender, Matthys, van de Wiel, & Lochman, 2007). Analyses of the cost effectiveness of UCPP found that the Coping Power Program produced reductions in children's conduct problems at the end of intervention for 49% less cost than in a care-as-usual condition (van de Wiel, Matthys, Cohen-Kettenis, & van Engeland, 2003).

In a larger-sample effectiveness study, the effects of the Coping Power Program (the combined Child and Parent Components) as an indicated preventative intervention directed at high-risk children were examined along with the effects of a universal classroom-level preventative intervention (Lochman & Wells, 2002b). A total of 245 male and female aggressive fourth-grade students were randomly assigned to one of four conditions. Children were selected from 17 elementary schools, and the study had a greater proportion of schools located in inner-city high-poverty areas than was the case with the earlier efficacy study. Intervention began in the fall of the fifth-grade year and was delivered by personnel more equivalent to counselors and social workers in school settings, with higher caseloads and less opportunity for home visits. At postintervention, the three intervention conditions (Coping Power alone; Coping Power plus Classroom intervention; Classroom intervention alone) produced lower rates of substance use than did the control cell (Lochman & Wells, 2002b). Children who received both interventions displayed improvements in their social competence with peers, and their teachers rated these children as having the greatest increases in problem-solving and anger coping skills. The Coping Power Program also produced reductions in parent-rated and teacher-rated proactive aggressive behavior as well as increases in teacher-rated behavioral improvement. A 1-year follow-up of this sample replicated the findings of the prior efficacy study. Coping Power children were found to have lower rates of self-reported substance use and delinquency and lower levels of teacher-rated aggressive social behavior at school than control children (Lochman & Wells, 2003).

Dissemination Study

Finally, a study of the dissemination of the Coping Power prevention program funded by the National Institute on Drug Abuse has been implemented in a field trial in 57 schools within five school districts. This field trial is examining whether the Coping Power prevention program can be usefully taken "to scale" and delivered in an effective manner by existing staff in a range of urban school sites within Tuscaloosa, Alabama, and the Birmingham, Alabama, metropolitan area. In this field study, existing school staff members (school counselors) have been trained to use the Coping Power Program with high-risk children at the time of transition to middle school.

During screening, third-grade teachers were asked in the spring of the year to rate how reactively and proactively aggressive all of the children in their classes were using a six-item scale. Based on these ratings, we determined the 30% most aggressive children across all classes. Consent was obtained for 531 (79% of those contacted) of these participants, and they were assessed at baseline; 65% being males, 84% African Americans, 14% Caucasians, and 2% of another race or ethnicity. Retention was 95% at postintervention assessment 2 years after the baseline assessment. The field trial randomly assigned counselors in 57 elementary schools to one of three conditions: Coping Power—Intensive Training for Counselors (CP-IT), Coping Power—Basic Training for Counselors (CP-BT), or care-as-usual comparison. Nineteen schools were in each condition, with 183 children in CP-BT, 168 children in CP-IT, and 180 in control groups. The Coping Power Program was delivered during the fourth- and fifth-grade years.

Counselors in both conditions for training of the Coping Power Program attended a 3-day initial workshop in the fall prior to the beginning of the intervention and participated in monthly ongoing training sessions (2 hours) in which the trainers provided concrete training for upcoming sessions, debriefed previous sessions, and problem-solved about barriers and difficulties involved in the implementation of the program. The counselors in the CP-IT condition had two additional training elements. First, individualized problem solving about barriers and difficulties in the implementation of the program was available only to school site intervention staff in the CP-IT condition through a technical assistance component. This component included access by the implementation staff to an email account in which the members could raise implementation concerns and problems and through which they could receive trainers' responses, and also included a telephone "hotline" in which trainers were available for telephone consultation about these same concerns. Second, research staff coded the audiotapes of child and parent group sessions for completion of objectives and quality of implementation.

A first set of research questions involved whether the counselor and school characteristics were related to the implementation of the Coping Power Program. Indicators of quality of implementation (quality of engagement by counselors with children in child groups and with parents in parent groups, rated from audiotapes of sessions); program delivery (as indicated by the proportion of sessions' objectives completed and by the number of sessions scheduled) have been examined using research assistants' ratings of audiotapes of sessions (Lochman, Powell, et al., 2009). Two broad categories of predictor factors, school-level characteristics and individual interventionist characteristics, were explored in this study. Counselors' agreeableness and conscientiousness were positively associated with facets of the implementation process, including the number of sessions scheduled and the quality of engagement with children and parents. Counselors who were cynical about organizational change and who were in schools that had rigid managerial control and little autonomy for school professional staff were less likely to implement the program with the requisite degree of high quality. Counselor characteristics and school climate characteristics were both linked to the counselors' ability to implement the intervention with a high level of quality.

In hierarchical linear modeling analyses, the intensity of training provided to counselors has been found to have a notable impact on outcomes, with children of intensively trained counselors having significant lower levels of externalizing behavior relative to control children, according to parent, teacher, and youth ratings (Lochman, Boxmeyer, et al., 2009). Children who had worked with intensively trained counselors also had better social and academic skills at school and improved social-cognitive abilities. Children who received intervention from only minimally trained counselors did not demonstrate behavioral improvement. Significant behavioral improvements only occurred when the Coping Power training was provided in an intensive way, with immediate feedback to counselors from audiotapes of sessions.

We have collected information about the sustained use of the Coping Power Program 1 year after completion of training for the first cohort of counselors. Some 83% of the counselors continued to use at least portions of the Child Component of the Coping Power Program in the next year, with the greatest use of the components addressing goal setting, peer relationships, organizational and study skills, and emotional awareness and management. Counselors had found it more difficult to get parents to attend parent sessions during the field trial, and the counselors had lower rates of sustained use of the Parent Component of the Coping Power Program, with 55% of counselors using at least some portion of the parent program. Overall, it appears that counselors are generally sustaining use of most of the Child Component of the program, with some adaptation, providing policy-level support for the importance and utility of training regular school counselors in these procedures (Boxmeyer, Lochman, Powell, Windle, & Wells, 2008).

CONCLUSION

Overall, these results support the efficacy of the Anger Coping Program and of the related Coping Power Program. These programs produce immediate postintervention effects on children's aggressive behavior at home and in school and on their social competence and social-cognitive skills. The programs' effects on social-cognitive processes have been maintained through a 3-year follow-up, and their effects on children's behavioral problems have been maintained through follow-ups up to 4 years after the end of intervention. The Anger Coping and Coping Power programs have produced significant reductions in children's substance abuse and have notable preventive effects in this area of negative adolescent outcomes. Booster interventions in subsequent years appear to be important in sustaining children's behavioral improvements. This series of outcome studies indicates the value of using these interventions in school-based settings to reduce the conduct problems of preadolescent children.

In addition to the inclusion of booster programs in subsequent years, other possible methods for enhancing the effectiveness of the Anger Coping Program, and of related cognitive-behavioral programs for aggressive children, have been suggested (Lochman, Dane, et al., 2001). First, group leaders have to be sensitive to negative group processes. In regard to selecting group members, we believe that the potential for creating a productive group increases when group members have at least some motivation for working on their anger management difficulties and when the group contains at least some group members who can be solid peer models of how to enact more competent verbal assertion and negotiation strategies. During the course of the intervention, a positive group process can be enhanced by maintaining clear rules and consequences for group behavior, by reinforcing children for positive prosocial behaviors outside the group, by transferring a child from group to individual intervention when necessary, and by developing positive therapeutic bonds between group leaders and the children.

Second, intervention research indicates that cognitive-behavioral interventions with aggressive children produce broader positive effects and better maintenance of behavioral improvements over time if they address both children's social-cognitive processes and parents' parenting practices than do interventions that focus on children or parents alone (e.g., Kazdin, Siegel, & Bass, 1992; Webster-Stratton & Hammond, 1997). Interventions that have both child and parent components can address a wider set of risk and protective factors than interventions with single components (Lochman, 2000a). Preventative interventions for children at high risk for early-starting conduct problems can address the children's school context, academic skills, and social competence and parent-interaction skills across multiple years from elementary school through early high school (Conduct Problems Prevention Research Group, 1992, 1999a, 1999b, 2004).

Third, the anger coping intervention should be individualized in several ways (Lochman, 2000b). Even though there is a guiding social-cognitive model indicating the targeted goals for this structured intervention, the intervention should be adapted to address the specific social-cognitive deficits and strengths of the specific aggressive children being helped. As we learn more about meaningful subtypes of aggressive children (e.g., Dodge et al., 1997), we can generate individualized treatment plans that emphasize certain aspects of the Anger Coping Program more than others for particular children. In addition, the Anger Coping Program can be flexibly delivered by adjusting the structured protocol to meet emerging clinical issues. When children begin discussing a current or recently encountered social problem, group leaders can respond by shifting to a problem-solving set, and modeling and reinforcing problem-solving skills directly, rather than rigidly sticking to all of the planned activities for the day. It is critical that group leaders keep the longer-term objectives of the programs uppermost in mind so that their flexible responses can more readily have a direct strategic impact on the specific targeted social-cognitive difficulties of the children in their groups.

The next chapter presents the Anger Coping Program in session-by-session detail, with a complete manual for its implementation along with group leader guidelines that should prove helpful.

CHAPTER 8

The Anger Coping Program Manual

What follows in this chapter is the complete updated text of the Anger Coping Program, including new individual session-by-session "notes" and helpful hints for group leaders. This newest version of the intervention is closely adapted from earlier manuals found in Lochman, Lampron, et al. (1987); Lochman, FitzGerald, and Whidby (1999); and Larson and Lochman (2002).

The term *session*, as used in this manual, should not be confused with *meeting*. "Sessions" contain the goals and objectives to be met, but very often multiple "meetings" are required to position the group to be ready to move on to the next session. Group leaders should concentrate on developing skills without undue concern about the time required, and they should avoid rushing the curriculum. For instance, scheduling an additional meeting time each week in order to "finish early" is highly discouraged. It is much better to extend the intervention further into the school year, maintaining the students' support and learning over time. In addition, there is no set time limit for a group meeting, but we have found that a minimum of 45 minutes per week is needed to accomplish a reasonable amount of training, given the time needed for transitions.

As leaders become familiar with the entire manual, it will become clear that flexibility and clinical judgment are important components. Very few "scripts" are presented that detail everything the leader should say or the students should do. Rather, objectives and training guidelines make up the bulk of what follows, and leaders are left to adapt them to the individual training experience. Most of the answers to "What should I do?" and "Did I do this correctly?" may be found by consulting one's own common sense and clinical experience. Maintaining clear, useful progress notes at the conclusion of each meeting and engaging in active co-leader debriefing help immeasurably in that regard. Some helpful questions to ask each other are:

- "What went well, what did not, and do we know why?"
- "What did we learn about the group dynamics and individual members that will assist us next time?"
- "Are we following our behavior management program as designed? Does it need to be adjusted?"
- "Are we ready to move on to the next session, or is more time needed on the current objectives?"

A session-by-session guide to help ensure treatment integrity is available in Appendix N.

The following manual assumes that group leaders have read the earlier portions of this book thoroughly, in which much information for a successful group experience can be found.

SESSION 1. INTRODUCTION AND GROUP RULES

Group Leaders' Notes

Have the group leaders:

- Completed all assessments?
- Secured informed parental consents?
- Consulted with the classroom teacher(s) to establish a collaborative effort?
- Informed administrator(s) of the group's purpose and the specific students enrolled?
- Prepared a behavioral management plan?
- Discussed and/or rehearsed transition behaviors with group members? (See Appendix I for a complete checklist.)

During this session, it is important to convey the purpose of the group, set up its rules and structure, have the members and leaders become familiar and fairly relaxed with one another, and begin to focus on perceptual and thinking processes. All these objectives may be difficult to accomplish in one session. As with all of the following sessions, *it is not necessary that all objectives for a session actually be completed within one meeting*; instead, an uncompleted objective can be carried over to the following meeting. Our experience is that such carryover is more often the rule than the exception. Leaders should be more concerned with skill development than with any need to adhere to any preset schedule. As in most therapy with children, it is all-important to make the experience *enjoyable*. Solid pregroup preparation increases that likelihood, as do plenty of smiles, verbal praise, and (we have found) a special treat at the meeting's conclusion.

Materials

A ball for pass-the-ball.

Session Content

Objective 1. Present the Group's Purpose and Structure

A. Present the group as a way to learn anger control or self-control, or use some other key words or phrase that can be a descriptive slogan of sorts. You may want to discuss how people in general sometimes have problems controlling their anger, or their tempers, moving toward the specific kinds of problems these children have. Encourage group members to volunteer examples of their own problems with anger control.

POSSIBLE SCRIPT: Welcome to Anger Coping. For the next few months, we will be meeting here every week to learn new ways to solve problems and how to get along better with everyone in school. In this group, we will be learning about how to control our anger. Let me see the hands of everyone who has ever gotten really angry at someone else. Right, everyone at sometime gets angry, and everyone at sometime loses his or her temper. That's why it's really important for us to learn how to control our own anger, and that's what this Anger Coping group is about. Now, who can give me an example of an incident when his or her lack of anger control created a problem?

B. Issue a statement about the time, frequency, and number of meetings of the group program and give a preview of some of the activities.

RULES

C. Discuss the need for group rules, and invite group members to suggest rules they think are appropriate. Areas to include are confidentiality, physical contact, paying attention and participating, proper demeanor, and so on. It is helpful to write the rules on poster paper or something that can be displayed each session and to convey them in an affirmative way to the greatest extent possible (e.g., "Keep your hands and feet to yourself" rather than "No physical contact").

POSSIBLE SCRIPT: People who work together in a group need rules to help them do their best job. What rules to you have in your classroom? ((In turn:) Why do you have that rule?) Okay, so now tell me: Why do we need rules for this group? Right, rules help prevent problems when people obey them. What are some rules that we should have for our group?

POINTS AND STRIKES

D. Discuss the group behavioral contingency system, both for rewards and response costs. As we discussed in Chapter 6, offering the opportunity during the group session to earn and lose *points* that can later be exchanged for a tangible reward or activity generally works well. Leaders may give some kind of token during group activities for good participation—such as checkers, playing cards, or pick-up sticks—that can be accumulated as points. Similarly, leaders can call *strikes*, which can also be accumulated to lose a point and may lead to a time-out if necessary. Points can also be accumulated by the group as a whole to earn a group reward, such as special treats or an activity of the members' choosing. (Figure 6.1 contains a list of suggested free or low-cost reinforcers.) Some permanent means of record keeping for points will also be needed, either a poster board or computer graphing program.

Objective 2. Get Acquainted

Make sure all group members and leaders know one another by name. If the enrollees are new to one another, a quick way of introducing everyone is to play a pass-the-ball game, with each member holding the ball until he or she can name the person to the immediate right and then giving his or her name and passing the ball, in turn, to the left.

Objective 3. Focus on Individual Perceptual Processes

A. Play the pass-the-ball game, with each person having to name something the same (e.g., "We're both boys") and something different (e.g., "He's taller") about the person who passed the ball to him or her. Continue the process until each member has had a turn.
B. Appendix O contains optional stimulus pictures—or leaders will have picked out one "DUSO" (American Guidance Service, 2001) or *Second Step* (Committee for Children, 2001) type of stimulus picture—that will be shown to the group but not discussed. Give the instruction that each member is to describe what he or she sees happening in the picture, putting the description on tape. Have the tape recorder in a location away from the group, and give each member a turn. After all have recorded their impression, have the group listen to the tape and then discuss:

- " Did everyone see the same thing?"
- "What similar things did people see? What different things did people see?"
- "Was there only one right way to see the picture?"
- "Can this be true in real life, too? Can people see the same thing differently?"
- "Who can give me an example of two people seeing the same event differently?"

Alternate procedure. Record the group members' responses to the stimulus picture individually in a meeting prior to the first group session, and have the tape ready to play. This approach is particularly recommended for groups with only one leader.

Provide Positive Feedback and Optional Free Time

- Have each group member identify one positive characteristic about him- or herself and/or one positive characteristic about another group member. Try to avoid compliments just about clothing. Model appropriate compliments, as needed.
- Following this activity, tally the points earned during the session. Members earning at least 1 point may be given free playtime if the schedule permits. Leaders should use this time to observe for possible conflicts and assist the members in using "prob-

lem solving in action." Reinforce any prosocial behavior that is observed (e.g., sharing, resolving conflicts appropriately).

Note. It may be that some or all of the members will get excited or upset during some of the sessions to come. It is very important throughout the remainder of the sessions that the leaders take steps to make certain that the children return to their classrooms in a "cooled-down" state. Free time or low-key structured play can serve as a transitional buffer well, as can 30–40 seconds of slow controlled breathing. Creating specific "transition points" to prepare the students for appropriate classroom return behavior may be a useful add-on, and teachers will definitely be grateful for the consideration.

Leaders: Debrief and Complete Case Notes

SESSION 2. UNDERSTANDING AND WRITING GOALS

Group Leaders' Notes

This session begins the goal-setting process (continuing throughout the Anger Coping Program) that enhances the transfer of treatment effects into the classroom. Goal setting and goal attainment monitoring help provide the real-life experiences of focusing on and dealing with problems within the classroom. In addition, the problems raised can often generate discussions and role plays during the group sessions. Goal setting also involves teachers more closely with the program and provides a very concrete indication of progress (see the section "The Generalization Link: The Goal Sheet Procedure" in Chapter 5).

Preplanning

Design a Goal Sheet (or use the model provided in Appendix F) that will be practical and workable in your school setting. Simplicity is helpful, and having teachers initial the sheet only once during the day is usually most feasible. Collaborate with each teacher who will be monitoring goals to explain the goal-setting and monitoring process, to explain how the Goal Sheet is to be filled out, and to ask for suggestions as to the goals the teachers would like the student to be working on. It is very important to convey an openness to the teachers' input and to make the goal-setting procedures as convenient for them as possible. Make it clear that the child is responsible for his or her Goal Sheet and for asking the teacher to initial it; the teacher is not responsible for remembering to do it. Some veteran teachers, wary of the forgetfulness of children and eager to collaborate, may want to infuse more structure to ensure a successful experience. This arrangement is perfectly acceptable if it is what the teacher prefers.

Because the Goal Sheets are one of the principal vehicles for the generalization of skills learned, care must be taken to ensure that group members understand the process. Leaders should not necessarily assume that each child understands what a "goal" is—nor even that the child understands why altering his or her preferred behavior to meet a goal is desirable.

Modeling goal setting and attainment from the leaders' own lives is a useful training procedure. Modeling should sometimes include instances of failure and coping with that failure by adjusting the goal(s). Differentiate between a child's "dream" (e.g., to play in the NBA) and "goals," which are the shorter-term objectives that may lead toward the dream (e.g., play on the school team). Leaders may model their own "dreams" that were never attained and explain why, in terms of their own personal unwillingness to accomplish necessary goals. The objective is not to deflate dreams but to teach useful goal setting and attainment.

Note. It is common in the first two or three group meetings for the children to test the group's governing structure to see where the real boundaries lie. Many a new therapist has been frustrated with this testing behavior. Our experience has been that if the leaders firmly adhere to the points-and-strikes system very closely, reinforcing positive behavior and calling strikes for any negative behavior, the vast majority of children will adjust their attitudes and behave accordingly.

Send home the first Parent Letter following this session (see Appendices K and L for both English and Spanish versions of all three Parent Letters).

Materials

Goal Sheet and Parent Letter.

Session Content

Objective 1. Review and Introduce the Concept of Setting and Realizing Goals

Review the group purpose, structure, and activities related to similarities and differences in perception. Have each group member recall something learned from the preceding session. Use reminders if needed.

A. Define *goal*. Most children understand it as something you work to get or do, or something you want and are willing to work for.
B. Review the overall goal of the group program, namely, to learn the smartest way to solve problems with other people and to improve one's ways of coping with anger.

POSSIBLE SCRIPT: Having goals in school is important. Who can tell me what a goal is? Good, a goal is something you want and are willing to work for. Both parts are important: you want it and you are willing to work hard to get it. I have a goal to _____, and I am willing to do the work to get it. The goal of our Anger Coping group is to learn how to control our anger to be more successful in school, and we are working hard at that.

C. Present the Goal Sheet and explain that, as part of the group program, each member will be working on a goal each week in his or her classroom that has to do with anger coping or self-control.

D. Have each group member identify a classroom problem that he or she wants to work on during the coming week:

- To minimize subjective judgments, help the members describe their goals in terms of observable behavior. For example, "being good in class" is very subjective, but it could be behaviorally defined in terms of "not talking back to the teacher," "no physical contact with other kids," and the like.
- Use information obtained from classroom teachers to indirectly influence the child's choice of goal (e.g., "How about something related to your behavior in art class?"). Strictly avoid simply prescribing the goal; clinically draw it out so that the child owns it.
- If the child's desired goal is unrelated to teacher concerns but reasonable, let the child go with it. There will be other opportunities.

E. Group members then "vote" to decide whether all the chosen goals are roughly equivalent in terms of difficulty. It is important to select a goal that is relevant but not so difficult as to preclude success. Have each group member write his or her goal for the week on his or her Goal Sheet.

F. Decide on the level of performance needed to reach the goal. Three out of five days is generally a good level to begin with, allowing for some lapses in behavior without ruining the entire week. Have the group members enter their required level of performance on the Goal Sheet as well as the date for the week.

G. Discuss the rules for the goal-setting procedure. The Goal Sheet is the group member's responsibility. He or she must keep track of it, make sure the teacher fills it out and signs it, and then bring it back to the group. No excuses are good enough for the Goal Sheet to "count" unless the rules are followed. Some group leaders have found greater success and reduced forgetfulness and loss by providing each child with a pocket folder to transport the Goal Sheet to and from the classroom. Within the classroom itself, some teachers prefer to keep the sheets at their desk.

H. Explain the consequences of meeting a goal. Group members can earn a point to apply to the already specified group reward system. Another idea that often enlists peer pressure as a motivator is to offer a group reward, such as 5 or 10 minutes of a fun activity if everyone in the group meets his or her goal for that week. The combination of individual and group rewards provides the greatest incentive.

I. Consult with the classroom teacher when difficulties arise concerning the goal activity. The teacher may be able to provide additional guidance as to the most appropriate goals and/or the smoothest procedure for obtaining signatures.

Positive Feedback and Optional Free Time

Leaders: Debrief and Complete Case Notes

SESSION 3. ANGER MANAGEMENT: PUPPET SELF-CONTROL TASK
Group Leaders' Notes

The main task in this session is to introduce the idea of thinking processes as helping to control feelings, such as anger. Children with undercontrolled or externalizing behavior problems such as aggression often suffer from *cognitive deficiencies*—lack of useful mediating cognitions to regulate anger and subsequent behavior (see Chapter 2). In this session group members are introduced to the concept of adding self-talk at the appropriate time to help them to control their anger and behavior.

The skill is introduced in an indirect fashion, through the use of puppets. It is the puppet, not the child, who will be "thinking" to control its feelings while the other puppets tease and provoke it. Using this procedure is less threatening to some children and serves as a useful lead-in to Session 4, in which group members will confront one another directly.

Leaders should obtain a puppet for each child ahead of time. (The kindergarten room is a good place to find puppets; animal or humanlike characters will do. With some older children, pasting magazine cutouts of popular media figures on a reinforced background and affixing them to stick holders has proven successful.) Leaders can also make puppets out of old sweat socks, varying their looks with magic markers, as needed. Using valuable group time to allow the children to make their own puppets is not recommended, as the taunts that are invited can readily shift to the quality of the workmanship, a criticism that is a little too direct for this activity.

Create a circle or square "safety zone" with tape on the floor ahead of time. The child with the puppet who will be teased will stand inside the zone, so it should be made large enough that puppet-to-puppet physical contact is not possible. Six to eight feet across is adequate. Alternatively, place two tape strips on the floor approximately 6 feet apart.

It is advisable to help the children come up with the self-talk they will use to keep their puppet under control—well before they take their turn in the safety zone. Leader modeling can assist in this effort. Avoid allowing the activity to become a game of "tit for tat" (e.g., "Oh yeah? Well, *you're* uglier than *I* am!"). The puppet in the middle is learning to use self-control language, not one-upmanship. In addition, because those who will tease *must refrain from using swear words or racial/sexual slurs*, they may need some "thinking time" to come up with appropriate taunts.

When a violation of the rules occurs, stop the activity immediately, inform the children of the correct procedure, and begin again. Chronic violations among children with average cognitive functioning indicate a lack of emotional readiness for this particular training exercise. Modifications such as having the child perform the activity with just the group leaders or with only one or two other group members may also be tried.

Repeat this exercise as often as necessary until group members appear to have a good understanding of the concept of using self-talk to avoid becoming angry. It is typical for this session to occupy more than one meeting time.

Send home the second Parent Letter following this session (see Appendices K and L).

Materials

Hand puppets, one for each group member, and Parent Letter.

Session Content

Objective 1. Review Last Session and Goals

Review each child's goals from the preceding week. Ask the child how many days were signed. If children have done particularly well, ask them to relate what they did that helped them to reach their goals on so many days.

Objective 2. Assess Group Problem-Solving Skills

A. In a central location place *one too few* puppets for each group member to have one, and then instruct everyone to get a puppet for the next activity.
B. Observe the problem-solving method the group uses, if any.
C. Ask the group to state the problem and discuss how they tried to solve it, what other ways could have been used to solve it, how well this way worked, and whether any rules were broken.

Objective 3. Introduce Self-Talk and Other Anger Management Techniques

Introduce the concept of self-talk, distraction techniques, and relaxation methods as affecting feelings and reactions.

> POSSIBLE SCRIPT: Which part of your body is responsible for making you angry—your brain, your stomach, or your foot? Right, and one of the best ways to control your brain is to tell it what to do. In Anger Coping, we call this "self-talk." Self-talk is a way for us to tell our brains to cool it, to calm down, to chill—to not get so angry. And it works! With self-talk, we are more in control of how angry we want to be by telling ourselves to stay in control and not lose our tempers. Who can tell me about a time when he or she used self-talk to stay in control? For the next few weeks, we are going to be practicing how to use self-talk to stay cool and avoid problems. Today, we will start out with puppets.

A. Have one of the leaders take a puppet and receive taunts, modeling self-talk that enhances anger coping such as:

- "I can tell I'm starting to get mad, and I want to be careful not to get too angry and lose my temper. I think I'll ask them to stop and see if that works."

Or, another possibility:

- "I don't want to let them make me angry and lose my temper, because then I might do something I'd be sorry for."

Or more simply:

- "Cool it. I can control my anger."

As additional anger coping methods, model ways to *distract* your attention from the provocation (e.g., focusing on a specific visual stimulus, thinking about something fun that is planned for later in the day) and how to count to 10 while breathing deeply (or other simple relaxation methods).

B. Have each member select a puppet for the self-control game. The essential rule for the game is that taunts are *directed at the puppets, not at group members.* In addition, no racial or sexual slurs or swear words are allowed. Each puppet takes a turn receiving and responding to taunts from the rest of the group. The taunting should go on for only 20 to 30 seconds, and ample space should be kept between group members to discourage physical provocations.

C. After each child's puppet receives taunts, the leaders should have the child discuss (1) how the puppet felt, (2) what the puppet was thinking or saying to itself, and (3) whether the puppet used anger coping or self-control in its responses.

D. Repeat the activity, with each group member's puppet again receiving taunts and trying to use anger coping. After each member's turn, emphasize what the puppet said to itself that helped in keeping self-control.

Note. Group leaders may request that the puppets use audible vocal (or overt) self-instruction for the first go-round, moving to silent (or covert) self-instruction in subsequent turns.

GENERALIZATION: What are some reasons why the puppets in this activity might have wanted to control their anger? Why were they successful? If you wanted to control your anger, what could you learn from what the puppets did? This week, we want everyone to count the number of times that they show anger control, and tell us about it when we meet again.

Positive Feedback and Optional Free Time

Leaders: Debrief and Complete Case Notes

SESSION 4. USING SELF-INSTRUCTION

Group Leaders' Notes

This session builds on the self-instruction skills introduced with the puppets in Session 3. If the leaders believe that the group members have started to grasp the concept of self-instruction to mediate anger arousal, and they can both demonstrate with puppets and verbalize the concept, then they are ready for the next level of training. At this point the puppets are put away, and the taunts are aimed by the group directly at each designated child.

It is important that the group leaders have a secure understanding of the purpose of this training procedure. Recall from Chapter 2 that angry, aggressive children often have a very limited repertoire of responses to emotionally trying situations and that their problem-solving skills become much less competent when they simply respond "automatically" rather than use a more deliberate style. If a child has had few or no experiences with the use of deliberating to seek a more adaptive response prior to acting, chances are he or she will simply continue to execute the same aggressive response—it is what the child knows how to do. Further, a child cannot use a deliberative problem-solving style if the level of anger arousal is prohibitive to any responses other than fight or flight.

Many efforts to help children control aggressive behavior fail because the interventions do not allow for even *in vitro* experiences with the skill. Simply explaining to the children what the skills are and letting them parrot back their understanding is destined for failure. This anger coping training procedure is an attempt to create a provocative situation, within the safety of the group room, that calls on the child to actually practice anger control. In other words, we want the child to *experience an anger-arousing situation* and then *to actively prevent* his or her anger from running its typical course. For many chronically aggressive children, this may be a first-time experience.

In this session, group members deliberately try to provoke one another to anger, and they also try to use self-instruction to maintain anger control. We have found it respectful to ask each child if there are certain sensitive provocations that he or she may not yet be ready to handle and to abide by those wishes. However, if a particular taunt commonly triggers a child's angry outburst, that child will need to confront it at some point in the training.

Note. Just as the three most important words in real estate are "location, location, location," the three most important words in behavioral change are "practice, practice, practice!" The more and varied the opportunities to practice the skill, the greater the likelihood that these new skills can be honed and generalized to other settings (see suggestions in Chapter 5: Meichenbaum's Procedural Checklist). Leaders should provide multiple opportunities for each child and, if possible, practice in multiple settings (e.g., the hallway, the restroom, the playground).

Materials

Deck of playing cards and dominoes, paper and pencil, a ball for pass-the-ball.

Session Content

This session again emphasizes the concept of self-talk and its role in improving anger control, using activities that emulate common daily classroom tasks.

Objective 1. Review Concepts of Anger Coping or Self-Control and Goals

Review each child's goals from the preceding week; ask the child how many days were signed. If some of the children have done particularly well, ask them to relate what they did that helped them to reach their goals on so many days.

Recall the self-control game with puppets from the preceding session, what self-talk the group members and leaders used and how that helped or hurt their anger coping. If some children are still struggling with the idea, the concept of self-talk can be explained to them as being a way we talk silently to ourselves and how we figure things out. Some children may have had more experience using self-talk to mediate fear, and leaders can make that connection to mediating anger. Recall who was most successful with anger coping in the puppet exercise and how he or she did it. Encourage group members to relate the taunting game to real-life experiences they encounter: "Does anyone ever try to make you angry by teasing you? What usually happens?"

Objective 2. Practice Using Anger Coping or Self-Control

A. Play a self-control memory game using playing cards. The leader picks 10 different number cards and arranges them as a fan so that all card numbers are visible. Before showing them to the selected group member, allow the other members to taunt and tease him or her for 15 seconds. *The same rules involving no racial/sexual slurs or swearing continue to apply.* Then expose the cards to the selected group member for 5 seconds while the other members continue to issue verbal taunts. The one trying to remember the numbers may talk aloud. That member then writes on a sheet of paper as many card numbers (ignoring suits) as he or she can recall. Repeat for each group member, keeping track of how many numbers each successfully recalls. The child with the most correct numbers wins. Be sure to keep sufficient physical distance between group members.

B. Discussion:

  • "Was it hard to concentrate on the numbers? How did you keep your attention focused?"
  • "Did you start to feel angry? Did that hurt your concentration?"

To the winner:

  • "Did you talk to yourself to help you win? Did you get angry? Why not?"

C. Play a self-control game using dominoes. One group member builds a tower or constructs a line *using one hand* for 30 seconds while the others taunt. Each member takes a turn, with the child constructing the highest tower or longest line winning.

D. Discuss this activity in a similar manner. Emphasize self-talk that helped, and model it if helpful.

E. Play the self-control game with taunts directed at group members in turn. *Leaders should model the activity first,* uttering anger coping "stay cool" self-statements while the group members taunt. Be sure to keep a safe distance between members. Use the same safety zone as in the previous sessions. The taunted one stays in the middle and responds, using anger-coping self-statements.

F. Discussion:

- "How did you feel? What bothered you most? What were you thinking or saying to yourself? How did you use self-control?"

Note. During this session, the leaders should model "stay cool" types of self-talk statements whenever deemed appropriate. In addition, group members may actually need some help in coming up with taunts that are within the rules—no swear words or racial/sexual slurs. Some may find it helpful to write them down on a sheet of paper for reference. For children who have difficulty with this exercise, leaders may want to vary the verbal taunting exercises by (1) having the targeted child face away from the taunters, (2) reducing the taunting time, or (3) allowing only one or two members to taunt.

GENERALIZATION: How was what we did in here like what really happens? What are some reasons why it important to keep yourself under control in those times? How will you use self-talk to keep yourself in control? We want each of you to remember how you used self-control and tell us about it next week.

Modification: For groups containing just girls, some group leaders have added the new element of also having the girls *outside* of the circle talk about the designated girl rather than directly at her, replicating relationally aggressive behavior. This option is utilized in addition to the direct procedure.

Positive Feedback and Optional Free Time

The need for "cool down" time prior to returning to class may be particularly critical following this session. A pass-the-ball exercise in which each group member states something he or she likes about another member can be useful. Relaxation exercises, such as deep breathing or pleasant imagery, are highly recommended.

Leaders: Debrief and Complete Case Notes

SESSION 5. PERSPECTIVE TAKING

Group Leaders' Notes

The main idea in this session is to help group members understand that situations can be seen from different points of view, all of which have some validity. In addition, it will be important for group members to understand that a person's view may lead him or her to certain thoughts and feelings.

This is the first "required" role play, and it is common for some of the group members to be hesitant or feel awkward. Modeling, social praise, and the awarding of points for participation can be effective motivators to get them involved.

Note. Those leaders who will be offering tangible reinforcers for points exchanged every fifth session should prepare for this activity. There will be no further reminders of this procedure.

Materials

Appendix O, *Second Step* (Committee for Children, 2001), or DUSO (American Guidance Service, 2001) type or other stimulus pictures found in a magazine, showing children interacting.

Session Content

Objective 1. Review Anger Coping Skills from Latest Session and Review Goals

Review each child's goals from the preceding week; ask the child how many days were signed. If some of the children have done particularly well, ask them to relate what they did that helped them to reach their goals on so many days.

Ask group members to describe how they used their anger coping or self-control skills that were practiced in the latest session. Where? How did the skills work? What might have happened if you did not use your skills?

Objective 2. Establish the Concept of Different Interpretations

A. Use a stimulus picture, such as shown on Appendix O or one of the DUSO or *Second Step* cards, to elicit as many perceptions of "what the problem is" as possible. Call on each group member, asking each person to come up with a different problem that *could be* happening in the picture. Repeat with other pictures if the group is interested or if it seems needed to get the point across.

B. Discuss the differences in group members' interpretations. Was there one real problem in each picture? Would all the people in the picture see the same problem? Did you change your mind about what the problem might be in listening to the other group members' ideas? How would the people in the picture act if they all saw the same problem? If they saw different problems?

Objective 3. Problem Recognition

Help group members to recognize at what point a problem starts, and reinforce the concept that each person involved in a social problem can see it differently.

A. Select a stimulus picture with a number of characters and some ambiguity, and assign a group member to portray each person in the picture. Perform a brief role play about the picture, beginning just before the scene in the picture, that is, with what led up to it. The leader assumes the role of a roving reporter and has group members freeze their action after the problem has occurred but before it is resolved. The leader interviews each actor individually to get his or her point of view: "What were you doing before the problem started? When did you first see a problem? Who had the problem? What were you thinking as the problem happened? How did you feel? What did you do? What were you planning to do next?"

B. Have group members resume their seats for a brief discussion. Did the people in the role play see things differently? Did they have different thoughts? Did they have different feelings? What caused those differences? Did their thoughts and feelings have an effect on what they were going to do next?

C. Ask group members to summarize the main idea from the day's activities. Preview the next session of more role play, and encourage members to bring in some real-life problems they have had, or saw others having, to use in a role play.

Positive Feedback and Optional Free Time

Leaders: Debrief and Complete Case Notes

SESSION 6. LOOKING AT ANGER

Group Leaders' Notes

This session is a continuation and elaboration of the preceding session, reinforcing the idea of perspective taking. It also begins to focus on the role of anger in social problems. A self-monitoring procedure is introduced.

Group leaders will now attempt to help group members understand the feeling of anger through role play and discussion. It is likely that one or more of the group members have been involved recently in an angry episode. Such incidents make excellent role plays in the effort to help the children gain a better understanding of the feeling of anger. It is important to have the children also play the roles of others in an incident (teacher, peer provocateur, etc.) so as to help them understand the concept of seeing things from another's perspective.

Group leaders may also choose to manufacture role plays around such common school themes as the following: a teacher blames you for something you did not do; someone accidentally rips your paper in class; someone cuts in front of you in line; someone takes your ball when you are playing. A useful insight to provide the children is that the perspective from the viewpoint of a peer provocateur is often "I have the power to make _____ angry and get him [or her] into trouble." Using anger coping strategies helps to prevent that trouble from actually occurring.

Materials

Stimulus picture, poster paper and markers, and Hassle Logs (see Appendix J for a recommended model).

Session Content

Objective 1: Review Goals and Perspective Taking

Review each child's goals from the preceding week; ask the child how many days were signed. If some of the children have done particularly well, ask them to relate what they did that helped them to reach their goals on so many days.

Review the concept of perspective taking, recalling the last session's role-play activity.

Objective 2. Explore Situational Interpretations and Anger

Elaborate on the possibility of different interpretations of the same pictured situation, focusing on how anger becomes involved.

A. Use a stimulus picture or ask group members whether they have had or have observed a problem situation that they want the group to role-play. Repeat the role-play procedure, including the roving reporter, as outlined in the preceding session.
B. Using the same picture or problem situation, have group members exchange roles and then repeat the role play.
C. Discussion: Which characters in the situation were angry? How could you tell they were angry? Was there anything about their facial expressions, their tone of voice, their body reactions, what they said, or what they did that showed that they were angry?
D. Repeat the role play, asking for "Academy Award-winning" portrayals of anger by the characters who were angry, including nonverbal as well as verbal indications of anger.
E. Discuss the concept of anger. Have the group list descriptors in trying to arrive at a definition, and write these on a board or poster paper. *Suggest the idea of anger being the feeling you have when you think you cannot get something you want or do something you want to do, or when you feel provoked.*
F. Elicit from the group examples of situations in which the children feel angry at school. Try to have the group figure out what the angry person is thinking he or she can't get or do. Talk about how the anger is a problem in itself. Generate examples of how anger gets involved in situations and how it affects what the person then chooses to do.
G. Introduce the idea of self-monitoring as presented in the Hassle Log (use the model shown in Appendix J or create your own). Group members should be encouraged to examine their incidents of anger following this simple format. Hassle Logs may be filled out in subsequent meetings and used as the bases for role plays.

GENERALIZATION: What are some reasons for knowing when another person is getting angry? Name some persons in school who get angry and how you can tell they are angry. Name some persons in school who almost never get angry. Why is that? This week, pay attention to the things that make other people angry. We will expect you to discuss what you observed next week.

Positive Feedback and Optional Free Time

Leaders: Debrief and Complete Case Notes

SESSION 7. WHAT DOES ANGER FEEL LIKE?

Group Leaders' Notes

The physiological aspects of anger are identified in this session, with emphasis on how they can serve as a warning sign or indicator that the person is angry and needs to mobilize anger coping strategies. The impact of thoughts or self-statements on angry feelings and behavior is also explored.

In this session, leaders will ask the children to get in touch with the physiological sensations that accompany anger. Most adults can "sense" when they are getting angry by monitoring their physiological responses (e.g., accelerated heartbeat or breathing, muscle tension, involuntary clenching of the jaw, etc.). The "early warning system" serves as a cue for the individual to begin to cognitively deliberate the most adaptive response. It is the capacity to recognize and monitor these bodily responses—so that they may serve as a cue for the child's anger control—that will be taught in this session.

The early warning system is a difficult concept for young children, especially boys, to master, unaccustomed as they often are to monitoring their emotional state. Nonetheless, it remains an important component in the effort to control one's anger. One must be aware that he or she is becoming angry before a decision to control that anger can be made. Abundant group leader examples and modeling help in this training (e.g., "A fellow cut me off on the highway this morning, and I could feel my teeth clench and my heart start to race"). In addition, the children may be more familiar with physiological sensations that accompany fear, which may provide a training link.

Session Content

Objective 1. Review Goals and Concepts of Anger from Last Session

Review each child's goals from the preceding week; ask the child how many days were signed. If some of the children have done particularly well, ask them to relate what they did that helped them to reach their goals on so many days.

Recall the definition of anger and the examples used in the last session.

Objective 2. Identify Physiological Reactions to Anger

Explore the physiological aspects of anger arousal and how these can serve as warning signals that a problem is starting.

A. Discussion:

- "How can we tell when we're feeling angry?"
- "How does your body feel when you are getting angry?"
- "What do you notice when others are getting angry that tells you how they might be feeling?"

POSSIBLE SCRIPT: Very often, you and I can tell that we are getting angry by signals in our bodies. These signals or warning cues may be different for different people. For instance, I can tell when I am starting to get angry because I feel _____ (rapid heart rate, or face getting warm, or muscles tightening, or _____. The signals tell me that it is time for me to use anger control. Let's talk about the warning signals that you feel in your bodies.

B. Optional: View a video that portrays the physiological aspects of anger arousal (see the end of Chapter 12 for a sample videotape that may be ordered).

C. Discussion: People have different kinds of bodily reactions when they're having strong feelings. Have each group member describe his or her bodily changes when he or she is getting angry.

- "Do these bodily changes create any problems for you or lead to any particular behaviors?"
- "Can these bodily changes be signals that you're angry and that there is a problem to be solved?"

Objective 3. Explore Self-Statements

Explore the role of self-statements in coping with anger and redirecting behavior in a problem-solving manner.

A. Discussion:

- "What thoughts usually go along with angry feelings?"
- "What do you say to yourself when you're angry? Do these thoughts make you get angrier or stay angry? Do they help you calm down and try to solve the problem?"

B. Optional: View a videotape that portrays two different types of self-statements (see the end of Chapter 12). After the first set of angry self-statements, discuss whether group members say these kinds of things to themselves when they're angry. Do these self-statements help them control their anger or solve the problem? View the second set of self-statements. Discuss whether the group members agreed with these thoughts. Did these self-statements help the child solve his or her problem, help the child cope with the onset of anger?

    Have group members specifically identify the problem the child had and tell what the child's feelings were, what choices the child had to solve the problem, and how what he or she said to him- or herself helped in making the right choice.

C. Discuss incidents during the past week when someone got angry at school. Use the Hassle Log (see Appendix J) to guide the discussion. What did the child say to him- or herself, or what thoughts did he or she have? Did the thoughts or self-statements help with anger control? Were there things the child could have said to him- or herself that would have helped with anger control? Can self-statements help with anger control at school? Is there any way to remember to use them? Can the body's warning signs help you remember?

D. Role-play Hassle Log incidents by using anger signal recognition *plus* self-talk. Children should vocalize their anger signal feelings and then orally rehearse responsive self-control statements. For example: "I feel my muscles starting to shake. Chill. Cool it. Stay in control."

GENERALIZATION: What are some reasons why knowing your anger signals will help you in school this next week? How do anger signals and self-talk go together? This week, pay attention to your own anger signals and use self-talk to stay in control.

Positive Feedback and Optional Free Time

Leaders: Debrief and Complete Case Notes

SESSION 8. CHOICES AND CONSEQUENCES

Group Leaders' Notes

The concepts presented in this session are in some ways the most important components of the Anger Coping model in terms of helping to make changes in behavior. It is essential that group members conceive of being angry as a problem with which they need to cope, that they have different choices of things they can do when they're angry, and that they realize there are fairly predictable consequences for their behavior.

    Recall from Chapters 1 and 2 that one of the common cognitive characteristics of highly aggressive children is their deficiency in problem solving. Aggressive children demonstrate deficiency in both the quality and quantity of their problem-solving solutions (Lochman, White, et al., 1991). These differences are most pronounced in the quality of the solutions offered, with aggressive children offering fewer verbal assertion solutions (Asarnow & Callan, 1985; Joffe et al., 1990; Lochman & Lampron, 1986), fewer compromise solutions (Lochman & Dodge, 1994), more direct-action solutions (Lochman & Lampron, 1986), a greater number of help-seeking or adult intervention responses (Asher & Renshaw, 1981; Dodge et al., 1984; Lochman, Lampron, et al., 1989; Rabiner et al., 1990), and more physically aggressive responses (Pepler et al., 1998; Slaby & Guerra, 1988; Waas, 1988; Waas & French, 1989) to hypothetical vignettes describing interpersonal conflicts.

In this session, leaders begin to help the group members address these problem-solving deficiencies through activities that encourage them to generate multiple "choices" to previous problem incident. The group will then review each choice and connect it to the most likely consequences that would ensue.

Note. This session is very didactic and can be too abstract for some children. Having group members participate as actively as possible is helpful in maintaining their attention. For example, let group members take turns in writing the choices or consequences they come up with on the board, determining the "good or bad" quality of the rankings, and so on. Be sure to award points for good participation as well as pass out abundant verbal praise.

Materials

Hassle Logs, poster paper and markers, or chalkboard.

Session Content

Objective 1. Review Goals and Physiological Reactions

Review each child's goals from the preceding week; ask the child how many days were signed. If some of the children have done particularly well, ask them to relate what they did that helped them to reach their goals on so many days. Review the physiological aspects of anger and the self-statements associated with anger discussed during the preceding session.

Objective 2. Generate Alternatives

Encourage the process of generating alternatives, including all possible alternatives.

A. Using the Hassle Log as a guide, have group members bring up problems that aroused anger either during the preceding week or previously. Taking one problem at a time, have the group brainstorm all the possible choices the person could have made. Emphasize the idea of *all possible choices*; leaders should offer desirable or undesirable alternatives if the group members' ideas are skewed in one direction of another. List the alternatives that are generated on the chalkboard or on poster paper under the heading "Choices" or "Alternatives."

POSSIBLE SCRIPT: We all have problems, but do you know what is similar about every problem? They all give us more than one choice about what to do. Sometimes the choices are easy. For instance, if you're about to get hit in the head by a baseball, you could choose to stand there or choose to duck. Easy choice. But with some problems the choices are much more difficult. Learning to make good choices starts with learning to take the time to think about what they really are. The more choices we can think of, the better the chances are that we will select the best one.

B. Once the list has been generated, go back to each choice listed and have the group decide whether the choice involved anger coping or self-control. Were there any self-statements that led to the choices? What were they? How did they affect the choices made?

Objective 3. Identify Consequences

Establish the idea of consequences as what happens after a choice is made—what others do and what happens to you—and as something to be considered in deciding on a choice.

A. Discussion: What is a consequence? This term is sometimes too sophisticated for the children, and they can more easily refer to the idea of *what happens as a result of something you do.* It can be positive or negative. Are consequences important to us? Are they one of the reasons we want to learn anger control?

POSSIBLE SCRIPT: All choices have consequences. This means that when you act on your choice and do it, something happens. What happens is the consequence. It can be a good consequence or a bad consequence. For example, if you choose to do your work in class rather than fool around, would there be a good consequence or a bad consequence for you? We always want to try to make the choice that will bring us good consequences. Learning anger control will help us to make good choices and get good consequences.

B. Consider one of the problem situations discussed in Objective 2 and look again at all the choices listed. Go through the list again and predict, for each choice, the consequence, or what would happen, if that choice was made. It may be particularly instructive to list the predicted consequences in another column to the right of "Choices," under the heading "What Happens."

C. Have the group rate each consequence as good or bad. Did the good consequence(s) involve anger coping or self-control? Who decides what consequence will happen? Who decides what choice is made? How are self-statements or thoughts involved in making choices and considering consequences? Can they help you make choices that lead to good consequences?

GENERALIZATION: What are some reasons why each of you wants to learn to make good choices? After you leave here today and during this week, what is one important time in which you will have to make an important choice? How will you know what to choose? What will be the good and bad consequences of your choices?

Positive Feedback and Optional Free Time

Leaders: Debrief and Complete Case Notes

SESSION 9. STEPS FOR PROBLEM SOLVING

Group Leaders' Notes

The problem-solving model is presented in its entirety in this session, helping group members to understand the decisional sequence as an integrated process. It is important for members to grasp the idea that this model deals with *how to think about problems*, not what to do. What happens—the content and context of problems—varies from one situation to the next, but the process of how to think about problems remains the same.

Group members have learned to recognize the existence of a "problem" by considering that there may be both good and bad consequences following the possible choices. For example, they have learned that if their anger is provoked on the playground, response choices may include: (1) aggression, with possible school administrative consequences; (2) nonaggression, with possible negative peer consequences; or (3) a third choice that may avoid both types of negative consequences. Explain that the existence of these tough choices is one type of *problem*.

In this session, group members are provided with a step model, a "cognitive map" to assist them in selecting and implementing the best choice. This session addresses the knowledge-level aspect of building applied problem-solving skills; so, multiple repetitions and examples with numerous situations and contexts will assist group members in learning the steps.

Send home the third Parent Letter (see Appendices K and L) following this session.

Materials

Poster paper and markers, Parent Letter.

Session Content

Objective 1. Review Goals and Problem Solving

Review each child's goals from the preceding week; ask the child how many days were signed. If some of the children have done particularly well, ask them to relate what they did that helped them to reach their goals on so many days.

A. Review the steps of social problem solving, beginning with determining that there is a problem and proceeding through consideration of consequences. Ask group members to recall the ideas discussed during the last session, prompting them when necessary. On a piece of poster paper, write the steps in words the students can understand and use for themselves spontaneously. An example of steps might be as follows:

1. "What is the problem?"
2. "What are my feelings?"
3. "What are my choices?"

4. "What are the likely consequences?"
5. "What will I do?"

A flowchart format can be used. Discuss each option, and ask for examples of each step.

B. Ask for examples of problems the group members had during the week, and go through the steps identified. Group members should be able to relate the steps in sequence and provide an appropriate example before moving to the next objectives in Session 10.

EXAMPLE

1. "What is the problem?" *John pushed ahead of me in line at the kickball game.*
2. "What are my feelings?" *I'm pretty angry.*
3. "What are my choices?"
4. "What will happen?"

Choices	Consequences
I could shove him.	*He might shove back. We might fight and get suspended.*
I could call him a name.	*He might get mad and start fighting, and we'll get suspended.*
I could ask him to move.	*He might move.*
I could tell the teacher.	*He would get in trouble and blame me.*

GENERALIZATION: What are some reasons for taking your time to solve a problem? What things make it hard to solve problems this way? How will you remind yourself this week to use the steps for problem solving?

Positive Feedback and Optional Free Time

Leaders: Debrief and Complete Case Notes

SESSION 10. PROBLEM SOLVING IN ACTION

Group Leaders' Notes

This session begins the portion of the training in which group members take a more active role in rehearsing skills intended to address their own particular anger-related needs. Over the course of the remaining weeks, the children will create, rehearse, and videotape one or more vignettes that depict the skills they are learning. It is important that the problems that are created by the group members reflect actual and recurring difficulties that they encounter in the school setting. This session prepares group members for this task by presenting a common problem and discussing alternative responses.

Session 10 assumes that the leaders have prepared a sample video ahead of time or have a copy of *The Anger Coping Video*, available from author Larson at *larsonj@uww.edu*. An effective sample video can be made very simply before the start of this group session. Position a volunteer child who is the same age or slightly older than group members at a desk with the camera on just him or her so that the child takes up most of the frame. The child ("Terry") should be writing in a workbook or on a piece of writing paper, obviously engaged in the assignment, not talking. Off camera, an adult's voice barks, "That's enough talking back there. Terry, that was your last warning. You go to the principal's office right now!" With that same setup, tape three different responses to the problem: (1) poor anger control, disrespectful; (2) passive, unassertive; and (3) good anger control, assertive and respectful. Alternately, this session may be completed by having group members role-play with the leader. The critical feature is analysis of the alternative responses.

Materials

Prepared sample videotape.

Session Content

Objective 1. Review Goals and Present the Problem-Solving Model in Action

Review each child's goals from the preceding week; ask the child how many days were signed. If some of the children have done particularly well, ask them to relate what they did that helped them to reach their goals on so many days.

A. Explain to the group that they will be making a videotape of themselves during the next 6 weeks that will show how anger coping works. Point out that you have a model for them to watch that will give them an idea of what they will be trying to do.
B. View the sample video in which a child is blamed by the teacher for something he or she didn't do. It will be important to stop the video between each alternative solution that is acted out to help group members understand that after each pause the scene returns to the point when the child is angry and deciding what choice to make.
C. After the *first alternative* is shown, stop the video for a brief discussion. What is the problem? When did it start? Whose problem is it? How is the child feeling? How can he or she tell—and how can you tell—that he or she is angry? What angry thoughts might the child be having? What could he or she be telling him- or herself? What choice did he or she make? What was the consequence? Did he or she make a smart choice?
D. After the *second alternative* is shown, pause for another discussion. Did the child have the same problem? Did he or she have the same feelings? What choice did he or she make (called the teacher a name; gave up; failed to be assertive)? What happened? Did he or she make a smart choice?
E. After the *third alternative*, again have the group discuss the tape. What were the three choices on the tape? Which one was the smartest choice? Which choices used anger con-

trol? What did the child say to him- or herself that helped him or her use anger control? (Emphasize a motto such as "Stop, think, what should I do?".) Can the children think of any other choices? What would happen as a result of those choices?

F. Remind the group that at the next meeting they will begin working on a script for the video they will make. Encourage group members to come up with ideas for their video.

Positive Feedback and Optional Free Time

Leaders: Debrief and Complete Case Notes

SESSION 11. VIDEO PRODUCTION I

Group Leaders' Notes

This session marks the beginning of the actual effort to produce a video that demonstrates what is being learned in the Anger Coping group. This process helps to consolidate the integrated problem-solving model begun in Session 9. By writing their own script, the group begins to acquire a working knowledge of the social problem-solving process. Another important goal for this session is to defuse some of the anxiety and impulse-control problems often spawned by the videotaping process. *Group leaders are strongly urged to consult the recommendations for parent/guardian consent and video distribution that are found at the end of Chapter 6.*

Our experience with this phase of the training program prompts us to advise the following:

1. Group leaders should become proficient with the video equipment ahead of time and make certain that it is in working order.
2. Leaders should resist group members' desire to rush to on-camera production. Be certain that they rehearse sufficiently so that the vignette is "camera-ready" before beginning to tape. Be prepared for multiple "takes," however.
3. Moving the shooting to the real-life setting (e.g., the gym or outside on the playground) and including such salient individuals as a teacher or administrator adds greater realism and offers potentially wider generalization possibilities.
4. Large poster-sized signs may be used to introduce scenes or video segments (e.g., "What Is the Problem?").
5. The use of written cartoonlike "thought bubbles" on a stick held over an actor's head can portray self-instruction. Alternatively, one of the off-camera group members can speak into the microphone of the video camera as the on-camera actor portrays "thinking."

Materials

Poster paper and markers, Hassle Logs, and video equipment.

Session Content

Objective 1. Review Goals and Identify Problems in School

Review each child's goals from the preceding week; ask the child how many days were signed. If some of the children have done particularly well, ask them to relate what they did that helped them to reach their goals on so many days. Identify one of several problems in school that the group believes would be good to video, establishing one problem as first priority for filming.

A. Remind the group of the sample video shown during the preceding session. Ask for suggestions of problem situations in school involving anger arousal that group members think would be good for making a video.
B. Write down on a piece of paper or poster board each problem suggested, determine whether it does involve anger, and ask for three or four choices the person with the problem might make and the consequences that would occur. Be certain to have the group include choices involving self-control as well as at least one that does not. The Hassle Log can provide possible scenarios.
C. Once choices and consequences have been outlined for each problem, have the group decide which problem they would most like to videotape first. Explain that if the taping goes well there will be an opportunity to make more than one video. Having the group reach this decision can prove to be a real-life demonstration of problem solving. Point this out, and see what choices the group can find as a whole.

Objective 2. Desensitize the Group to Being on Camera

Give each group member a chance to be on camera informally, allowing the laughter and silliness that invariably occur. It will still be necessary for members to retain some degree of self-control. In addition, it can be fun to practice some close-up shots, with the group members asked to portray different emotions. At the end of the session, play the tape back so that the group members can watch themselves. It is also important to establish a policy about handling the equipment to prevent damage.

Positive Feedback and Optional Free Time

Leaders: Debrief and Complete Case Notes

SESSIONS 12–18. VIDEO PRODUCTIONS II–VIII

Group Leaders' Notes

During the early sessions, the group should begin to work more seriously on producing part of their video. Although it is important to encourage the children to do their best job of acting so as to make a good product, leaders should continue to keep in mind that this taping activity is primarily a *training* activity. The goal is to help the children internalize the problem-solving model, and the video project is the vehicle to help reach that goal. Our experience—and that of many of our students and trainees—is that it is easy to get swept up in the novelty and high-tech aspects of video production, sometimes losing sight of that primary goal. Consequently it is advisable for leaders to remain particularly observant of the developing skill levels of each group member as rehearsals progress and to develop refined training objectives prior to each session.

Materials

Video equipment, paper and pencil.

Session 12. Content: Video Production II

Objective 1. Review Goals and Tape the Problem Situation

Review each child's goals from the preceding week; ask the child how many days were signed. If some of the children have done particularly well, ask them to relate what they did that helped them to reach their goals on so many days. Videotape a clear representation of the "problem stem," which leads into an initially inappropriate angry/aggressive action that has negative consequences for the individual.

A. Review the problem decided upon by the group. Lay out the scene and how to depict the circumstances leading up to the problem. Assign roles (which can be another group problem-solving process) and arrange scenery. Decide on the actions and words used by each character, writing them down if necessary (although it usually is not).

B. Have several "dress rehearsals" of role plays of the problem. Begin with setting the stage, what leads up to the problem, then have the problem occur, and stop when the person with the problem is looking very angry. (One of these taped rehearsals may be good enough for a final version.) The group continues to do these "dress rehearsals" for subsequent segments of the video as well.

C. Allow the group to watch the replays of their video rehearsals, keeping these questions in mind: Is the problem presented clearly? Can the actors be understood? Is there too much extraneous noise or silliness? How is the anger displayed? Did the most important actions of the sequence get on camera? Would someone from outside the group understand the problem merely from watching the tape? After watching the replay, decide what changes need to be made on the next taping, giving specific suggestions.

D. An additional feature that may be added to the problem stem is a roving reporter or narrator who interviews the actors while the action is frozen, as in the role-play activities for Session 5. Get a close-up of the person being interviewed, having him or her respond as an aside to the audience, telling what he is thinking, feeling, and so on.

E. Select and tape a solution choice that demonstrates lack of anger control.

Positive Feedback and Optional Free Time

Leaders: Debrief and Complete Case Notes

Session 13. Content: Video Production III

This session continues the videotaping efforts, moving to the various alternatives and consequences in the script.

Objective 1. Review Goals and Prepare for Taping of Alternatives and Consequences

Review each child's goals from the preceding week; ask the child how many days were signed. If some of the children have done particularly well, ask them to relate what they did that helped them to reach their goals on so many days.

A. Watch the group's video of the problem stem and the angry/aggressive solution that was selected as the final version.
B. Prepare any props that the group decides to include in its tape, such as signs saying "Stop, think, what should I do?" or listing the steps in the problem-solving process the group has outlined.

Objective 2. Tape the Alternative Solutions

Videotape a clear representation of each alternative and associated consequence, using only alternatives that involve self-control of anger arousal.

Positive Feedback and Optional Free Time

Leaders: Debrief and Complete Case Notes

Sessions 14–18. Content: Video Productions IV–VIII

These sessions review the group's video product and the concepts presented during the group's meetings and apply the concepts to group members' anger arousal problems. Leaders should continue with the goal reviews through the conclusion of the intervention.

Objective 1

View the "finished products," giving comments about strengths and weaknesses.

Objective 2 (Optional)

Produce videos of other problem stems, alternatives, and consequences. These videos can focus on different types of anger arousal problems, such as with adults rather than peers.

Objective 3

Review the steps of social problem solving, giving group members an opportunity to offer what they recall before the leaders fill in.

Objective 4

Review the progress group members have made in anger coping, asking for many specific examples of situations in which group members have used their skills. Reference to the Goal Sheets may be helpful.

Objective 5

Preview how group members anticipate being able to use their newly acquired anger coping skills in the future.

Objective 6

Train for the eventuality of setbacks, such as how to cope with possible situations in which the newly acquired skills may be neglected in favor of aggression (see suggestions in Chapter 5, Meichenbaum's Procedural Checklist). Remind group members that they are learning to "cope" with anger, not "master" it, and sometimes they will not be successful. Remind them that one doesn't quit a basketball game after a missed shot or a bad pass—rather, one learns from the error and continues playing. Coping with anger and aggression requires the same kind of commitment to learning from errors and moving on. Coping with setbacks specifies that the group member engage in:

Self-coaching: "What did I forget to do?" "How can I handle this issue better next time?" "What step did I forget?" "I know how to do it, I just need practice." "One mistake doesn't spoil all the work I've done." "I'll do better next time."

Seeking help: Ask to see one of the group leaders for an individual session to help you improve your skills.

Objective 7

Plan a "graduation" ceremony. Our experience has been that group members appreciate a closing ritual, which may include personalized Anger Coping Program certificates (made with a word processing certificate-maker program), invited adult guests, snacks, and the opportunity to show their videotape and talk about what they have learned.

Objective 8

Schedule "booster" sessions. Depending on the time left in the school year, booster sessions should be scheduled at 2 and 4 weeks from the graduation ceremony. During these meetings, goals may be examined, and efforts at and barriers to generalization may be addressed. Any need for more intensive or continuing intervention should also be explored and plans made accordingly.

CHAPTER 9

Considerations When Treating Girls and Treating Children from Diverse Cultural Backgrounds

Recent years have seen the publication of numerous books addressing the subject of aggression in girls. Both relational aggression (e.g., Wiseman, 2003) and physical aggression (e.g., Garbarino, 2006) received "best seller" public attention, and the issue has even spawned popular movies such as *Heathers* and *Mean Girls*. Although most of the recent attention to girls' aggressive behavior has focused on relational aggression, there is growing concern, fueled in part by the popular media, regarding what has been observed to be an increase in physical aggression. For example, a 2005 article in *Newsweek* trumpeted: "Bad Girls Go Wild: A Rise in Girl-on-Girl Violence Is Making Headlines and Prompting Scientists to Ask Why" (Scelfo, 2005).

Are girls really "going wild"? On examination, data from the FBI indicate that juvenile arrests generally declined between 1996 and 2005. The lone exception to the general trend was found in arrests for simple assault, which increased for girls while decreasing for boys (Federal Bureau of Investigation, 2006). During this period, boys still well outpaced girls in the more serious category of aggravated assault, due in part to boys' greater use of weaponry (Zahn et al., 2008). However, Garbarino (2006, pp. 3–4) observed:

> According to the U.S. Department of Justice, while criminal violence among teenage boys today still far exceeds criminal violence among teenage girls, the gap is narrowing. Twenty-five years ago for every ten boys arrested for assault, there was only one girl. Now there are four boys arrested for each girl arrested. Put simply, the official arrest data indicate that girls today assault people and get arrested more often than did the girls in generations past.

The critical element in these data is that the focus is on *arrest*, which accounts for those individuals who behavior creates an official record. However, when other metrics are included, such as those from nationwide victimization surveys and girls' self-reports, one finds that "although girls are currently arrested more for simple assaults than previously, the actual incidence of their being seriously violent has not changed much over the last two decades" (Zahn et al., 2008, p. 15). The reasons that girls are being arrested for simple assault at higher frequencies than in prior years is undeniably a cause for further study, but there does not appear to be a crisis of girls going "wild."

However, as more than a few school administrators would attest, girls do indeed engage in aggressive physical violence in the school setting. In the many years that the Anger Coping Program has been available for use in schools and clinics, the question regarding its applicability to the treatment of girls' anger and aggression problems arises regularly. The amount of research that addresses the treatment of physically aggressive girls pales in comparison to that of boys, and studies that focus on school-based interventions are virtually nonexistent. One of the distinguishing elements of the Anger Coping Program is its solid research foundation (see Chapter 2). Since all of the research support underlying the Anger Coping Program reflects work undertaken only with boys, one might ask if the intervention can be reliably used in working with girls. The short (and admittedly too easy) answer is that it depends largely on how closely the reactive anger problem of the girls resembles that of their male counterparts.

In this chapter, we expand on that brief answer and provide guidance for group leaders who wish to conduct Anger Coping groups with girls. First, we begin with a brief review of the relevant research.

DEVELOPMENTAL PATH OF PHYSICAL AGGRESSION IN GIRLS

As infants, boys and girls display a similar pattern and frequency of aggressive behavior. Somewhere between 2 and 3 years of age, gender differences begin to emerge, particularly for more serious and stable aggression (Dodge, Coie, & Lynam, 2006). As examples, Alink et al. (2006) examined gender differences in physical aggression in a sample of children initially recruited at 12, 24, and 36 months ($N = 2,253$). Using mother and father reports of physical aggression, these authors found that there was no gender difference in levels of physical aggression at 12 months of age. However, at 24 and 36 months of age, a significant gender difference emerged such that boys displayed higher levels of physical aggression than girls. Broidy et al. (2003) used data from six sites and three countries to examine the developmental course of physical aggression between boys versus girls. These authors also concluded that over the developmental course girls exhibited lower levels of typical aggression than did boys, and that even among the most aggressive girls "their mean levels of aggression are notably lower than those of chronic physically aggressive boys in the same sample" (p. 232).

One exception to this pattern may come in high-poverty central-city neighborhoods. Examining physical aggression in first, fourth, and seventh grades, Xie, Farmer, and Cairns (2003) found that fourth-grade African American girls in the inner city displayed the same levels of physical aggression as boys. However, boys in this sample displayed higher levels of physical aggression than girls in both the first and seventh grades. Schaeffer et al. (2006) studied a city of Baltimore sample, beginning in the first grade and ending when the participants were 19–20. They combined aggressive and disruptive behaviors into a single variable and identified three pathways in girls: (1) early-starter with consistently high levels of aggression/disruption, (2) low/moderate aggression/disruption, and (3) low aggression/disruption. Unlike previous studies in which the samples of girls were mostly nonaggressive, a majority of girls (67%) in this sample belonged to the low/moderate aggression/disruption group. On this higher level of normative aggression, the authors hypothesized that the high levels of violent crime and disorganization in urban neighborhoods was a contributing factor: "It may be that aggressive-disruptive behavior among girls is more normative in these communities and thus is more likely to be accepted or tolerated by peers and adults" (Schaefer et al., 2006, pp. 507–508).

As their developmental trajectories bring them into adolescence, the paths of aggressive boys and girls begin to diverge. Aggressive boys are more likely to become involved in delinquency and violent crime, while aggressive girls experience more co-occurring emotional problems such as depression (Moffitt, Caspi, Rutter, & Silva, 2001). In addition, when compared to adolescent boys, aggressive girls demonstrate a higher risk for heavy episodic drinking, marijuana use, and early sexual activity (Prinstein & La Greca, 2004). This potential for sexual precocity also places girls at risk for early parenthood responsibilities for which they may be woefully underprepared (Pepler, Walsh, & Levene, 2004).

PROBLEMS ASSOCIATED WITH PHYSICAL AGGRESSION IN GIRLS

The individual and family risk factors that contribute to the development of problem aggression in boys and subsequent negative life outcomes (see Chapter 2) appear to pertain comparably to girls (Fergusson & Horwood, 2002; Moffitt et al., 2001; Pepler et al., 2004). Like their male counterparts, girls who experience poverty, physical or sexual abuse, criminal behavior within the family, and ineffective parenting are at increased risk to develop problem aggression, peer rejection, academic underachievement, truancy, and school failure. Pepler et al. (2006) found that, compared to girls who were nonaggressive, girls who were highly aggressive experienced significant physical and emotional health problems and were at higher risk of having problems in their relationships with their parents.

Meichenbaum (2006, p. 22) reviewed the literature and concluded:

Girls who display aggressive behavior at an early age are prone to experience major difficulties throughout their lives. The likelihood of becoming serious violent offenders is increased if the girls have been maltreated and victimized, enter puberty early, have learning problems, a depressed mood, associate with antisocial peers, and partner with antisocial males. In addition, such girls with a history of aggression are likely to experience a number of clinical problems including PTSD and substance abuse. They are likely to engage in a number of risk-taking behaviors including early sexual activity, unprotected sex and becoming teenage mothers for which they are inadequately prepared, demonstrating poor parenting skills. This contributes to their children being at high risk for developing externalizing problems and a greater risk for their children to be victimized. Thus, the cycle continues!

RELATIONAL AGGRESSION

Continuing since the seminal work of Crick and her colleagues during the 1990s (e.g., Crick & Grotpeter, 1995, 1996; Crick & Bigbee, 1998), researchers and educators alike have been striving to better understand the development, identity, and treatment of relational aggression. Observed predominantly although certainly not exclusively among girls, relational aggression refers to the purposeful manipulation of social relationships. This type of aggression occurs most often through malicious gossip and planned exclusion, the intent being to hurt another person. It has been observed to occur as early as preschool (Crick, Casas, & Ku, 1999) and can continue into adult relationships. Although an in-depth treatment of relational aggression is well beyond the scope of this book, interested professionals may find a useful discussion in Young, Boye, and Nelson's (2006) treatment of the subject.

Most relevant to concerns about physical aggression has been the finding that relational and physical aggression tend to be highly correlated (Henington, Hughes, Cavell, & Thompson, 1998; Leschied, Cummings, Van Brunschot, Cunningham, & Saunders, 2000; Schaeffer et al., 2006). Indications are that girls manifesting one phenomenon are at increased risk for manifesting the other, as well. This linkage has important implications for anger management treatment that we will discuss later in this chapter.

GENDER-SPECIFIC INTERVENTIONS FOR PHYSICALLY AGGRESSIVE GIRLS

The development and research of anger management interventions for girls lags far behind that of boys. Probably the most impressive research-supported intervention work with physically aggressive girls is being conducted currently by the Child Development Institute in Toronto, Canada. The SNAP® Girls Connection (formerly the Earlscourt Girls Connection) is a cognitive behavioral treatment program for girls under the age of 12 who display aggressive and antisocial behavior problems (Augimeri, 2008). It uses a developmental model of risk and protective factors to guide intervention in three primary areas: individual behaviors, multiple relationship contexts (including parent–child and family), and environmental contexts (including school and community). SNAP (which stands for "Stop Now and Plan") is a manualized small-group intervention that is informed by the sociocognitive information-processing deficits of aggressive children (e.g., Crick & Dodge, 1994) and has been designed to meet the gender-specific needs of girls. In contrast to similar interventions for boys, SNAP Girls Connection places increased emphasis on girls' propensity for social and relational aggression and directs focused attention on improving the parent–child bond.

The stated goals of the intervention include:

- Teach girls effective anger management skills by using SNAP (Stop Now and Plan as well as self-control and other problem-solving techniques).
- Teach parents effective child management skills by using SNAP parenting.
- Teach effective ways of recognizing and coping with social forms of aggression.
- Facilitate positive relationships with primary attention given to the mother–daughter relationship and same-sex modeling.
- Teach girls to engage in prosocial peer relations.
- Facilitate success in school.
- Prevent teen pregnancy. (Augimeri, 2008)

Ongoing research on this intervention found reductions in conduct problems and oppositional behaviors (Walsh, Pepler, & Levene, 2002), improvement in relationships with both parents and teachers (Pepler, Levene, &Walsh, 2004), and reduction in criminal offending (Levene, Walsh, Augimeri, & Pepler, 2004). A review of the research is available at *www.stopnowandplan.com/research.php*. Interested professionals can find complete program information at *www.stopnowandplan.com/index1.php.*.

TREATMENT ADAPTATIONS WHEN USING ANGER COPING WITH GIRLS

Screening, Identification, and Managing Grudges

A teacher friend who recently began his first year as a girls' fifth- and sixth-grade basketball coach remarked that he found girls to be every bit as eager and athletic as boys, with the only significant difference occurring at game time. "I have to get a quick read on the social situation of that particular day," he said. "For instance, if Emily and Tanesha aren't speaking, then I know certain plays are out because Emily simply won't throw her the ball."

Girls' tendency to hold prolonged grudges can at times wreak havoc on the best intentions of group skills training. Our experience is that boys, too, have and hold grudges against others, but in comparison to girls they seem more inclined to set them aside, at least temporarily. Perhaps boys' preference for direct physical responses to anger arousal helps prevent the kind of group meeting more characteristic of girls in which members sit silently, arms folded, lips pursed, not looking at one another.

In general, the screening and identification of girls for the Anger Coping group should follow the same guidelines described in Chapter 4 for boys. The goal is to identify girls who are experiencing chronic reactive aggressive anger problems in the school setting. Girls who are appropriate for this intervention typically demonstrate a *significant physical component* in their problem behavior that may include hitting, pushing, kicking, threatening, and/or destroying property. Girls displaying *only reactive aggressive behaviors* (i.e., with little or no physical eruptions or evident loss of temper) may be better served by involving them in one of the interventions identified in the Additional Resources section at the end of this chapter.

Recommendations

Our specific recommendations for screening and identification of girls with aggression problems are:

- When screening girls for participation in the Anger Coping group, discuss their friendship and "enemy" relationships with the classroom teachers. Teachers very often are clued into this information and can be especially helpful. Multiple short-duration tiffs with other girls are to be expected, but probe for those that have been longstanding and show no signs of abating. It may be advisable to place two girls who evidence acute animosity toward each other into separate treatment groups.
- When interviewing potential girls to include in the group, ask each one whom she "likes least" and "likes best" among the girls in the school. Take note of reciprocated instances of mutual dislike, and avoid pairing the two girls in the same group.
- Examine office discipline records and consult with the administrator in charge of discipline to determine the frequency of problem behavior between or among the same girls.
- Consider screening with the "Peer Nomination Scale" available by contacting the Outreach Center at the Crick Social Development Lab through the website *www. cehd.umn.edu/ICD/SocialDevelopment/*.
- Within the group, seek to establish a "peace zone" in which past problems can be temporarily set aside for the meeting time. This approach may constitute a struggle for some girls, but it can prove beneficial to openly acknowledge the legitimacy of their issues (rather than merely dismissing or diminishing them) and then to reinforce any of their efforts at cooperation.
- If a particularly problematic dyadic relationship persists, meet with the girls separately from the group and problem-solve their situation. Avoid forced "make-up" rituals in favor of patience, empathy, and small steps toward mutual toleration if not actual friendship.

Superior Verbal Skills

While boys tend to be action-oriented within the group context and often prefer to be on their feet "doing" something, girls tend to be comparatively more comfortable sitting and talking. Anecdotally, it is our observation that a group of young girls will often need only the smallest of encouragement to start a lively verbal exchange, but the potential for it to turn unproductive or even counterproductive is very high. Consequently, group leaders need to be watchful that the verbal skills of a few group members do not dominate the session and prevent actual behavioral skills training from occurring. Highly verbal girls can be a considerable force for both positive and negative group experiences, but—particularly when one is working with a time-limited treatment schedule—helping them to manage and focus those abilities is essential.

Our recommendations as they relate to girls' verbal skills are:

- If necessary, add a short time-limited "chat session" at the outset of each meeting that will enable group members to raise issues of immediate concern. Reinforce subsequent "on-task" behaviors, and use the "strikes" system to combat any efforts to sidetrack the session.

- Using a soft rubber "talking stick" or similar device that limits permission to speak to only its holder can be a helpful instructional aid.

- Verbal or nonverbal reminders to assist girls in focusing and remaining on the topic at hand can be helpful. For instance, when any of her group members began to head off in an unproductive direction, one of our interns would state the girl's name, tap her own nose, and say "topic." This cue was subsequently faded to a simple nose tap.

- Within the group itself, verbal and passive nonverbal aggression can become an issue, and group leaders are well advised to be proactive in setting behavioral expectations. As compared to boys, girls tend to evidence more frequent surreptitious and overt looks, gestures, and body language as aggressive communication devices. If these are left unmonitored, group meetings may sometimes deteriorate, with frequent interruptions of the "Tell her to stop doing that!" variety. Group leaders should use such incidents as opportunities to discuss and inculcate more effective ways of communicating anger or upset.

- In some instances, it may be necessary to include a rule against "sniping" or what is seen as under-the-breath disparagements or put-downs meant to get in the last shot or to show solidarity with another group member against a third. Compared to boys' use of overt, in-your-face digs and put-downs, this sort of *sotto voce* behavior may reflect girls' preference for more indirect aggression as well as to provide a handy option for a quasi-aggressive denial ("I didn't say anything—she's hearing things"). Further, with boys the verbal put-down can also be a type of bonding and affiliation gesture, containing an unstated "We're close enough that I get to say this without you becoming angry" agreement. In our experience, similar "agreements" or understandings among aggressive girls are exceedingly rare.

Co-Occurring Relational Aggression

Relational aggression tends to be particularly covert in nature and difficult for parents or school personnel to detect. In some cases, the existence of a longstanding and serious problem of relational aggression may not even come to light until after a physical fight has occurred (Young, Nelson, Hottle, Warburton, & Young, 2009). Although the Anger Coping Program is designed more generally for students who are demonstrating physical aggression in response to anger management problems, when working with girls the likelihood of co-occurring relational aggression must be considered (e.g., Schaeffer et al., 2006). Compared to physical aggression, relational aggression in its varying degrees of intensity is considerably more ubiquitous in the general population of schoolchildren, and particularly among girls. Consider the following admission:

> "When she did that, I was gonna beat her up right there at lunch, but instead, me and Nina texted her boyfriend that she was cheatin' on him."

The question arises as to whether a girl's reduction in reactive *physical* aggression and concurrent increase in reactive *relational* aggression can be considered a treatment gain. If she opts not to fight but instead turns to hurtful social manipulation, how should group leaders respond to that? Given the available evidence on the long-term outcomes of one versus the other, we are inclined to assert that when reactive relational aggression is purposefully substituted for physical aggression it can be viewed as a step forward for some girls. Of course, this is not to imply that group leaders should encourage such forms of aggression—quite the contrary.

In this instance, group leaders should not view the possible treatment gain to be the girl's choice of relationally aggressive behavior but rather *her inhibition of that first impulse to strike out physically.* As earlier noted, children who demonstrate reactive aggression tend to have a strong preference for direct action and often overrely on aggressive solutions. In this case, we have a chronically aggressive child who restrained herself from direct physical action and selected a nonaggressive response to a perceived provocation. That she replaced it with another socially undesirable option is a matter for further training, but clearly the child has expanded her response repertoire, and that in our clinical opinion is a net positive. Helping her to self-discover why she chose to select one option over the other would be an appropriate next step in treatment.

Assertiveness Training

Although the idea of flip-flopping from one form of aggression to another makes for an interesting scenario, our experience has been that most of the girls referred for anger regulation problems are already heavily engaged in both relational and physical aggression, and for the most part neither course is working out for them. It has been argued (e.g., Garbarino, 2006; Simmons, 2002) that girls frequently receive double messages on how anger should be expressed. On the one hand, parents, teachers, and certain media influences can send out the message that "boys will be boys" but girls need to be "ladylike" and shun unfeminine conflicts in favor of cooperation, friendship, and belonging. But simultaneously come media messages of aggressive "girl power" from both television programming and the many lethal action adventure films of the past two decades, such as *La Femme Nikita, Laura Croft: Tomb Raider,* and the *Kill Bill* series. In addition, recent years have seen girls' emergence into aggressive, physically demanding sports through Title 9 opportunities, in the process "learning the very positive message that their bodies can be physically powerful in ways that are not sexual" (Garbarino, 2006, p. 17). Add to this confusion neighborhood or street "codes" with their aggressive imperatives ("Don't let nobody talk about your family") that send yet additional negative messages to girls and boys alike.

Young people often respond to group leaders by saying "Oh, you want me to just stand there and do nothing, right?" Experienced professionals as well as many experienced parents will recognize this often-used straw man rejoinder when they hear it. However, girls who engage in chronic fighting and other aggressive behaviors genuinely may believe that their choices in highly charged situations are either punching or doing nothing. The treatment objective is to help them to consider and then enact a more efficacious third way.

A caveat: There are some young people who doggedly adhere to the "I have to hit them" imperative regardless of any negative consequences that are brought to their attention. Group leaders should avoid getting pulled into what is usually a fruitless back-and-forth in the context of the group meeting. Aggressive posturing such as this can be as much about the child communicating to the other members as it is about defending her own sense of self. Meeting with the group member individually later in the day or week may allow her to problem-solve more openly and/or less fearfully.

The following instructional procedures are recommended for inclusion in the second half of the Anger Coping Program:

- Divide a flip chart or white board into two columns, with the heading on one side "The Possible Good from Fighting" and the heading on the other "The Possible Bad from Fighting." Brainstorm the two lists, noting that any "good" outcomes will occur only if you win the fight. Invariably, the number of possible bad outcomes will far outweigh the good outcomes accruing from violence. Discuss the implications with the students.

- Have the group come up with a definition of what *being assertive* means when viewed in comparison to *being aggressive*. Examples might include:
  - "Being assertive means standing up for what you think is right without fighting."
  - "Being assertive means defending yourself without fighting."
  - "Being assertive means letting the other person know what you think and feel *without* fighting."

- Some common assertiveness techniques include:
  - Using "I statements": *I don't like it when you _____, and I get angry when you do. I want you to please stop.*
  - Fogging: This technique is used to help de-escalate verbal provocations by refusing to become angered by them. Other girl: *You are such a bitch!* Group member: *Yeah, I know I can be sometimes, but I'm working on it.* Other girl: *Want me to kick your ass?* Group member: *No, I have a lot of other things I have to do right now instead.*
  - Escalating assertion (Feindler & Ecton, 1986): This is a sequence of responses that start mild (the initial one) and increase in assertiveness, leading to a final contract option (the fourth one). Group member: 1st—*Please stop doing that.* 2nd—*I asked you to stop doing that.* 3rd—*I want you to stop doing that* now. 4th—*If you don't stop doing that, I am going to tell the playground supervisor, and you will have to deal with* her.

- Have the group members all recall incidents in which they chose to be assertive rather than aggressive and then describe the outcome.

- Construct scenarios that may have or actually have led to fighting, and use role play to have the group members enact "being assertive" rather than aggressive.

- Throughout this effort, it is important that historically aggressive girls understand that fighting is almost always a choice and that the best times to be assertive come well before someone throws the first punch. Fights don't "just happen" but rather evolve through a series of escalating provocations and responses. Being assertive is also about timing, and this will require discussion, role play, and feedback.

Victimization Issues

Early childhood physical and sexual abuse has been found to be associated with aggressive, antisocial behavior in children and youth (see Dodge, Pettit, & Bates, 1997, and Horton & Cruise, 2001, for reviews). This is as true for boys as it is for girls, but chronic, reactive aggressive behavior among girls, particularly in combination with other warning signs, should signal the need for a closer investigation. With both boys and girls, it is essential for group leaders to be sensitive to the warning signs that are most evident in the school setting and if warranted, proceed as required under state-mandated reporter statutes. Although a comprehensive exploration of this issue is beyond the scope of this chapter, useful guidance may be found online at Prevent Child Abuse America (*www.preventchildabuse.org*) and in Horton and Cruise's volume (2001).

Our recommendations on victimization issues include:

- Group leaders should take steps to ensure the safety of the child in question if there is suspicion that abuse may be taking place currently. Group leaders are reminded that interviewing a child for suspected physical or sexual abuse requires specific skills generally beyond those of traditionally trained school personnel and should be left to professionals with the appropriate clinical training. The potential pitfalls, both legal and clinical, are numerous and serious.
- Some training activities in the Anger Coping Program (e.g., the taunting exercise) may be contraindicated for children with PTSD. Consequently, the potential that a victimized child may be experiencing PTSD symptoms or those of a related anxiety disorder should be confirmed through a comprehensive clinical evaluation prior to enrollment in an Anger Coping group. Alternative treatment strategies are available to address the needs of children engaging in trauma-related problem behavior (see Additional Resources at the conclusion of this chapter).
- For some children and youth, the aggressive behavior seen in school may be an adaptive mechanism of self-defense against abuse in the home or community. With girls in particular, consideration may be give to providing physical self-defense training along with other protective skills and information (see Additional Resources at the conclusion of this chapter).

Treating Boys and Girls in the Same Group

Deciding whether or not to run a combined girls and boys group depends entirely on the children involved. For instance, is their aggressive behavior limited to members of their own sex, or does it cross over to members of the opposite sex as well? Is the problem primarily reactive aggressive behavior, or are there significant elements of relational aggression? In other words, the more alike the presenting problems are, the greater the likelihood that group leaders will find common training goals. Ultimately, the decision to include or exclude any child in a treatment group is an informed judgment that reflects the needs of the child and the context of treatment.

In our experience, blended groups are least problematic with younger children. As children mature sexually, group leaders need to be very sensitive to the issue of "deviant peer influence" by inadvertently contributing to a potentially problematic "romantic" relationship (see Chapter 10 and Dodge, Dishion, & Lansford, 2006, for additional information). Aggressive students tend to be attracted to and affiliate with one another (Farmer et al., 2002). When a treatment group brings together young people of both sexes who otherwise do not associate as peers in the larger school environment, the potential for iatrogenic matchmaking arises. Early maturing aggressive girls may be particularly at risk (Pepler & Craig, 2005).

Our recommendations in this area include:

- In general, normally opt for the use of same-sex groups.
- Organize blended groups only with younger, prepubescent students who are demonstrating similar problems with reactive aggressive behavior, particularly if aggressive incidents cross over to members of the opposite sex.
- With blended groups, maintain a balance of girls and boys to avoid the potential for bullying or rejection within the group.

Anger management interventions with physically aggressive young girls present a unique set of challenges, but the need to help remove them from a potentially very serious antisocial trajectory is critical. The flexible adaptation of the Anger Coping Program can provide a potentially effective treatment vehicle to assist in this effort. In addition, adaptations by group leaders should be informed by the finding at the Child Development Center in Canada (see SNAP Girls Connection research) of the positive effects associated with enhancing parent–child relationships, with primary attention to the mother–daughter relationship and same-sex modeling. Although involving parents can be particularly challenging with school-based treatment, it may well be an important component when working with young girls, and one may have to seek out creative ways to make it happen.

CHILDREN FROM DIVERSE CULTURAL BACKGROUNDS

The Anger Coping and related Coping Power programs have been implemented and evaluated with samples that have included large representations of African American as well as white children. The Anger Coping and Coping Power programs' efficacy, effectiveness, and dissemination research studies have all tested, as a matter of course, for whether the intervention effects were moderated by children's racial status. Racial moderation of intervention effects have not been found. It appears that the social-cognitive and social skill risk factors that are related to children's aggressive behavior problems are similar across racial groups and that an intervention targeting active risk mechanisms is roughly equally effective among children of various races and ethnicities.

However, interventions must be delivered in ways that make them relevant and appropriate for the various types of populations that can be found in urban, suburban, and rural settings. Lochman, Whidby, and FitzGerald (2000) noted that the effects of a cognitive-behavioral intervention like the Anger Coping Program could be limited by certain cultural constraints. Within African American low-income populations, children's abilities to accept and use nonaggressive strategies to solve problems may be limited by their parents' modeling of physical aggression through their greater use of corporal punishment and by their parents' direct advice to retaliate when confronted by certain types of threatening situations. These parental responses can often be the result of the parents' desire to protect their children within a threatening violent environment within a low-income community. Intervention may need to explicitly advocate the use of "code switching" among these African American youth (Lochman, Whidby, et al., 2000) so that children can acquire a different code of behavior depending on the environment they are in (e.g., a violent, crime-ridden neighborhood vs. a relatively orderly school).

Anger Coping clinicians should be sensitive to children's cultural background. Culture and ethnicity are sometimes used interchangeably, but they are qualitatively different constructs (Jones et al., 2001). Culture involves the norms and values, influenced by society, that influence how someone thinks, feels, and behaves, while ethnicity is a set of genetic, morphological, and anthropological characteristics (Parron, 1994). Appreciation of diversity is a core foundation of clinicians' respect for people's rights and dignity. The American Psychological Association states this principle as follows:

> Psychologists are aware of and respect cultural, individual, and role differences, including those based on age, gender, gender identity, race, ethnicity, culture, national origin, religion, sexual orientation, disability, language, and socioeconomic status, and consider those factors when working with members of such groups. Psychologists try to eliminate the effect on their work of biases based on those factors, and they do not knowingly participate in or condone activities based upon such prejudices. (American Psychological Association, 2002a, Principle E)

The emphasis on cultural competency for professional therapists is especially important, as the United States becomes more racially and ethnically diverse and thus requires more culturally responsive practices and services (American Psychological Association, 2002b).

At the level of the clinical provider, clinicians' appreciation of diversity permits them to more effectively understand the experiences of those clients and to more accurately assess the appropriate use of intervention procedures (Falender & Shafranske, 2004). Clinicians working with minority children may be challenged to earn the trust of the child and the family, which is essential for a strong viable therapeutic relationship (Jones et al., 2001). Key components of clinicians' cultural competence include: (1) knowledge about individual and cultural diversity; (2) sensitivity and responsivity to individual and cultural diversity during intervention; and (3) awareness of the interaction between clinican's own diversity characteristics and those of the people with whom the clinician is working professionally.

When working with minority children and families, clinicians should attend to how contextual variables may have an effect on the expression of psychopathology and on the level of impairment involved (Jones et al., 2001). Culture affects children's and families' schemas and beliefs about issues such as the value and utility they place on aggressive behavior (Lochman, Holmes, et al., 2008), and children's ethnic identity can influence their social goals (Holmes & Lochman, 2009). When working with African American children and families, attention to an Africentric worldview can assist the clinicians' understanding of strengths in African American children and families. Some of the Africentric values and beliefs that may be important (Council of National Psychological Associations for the Advancement of Ethnic Miniority Interests, 2009) are: (1) spirituality, involving a belief in a being or force greater than self; (2) collectivism, interdependence, and cooperation, which motivate a person to work for the well-being of the group rather than oneself; (3) time orientation, as time is viewed as subjectively flexible rather than being bound concretely by clocks, and as being more focused on the past and present rather than the future; (4) sensitivity to affect and emotional cues ("I am well if you are well"); and (5) being in balance and harmony with nature. Clinicians should attend to the worldviews relevant for the specific types of minority children they see, although some of these worldviews, such as collectivism, spirituality, and harmony with nature, are found among Latino and other minority groups in the United States as well. (See Additional Resources, below.)

ADDITIONAL RESOURCES

Treatment of Trauma-Related Problem Behavior

Smith, P., Perrin, S., Yule, W., & Clark, D. M. (2010). *Post traumatic stress disorder: Cognitive therapy with children and young people.* New York: Routledge.

Contains assessment, case formulation, and treatment procedures.

Cognitive-Behavioral Intervention for Trauma in Schools (C-BITS)
www.rand.org/health/projects/cbits

Provides mental health screening and a brief standardized series of therapy sessions in schools aimed at reducing a child's symptoms related to existing traumatic experiences and enhancing skills to handle future stresses.

Treatment of Relational Aggression

Dellasega, C., & Nixon, C. (2003). *Girl wars: 12 strategies that will end female bullying.* New York: Fireside. (*www.simonandschuster.biz/content/book.cfm?tab=1&pid=423782&er=978074324 9874*)

An especially useful text for parents and teachers who desire to become more informed.

Kupkovits, J. (2008). *Relational aggression in girls.* Chapin, SC: Youth Light, Inc. (*www.youthlight. com/products/1437.html*)

A prevention and intervention curriculum with activities and lessons for small groups and classrooms.

The Ophelia Project
www.opheliaproject.org/main/index.htm

Organization dedicated to providing programs and training to address nonphysical forms of aggression.

Self-Defense Training for Girls—"Just Yell Fire"

www.justyellfire.com/index.php

> *Organization dedicated to providing programs and training to help girls learn to fight back against predators and attempts at date rape.*

Working with Diverse Populations

Pederson, P. B., Draguns, J. G., Lonner, W. J., & Trimble, J. E. (Eds.). (2008). *Counseling across cultures* (6th ed.). Thousand Oaks, CA: Sage. (*www.sagepub.com/cac6study*)

> *Becoming a classic text in understanding the many issues that surround counseling individuals from diverse ethnic and cultural backgrounds.*

CHAPTER 10

Possible Negative Group Effects and Alternative Use as an Individual Format

The Anger Coping Program was developed to be used in small groups, and some outcome research has focused on this particular intervention format. Although, overall, the Anger Coping and related Coping Power programs have significantly reduced children's problem behaviors, in some cases the positive effects are reduced or at least obfuscated by deviant peer effects and other behavioral management problems. Based on the emerging studies, researchers have concluded that behaviorally disordered children in largely homogeneous groups are likely to affiliate well with one another (Arnold & Hughes, 1999). However, research results are sufficiently tenuous to lead some researchers to recommend that practitioners be cautious in how they provide group interventions (Dishion, McCord, & Poulin, 1999), generally avoiding any concentration of truly high-risk youth in groups within clinical, educational, or correctional settings (Poulin, Dishion, & Burraston, 2001; Weaver, 2000). Other research has found no specific evidence for iatrogenic deviancy training effects in group interventions with disruptive youth (e.g., Lipsey, 2006; Weiss et al., 2005). While all agree that the potential for deviancy training is present in group interventions with disruptive youth, this potentially adverse iatrogenic effect can be manageable in properly structured interventions.

As a result of these concerns, it has become increasingly important to explore whether the Anger Coping and Coping Power programs can be effectively and usefully delivered in a one-to-one format and how deviant peer effects in groups should best be addressed. In this chapter, we discuss the relative merits of group formats for intervention programs, research on deviant peer effects in general and in interventions, the mechanisms that account for these deviant peer effects, and how potential group leader actions can avoid deviancy training effects within groups. Ways in which Anger Coping group sessions can be adapted to an individual one-on-one format are also discussed.

DEVELOPMENTAL RESEARCH ON DEVIANT GROUP EFFECTS

Adolescents' problem behaviors are often embedded in their close involvements with peer groups (Dishion et al., 1999). Research over the past 60 years has detected a strong association between children's antisocial behaviors and those of their peers (Arnold & Hughes, 1999; Sutherland, 1939). When adolescents join a deviant peer group, they often increase their rates of school truancy and dropout, placing themselves in even closer contact with one another, which may lead directly to increased rates of delinquency (Coie et al., 1995; Lochman, 2003). Children's association with deviant peers in adolescence becomes one of the strongest proximal risk predictors for growth in subsequent delinquency (Miller-Johnson, Coie, Maumary-Gremaud, Lochman, & Terry, 1999; Patterson, 1993; Tremblay, Kurtz, Masse, Vitaro, & Pihl, 1995). Moderately aggressive boys have been found to be most susceptible to the negative effects of aggressive friends (Vitaro, Trembly, Kerr, Pagani, & Bukowski, 1997). Exposure to high levels of peer drug abuse within the deviant peer groups is also associated with high levels of concurrent drug use by adolescents (Dishion, Reid, & Patterson, 1988) and with escalating drug use over time (Wills, McNamara, Vaccaro, & Hirkey, 1996). The steepest growth of substance use occurs among adolescents with drug-using peers (Chassin, Curran, Hussong, & Colder, 1996; Curran, Stice, & Chassin, 1997).

The effect of the deviant peer group on individuals' behavior is evident in other social contextual research on gang involvement and on the influence of aggressive children in classroom settings as well. Youth's rates of violent delinquent behavior have been found to increase sharply when they first become involved in gangs and to decline when they leave the gangs (Thornberry & Krohn, 1997). Similarly, aggressive children in classrooms with high proportions of other aggressive children are more likely to increase their aggression during that academic year than is the case for aggressive preadolescents in classrooms with lesser proportions of antisocial children (Barth, Dunlap, Dane, Lochman, & Wells, 2004). These classroom contextual effects likely influence children's behavior for several years when the antisocial classroom experience occurs in the early years of elementary school (Kellam, Ling, Mersica, Brown, & Ialongo, 1998). However, the antisocial classroom effect is likely to have only a concurrent effect on children's behavior in later years (Barth et al., 2004), much like the gang involvement effect (Thornberry & Krohn, 1997). These findings raise questions about the mechanisms by which deviant peer group effects occur, and whether they also occur during group interventions that aggregate antisocial youth.

MECHANISMS UNDERLYING DEVIANT PEER INFLUENCE

Social Norms

Prominent explanations for the effect that deviant peer groups have on individuals' behavior include the influence of social norms and the separate influence of deviancy training through greater interaction (Lavallee, Bierman, Nix, & Conduct Problems Prevention Group, 2005; Patterson, Dishion, & Yoerger, 2000). Using the person–group similarity model, Wright, Giammarino, & Parad (1986) found that a high proportion of aggressive youth in a group may cause the social norms underlying aggression to shift to a higher level for individuals within the group, effectively increasing the social acceptability of aggressive and antisocial behavior. The influence of deviant peer groups' norms on individual children's behavior has also been evident in findings that elementary school children's aggression may be influenced by peer rejection only when aggression is relatively rare in the classroom (Boivin, Dodge, & Coie, 1995; Stormshak et al., 1999).

Deviancy Training

In addition to being exposed to others with high levels of aggression, members of a deviant peer group may directly reinforce one another's antisocial attitudes and behaviors. Delinquent adolescent dyads have been found to provide high rates of positive reinforcement for their partners' deviant talk, while nondeviant dyads provide reinforcement for each other's normative nondeviant discussions (Dishion et al., 1999; Patterson et al., 2000). This pattern of reinforcement of rule-breaking talk among deviant dyads directly affects these youth's subsequent substance use and delinquency (Dishion & Andrews,1995; Dishion, Eddy, Haas, Li, & Spracklen, 1997). In a key study that demonstrated how deviancy training could be a primary mechanism accounting for the negative effect of aggregating antisocial youth, Patterson et al. (2000) found that deviancy training in dyadic interactions partially mediated the effect of boys' involvement with deviant peers in the fourth grade and their substance use, police arrests, and number of intercourse partners in the eighth grade.

Modeling

In addition to receiving direct reinforcement for deviant behavior, modeling and imitation, especially of older peers, might account for deviant peer effects (Dishion & Dodge, 2006). Some youth may perform deviant behaviors at a higher rate because they are being modeled by deviant peers.

Increased Exposure and Opportunity

Deviant peers may provoke fights among group members, increasing the opportunities for aggression (Dishion & Dodge, 2006). Outside of a group intervention setting, deviant peers can bring a child to new neighborhoods where new opportunities for deviant behaviors exist (Thornberry, Krohn, Lizotte, Smith, & Tobin, 2003).

INTERVENTION RESEARCH ON DEVIANT GROUP EFFECTS

During the past decade research has actively explored whether these deviant peer group effects operate in intervention groups as well. An early indication that grouping together various problem-ridden children may have untoward iatrogenic effects was evident in follow-up analyses of the Cambridge–Somerville Study (Dishion et al., 1999). This long-lasting multicomponent intervention for conduct problem children continued through age 16. At the end of the program, there were no differences between the intervention group and the randomized control group. However, the intervention was found to have produced *harmful* effects when the participants were followed up in middle age, and the worst outcomes were evident for those who attended summer camp as part of the intervention (Dishion et al., 1999). Although this iatrogenic effect may have been attributable to additional group attention that participants had received for misbehavior, more carefully planned research was required to document the nature and source of these iatrogenic effects. The efforts by Dishion and colleagues have had a significant effect on spurring systematic research relating to deviant group effects in interventions.

Dishion and Andrews (1995) randomly assigned high-risk young adolescents to one of four conditions that varied as to whether (1) the youth received 12 youth-only sessions, (2) their parents received 12 parent-only sessions, (3) the youth and parents both received combined intervention, or (4) the youth and parents received no intervention. All three of the adolescent transition program intervention cells (conditions 1–3) manifested some positive effects at postintervention, and the conditions providing youth intervention (1 and 3) produced reductions in negative family interactions and good acquisition of the concepts presented in the intervention. However, by the time of a 1-year follow-up, the youth who had received youth sessions had higher rates of tobacco use and of teacher-rated delinquent behaviors than did the control children, and these iatrogenic effects were evident even if the parents had also participated in the combined intervention. At a 3-year follow-up, the teen intervention conditions continued to reflect more subsequent tobacco use and delinquency (Poulin et al., 2001). Analyses of the iatrogenic group conditions revealed that the subtle dynamics of deviancy training during unstructured transitions in the group sessions predicted subsequent growth in self-reported smoking and teacher ratings of delinquency (Dishion, Poulin, & Burraston, 2001). Group effects were minimal, and negative effects of the intervention seemed largely attributable to errant individuals dispersed across groups. This finding is consistent with the conclusion of several studies in a recent special issue on this topic in the *Journal of Abnormal Child Psychology* (summarized in Dishion & Dodge, 2006). If this finding holds up over time, it suggests that better group leader training is a critical component in increasing the effectiveness of group interventions with youth. Identification, proactive management, and appropriate placement of the group's worst offenders may be the best strategy for optimizing intervention effectiveness and minimizing future harm.

Planned Group Composition as a Moderator of Deviant Group Effects

Arnold and Hughes (1999) have suggested that the deviant peer group effects may be less apparent in child groups that are composed of *both* conduct problem and non-conduct problem children, based on suggestive findings from earlier research using children's self-reports and staff reports (Feldman, Caplinger, & Wodarski, 1983). However, empirical research suggests the opposite is true. In a recent rigorous test of this hypothesis, Mager, Milich, Harris, and Howard (2005) randomly assigned sixth- and seventh-grade children to either "pure" intervention groups of all conduct problem children or to "mixed" groups of children with and without behavior problems. Youth in the "pure" intervention groups had greater reductions in parent- and teacher-rated externalizing outcomes than did the children in the "mixed" groups. Results indicated that deviancy training occurred for children in the "mixed" groups, accounting for their comparatively poorer outcomes. These results accord with the findings of Poulin et al. (2001), lending greater support to the deviancy training explanations of deviant group effects than to the social norms explanations that are based on the simple aggregation of aggressive children.

Deviancy Training versus Social Norm Explanations of Deviant Group Effects

Lavallee et al. (2005) have also not found evidence for social norm explanations of deviant group effects. Examining high-risk first-grade children's responses to the multicomponent Fast Track intervention, children's outcomes were not influenced by the negative behavior of their peers. Lavallee et al. (2005) found that most children were positively engaged during group sessions, displaying high rates of on-task behavior with little disruptiveness, and, more importantly, that the degree of children's positive engagement in sessions predicted whether they would have positive teacher-, parent-, and observer-rated outcomes at the end of the first grade. There was evidence for deviancy training, in that worse teacher- and peer-rated outcomes were found for children who had received increased peer attention for their disruptive behaviors. However, whether a child received attention for his or her disruptive behavior was predicted primarily by his or her own baseline level of problem behaviors. Thus, the deviancy training that occurred appeared to be more attributable to the child's negative behavior than to the behavioral characteristics of the peer partners, and the inclusion of aggressive peers did not necessarily lead to deviancy training or to negative outcomes.

Deviancy Training Revisited: Alternate Views

Meta-analyses examining group versus individual formats across all types of interventions for children and adolescents have not detected iatrogenic effects for groups, although smaller effect sizes for group formats have sometimes been reported (Ang & Hughes, 2002; Lipsey, 2006; Tillitski, 1990; Weisz et al., 1987; Weisz, Donenberg, Han, & Kauneckis, 1995). Several meta-analyses specifically examining group versus individual interventions for antisocial youth (Ang & Hughes, 2002; Lipsey, 2006) have had divergent conclusions. A meta-analysis by Weiss et al. (2005) concluded that the risk of having iatrogenic effects may currently be overstated, supporting certain prior suggestions (e.g., Handwerk, Field, & Friman, 2000). Weiss et al. (2005) updated their prior treatment meta-analysis datasets with new studies and found that there was no difference in effect size for group versus individual treatment (group = 0.79, individual = 0.68). Surprisingly, group intervention studies had a significantly lower likelihood of creating negative effect sizes than did individual intervention studies, although the log odds for having a negative effect size peaked at age 11 for children in groups versus age 8.6 for individual interventions. This pattern suggests that groups tend to have worse effects as children approach adolescence, consistent with prior indications that group iatrogenic effects were most noticeable among early adolescents. Within studies of group treatments, homogeneity of group membership was not found to relate to outcome. This meta-analysis suggests that iatrogenic effects of group interventions are not universal effects but that it is critically important to research the potential iatrogenic effects of group interventions at key developmental points further.

A recent meta-analysis by Lipsey (2006) may have even more bearing on this planned study because of Lipsey's focus on community-based group treatments for delinquency. Lipsey's meta-analysis found no overall indication that group treatments had negative effects on youth, but rather they appeared to diminish the effects of comparable individually delivered interventions under certain conditions. The diminishing effect of group interventions was more evident with prevention programs with less disturbed youth, as these group programs had mean effect sizes that were about one-third less than for individually delivered programs. Similarly, Ang and Hughes (2002) found larger effect sizes for individual (0.78) versus group interventions (0.60 for groups combining antisocial and nonantisocial youth, 0.55 for homogenous antisocial groups). Lipsey (2006) concluded that the strongest likelihood of diminished effects occurred with relatively unstructured or ineffectually supervised groups consisting of a mixture of more and less antisocial youth. The results of these meta-analyses suggest that it is critically important to now test this difference between group versus individual formats in a randomly assigned trial, as is proposed in the current study.

It is evident that further research is required to address the relative effectiveness of group versus individual intervention formats, to examine the degree of deviant group effects, and to explore under what conditions variations in the deviancy of groups might influence preadolescent aggressive children's behavior (Weiss et al., 2005). This research would be most productive if it could test variations in format for an intervention that has already established an evidence base and has the potential for wide dissemination. The current application will use Coping Power as the focal intervention, and the conceptual framework, intervention structure, and outcome effects will be described in the following section.

POTENTIAL ADVANTAGES FOR GROUP FORMATS

Although there are concerns about deviant peer effects in interventions for aggressive and conduct problem children, there are also important potential benefits to using a group format for intervention delivery. The benefits fall into at least five areas. First, working with children in groups is more cost-effective than individually delivered interventions (Mager et al., 2005; Manassis et al., 2002). Cost is an important consideration at all levels of mental health service delivery and could certainly be a factor, from a public health perspective, in making preventive interventions readily available to a broad spectrum of the population. Second, group reward systems and peer reinforcement can play an important role in assisting children in attaining intervention-related goals and thus generalizing behavioral improvements resulting from intervention to the children's real-world school and home settings (Poulin et al., 2001). Third, groups can enable children to develop prosocial leadership skills (Flannery-Schroeder & Kendall, 2000). Fourth, the group format may be less threatening to conduct problem children, especially in the school setting (Schechtman &

Ben-David, 1999). Fifth, the group format enables the enrollees to practice learned skills (Poulin et al., 2001), and the small-group format has generally been considered better than individual formats for skills training (Landau, Milich, & Diener, 1998). Inclusion of peers in small-group interventions facilitates opportunities for learning social and emotional skills and for feedback on social and emotional skill performance, and it fosters children's abilities to generalize the use of these skills with peers (Bierman, 1986; Lavallee et al., 2005). Intervention techniques such as role playing, peer modeling, and peer reinforcement of adaptive behavior are available only within small-group formats (Mager et al., 2005).

Studies Using Group and Individual Formats

Because there are potentially unique advantages in working with children in interventions featuring group formats (in addition to the potential for negative deviant group effects), it is important to determine the types of outcomes produced by group versus individual formats. However, there are relatively few rigorously designed studies of child interventions that have compared these formats, and no such studies exist for disruptive children.

Nonexternalizing Problems

In studies of anxiety disorders, Flannery-Schroeder and Kendall (2000) randomly assigned 37 children and adolescents to cognitive-behavioral (CBT) individual treatment, CBT group treatment, or wait-list control. Both the group and individual versions produced significant reductions in diagnostic status and parent- and child-reported trait anxiety, relative to the control condition. However, children in individual CBT reported the greatest reduction in self-reported anxious distress. Similarly, Manassis et al. (2002) randomly assigned children to group versus individual versions of the CBT Coping Cat program, finding reductions in child- and parent-reported anxiety for both versions. With regard to moderator variables, children with high initial levels of social anxiety had greater improvement in individual CBT.

In studies of group treatments for child abuse effects, Trowell et al. (2002) randomly assigned 71 sexually abused girls to 30 individual or 18 psychoeducational group treatment sessions and found no differences between their relative improvement in psychopathology at posttreatment. The youth receiving individual treatment had greater reductions in PTSD symptoms such as re-experiencing of the traumatic events and persistent avoidance, although these effects might be attributable to the greater length of treatment in the individual format. In another study, Nolan et al. (2002) randomly assigned 20 abused children to either individual treatment (IT) or individual plus group treatment (IGT). The two conditions showed comparable improvements in parent-reported externalizing and internalizing problems and in child-reported depression and anxiety, and they were equally effective in treating the sequelae of child sexual abuse.

In sum, group and individual formats appear effective for nonexternalizing problems, and there may be some advantage for individually based interventions. While intriguing, these findings may be only modestly related to understanding this issue in antisocial youth, as we would expect the dynamics of a group of nonexternalizing children to differ in substantial ways from those of externalizing youth.

Externalizing Behavior Problems

In an early well-controlled study, Kendall and Zupan (1981) randomly assigned children referred by teachers for self-control problems to individual treatment, group treatment, or a nonspecific group treatment control. All three conditions demonstrated improvements on some outcome variables, but only the individual and group CBT produced improvements in teacher-rated self-control at posttreatment and in perspective taking at a short-term follow-up. At a 1-year follow-up, only the children who had received group treatment rated comparably to nonproblem children on hyperactivity ratings and in their recall of program materials (Kendall, 1982). However, on most measures both the group and individual formats produced lasting effects at follow-up.

Several studies by Schechtman have been more specifically focused on children with aggression problems. Schechtman and Ben-David (1999) compared 15 children seen in individual sessions to 71 children seen in 15 groups. Children were nominated by first-through ninth-grade teachers on the basis of their aggressiveness. The intervention used bibliotherapy and included psychodynamic and humanistic strategies during the early phases and cognitive-behavioral strategies during the later sessions. Children were randomly assigned to intervention or to wait-list control, and then intervention children were placed in the group or individual format, depending on the therapists' access to a sufficient number of children. Both the group and individual formats produced reductions in teacher-rated aggression at posttreatment, but only the individual format led to reduced levels of child-reported aggression. A second study by Schechtman (2003, 2004) assigned teacher-rated third- to sixth-grade aggressive children to individual versus group formats and found no differential impact for the two intervention formats in producing reductions in teacher- and child-reported aggression. Although these two studies suggest that aggressive children treated in group formats have adult-rated behavioral improvements that are similar to the outcomes for children provided with individual interventions, the lack of random assignment between the two formats, as well as the baseline differences in scores (Dodge, 1999), tempers the conclusions from these studies. Clearly, additional rigorously controlled research is needed to clarify the relative effectiveness of group versus individual treatment for disruptive youth.

Pilot Study of Individualized Administration of the Coping Power Program

During the past 2 years we have piloted an abbreviated individual version of Coping Power (ICP-A). We have carefully planned the 24-session ICP-A to precisely mirror the objectives of the 24-session CP group format (GCP-A). Session activities that could be accomplished between the child and interventionist were retained, and activities that required peer involvement were modified. ICP-A was designed to take place in 30- to 40-minute weekly sessions, compared to 45- to 60-minute weekly sessions for GCP-A. In the initial pilot project, we implemented ICP-A with 23 children in four schools and found the program to be well received by children and to be feasible to implement at school. Session objectives can be met within the individual format, with some 94% of session objectives completely met, 6% partially met, and less than 1% not met.

Intervention staff (who were also experienced in providing GCP-A) perceived certain advantages for ICP-A, including that it can be more easily tailored to the specific needs of the child, that it permits better assessment of children's comprehension, that fewer behavior management difficulties arise, that it is easier to maintain children's attention, and that it can more easily focus on specific examples of problems and skills from the child's life. Potential disadvantages of ICP-A are that it lacks group cohesion and friendship-building opportunities, that it may seem more didactic than a group discussion, there are fewer opportunities to directly observe the children's level of social skills, and there is no opportunity to practice successful interaction skills with peers.

Following completion of ICP-A, based on the teacher-rated Behavior Assessment System for Children (BASC), children had significant reductions in aggression (pretreatment, 24.3; posttreatment, 17.3) and hyperactivity (21.9 vs. 16.5) and tended to have improved social skills (9.7 vs. 14.7). As a pilot test of the effect size difference between the two conditions, we compared the 23 children who received ICP-A to 120 children who had received GCP-A. When the ICP-A and GCP-A pre–post changes in teacher-rated BASC aggression scores were compared to the control group, ICP-A had an intervention effect size of 0.6 versus GCP-A, which had an intervention effect size of 0.2. Thus, the pilot study suggests that ICP-A may have an advantage of 0.4 effect size in comparison to GCP-A. We also compared the parent group attendance for the two forms of intervention and found that the parent attendance at parent groups was lower for ICP-A (27%) versus GCP-A (36%), suggesting that differential parent group attendance could complicate interpretation of the differences between the two conditions. In this case, because GCP-A had the higher rate of parent attendance, the difference in parent attendance suggests that the 0.4 effect size difference favoring ICP-A is a conservative estimate and that the likely difference between conditions may be higher than that.

Using the GCP-A data from this same trial, we have also examined the degree of variability that exists across groups. Considerable differences were found to exist in the groups' average BASC behavioral improvement, indicating that some groups have better behavioral outcomes than others and that group composition, deviancy training, and/or group leader characteristics can impact group outcomes. Using GCP-A with 23 groups (at least three children per group), 5 groups fared worse than the control group (increases of 4.75–8.25 on the BASC Aggression Scale), 5 groups increased in aggression but at a lower rate than the control group (control group = +2.75) across the year (1.20–2.33), and 13 improved (–0.20 to –10.25, with 7 of these groups having decreases of at least –2.3). Thus, variability in outcomes does exist across GCP-A groups, and this variability provides support for further research to examine how group leader behaviors and child characteristics may influence the degree to which GCP groups might enhance or diminish the intervention's effectiveness.

Summary

Based on the current literature from randomized intervention trials, the relative effectiveness of group versus individual formats in the delivery of interventions for aggressive preadolescent children has not yet been conclusively determined. Existing limited evidence suggests that there may be generally similar results for individual versus group formats in intervention research with children, with some variation between these formats for certain types of outcome measures (e.g., child self-report measures may show more improvement when children are seen individually), although earlier reviews had suggested that there were advantages for individual interventions over group interventions (e.g., Weisz et al., 1995). The pilot data reported here suggest that individual administration of interventions like Coping Power and Anger Coping may have advantages over group administration in reducing children's aggression but that a controlled intervention research study is ultimately needed.

WHAT THERAPISTS MAY BE ABLE TO DO TO REDUCE DEVIANT GROUP EFFECTS

Although there is a relative dearth of rigorous research on the protective factors related to different types of group leader behaviors, it has been suggested that carefully managed and supervised groups may avoid iatrogenic effects (Dishion & Dodge, 2006). Leader behaviors considered to be important for the successful implementation of groups include certain behavior management strategies (attention to rules, rigorously correcting behavior, praising the child for compliance, the liberal use of rewards and punishments) and specific teaching strategies (reviewing the prior session, praising cooperative behaviors, reviewing activities when completed, introducing new concepts and activities carefully, providing examples, and discussing skills and the directions for activities; Letendre & Davis, 2004).

The group leaders' abilities to manage and structure peer interactions can assist in redirecting or stopping peers' reinforcement of deviant behaviors. The experience of group leaders in successfully handling deviant behavior in groups by redirecting attention, reestablishing appropriate norms, and respectfully controlling children can dissipate deviant peer contagion (Dishion, Dodge, & Lansford, 2006). For example, high levels of useful group structure result in tight time schedules that permit little opportunity for deviant talk, while providing too little structure may permit free discussion of all ideas but can also stimulate too much deviant peer contagion (Dishion et al., 2006).

ADAPTATION OF THE GROUP-BASED ANGER COPING PROGRAM TO INDIVIDUAL ADMINISTRATION

Individual sessions can typically be shorter (e.g. 30 minutes in length) than group sessions and yet accomplish the same objectives; of course, groups with four to six children are more time-efficient overall than briefer individual sessions with that same number of children. When working with an individual child, those Anger Coping session activities that can be accomplished between the child and interventionist (as indicated in the manual in Chapter 8) are retained, while those requiring peer involvement are modified.

A primary area of adaptation involves Anger Coping role-playing activities. Instead of having the children in a group engaging in role playing how they would handle teasing and other anger-arousing situations, the therapist and child role-play the same activity in individually administered Anger Coping. The therapist should first use the puppet receiving teasing while the child uses another puppet. The therapist can then model how to use various coping methods (distraction, deep breathing or relaxation, use of self-statements) in a manner similar to group administration of Anger Coping. Next, when the role play is reversed and the child's puppet is the one to be teased, the therapist has the "teaser" puppet. The therapist should carefully monitor the child's reaction throughout the puppet role play, and if the child becomes too aroused, then the therapist should quickly end the role play. Role playing actual, rather than puppet, teasing situations would proceed in a similar manner. The therapist models the procedure first, and then the child receives teasing. The therapist will be very careful not to proceed too quickly and will avoid arousing the child unduly. The therapist first identifies triggers that are on the lower end of the child's anger thermometer and then suggests to the child that those be used. The child should indicate which types of these lower-order "teases" are acceptable for use in the role play. As the child becomes more capable of handling arousing provocations, higher-order triggers from higher on the child's anger thermometer can be used to ultimately help the child manage the types of provocations that typically lead to their aggressive behavior in the school or community settings.

Similarly, the role-playing activities that occur as the child learns the problem-solving process need to be adapted. Problem-solving role plays can be conducted between the child and the therapist, with the therapist at times modeling by portraying the child client's role (and the child playing the role of a provocateur) and at other times reversing the roles. We still videotape children's enactment of role plays, but the therapist typically has to play a variety of roles in a single role play (e.g., a peer who is a provocateur and a teacher who provides consequences).

In the absence of a group, use of peer buddies to remind children of their goals during the week is not possible. Therapists can take a more active role in delivering reminders to the child about their goals by, for example, delivering reminder notes during the middle of the week to the child in his or her class.

Although working with a child individually removes many of the difficulties related to peer contagion and escalation in the group, the therapist has a much less enriched view of the actual social behaviors and problems that the child displays. Thus, more active contact is useful with adults (e.g. teachers) who do observe children's social behaviors, as is periodic observation of the child during classroom and less structured times of the school day.

CHAPTER 11

Case Example

Jenna was a first-year school psychologist who provided services to Lincoln Elementary School, located in a medium-sized, industry-based community in south central Wisconsin. One of the first things she noticed when she arrived at the school was the seemingly high volume of children who were referred for special education services. In particular, children at Lincoln were being referred at the highest frequency to programs for pupils with emotional and behavior disabilities. In fact, the referral and placement rates were well above the state and national averages for this category of disability.

A little investigation on Jenna's part turned up a possible contributing explanation: The recently retired previous school psychologist was of the "old school," and although he was very skilled at individual assessment, he offered little else in his service delivery model. In addition, there was no functional building consultation team to support the teachers. Children with behavior problems either adjusted to the school and classroom discipline structure or were routinely suspended or referred to special education. This model ran counter to everything that Jenna had learned in her training and was inconsistent with both the letter and spirit of the Individuals with Disabilities Education Act. Change was in order, she thought.

Following a number of meetings with key administrative, supportive services, and teaching staff, Jenna spent much of her first year setting up the structure for a more prevention-oriented approach to service delivery. The first order of business was to get a useful building consultation team (BCT) organized, trained, and functioning. This task was a real challenge, owing mostly to the teachers' comfortableness with the traditional "test and place" model they had grown used to, but Jenna persisted. Ultimately, the increased recurrence of effective classroom interventions made possible through the consultation process began to win over most of the staff.

Jenna knew that, along with indirect service delivery, an essential ingredient to an effective prevention-oriented model of service delivery was direct skill training for the children at highest risk. Her university education had included training and supervised practice in the Anger Coping Program; so, when an increasing number of referrals to the BCT began to include children with anger and aggression difficulties, she decided to see whether the situation warranted this type of intervention. Jenna consulted with several teachers and decided to form a group consisting of fourth-grade boys. She enlisted the support of the school guidance counselor as a co-leader.

Following the procedures she had learned in her university training, Jenna used the multiple-gate screening system (described at length in Chapter 4) and eventually came to select five fourth-grade boys for her group. Once parental consents were secured, she met with each of the boys individually, discussed the group, and asked them to complete the Children's Inventory of Anger (Nelson & Finch, 2000), a Likert scale measuring the affective component of anger in response to certain trigger statements (e.g., "Someone rides your bike without permission"). She then obtained from office records a count of the number of discipline referrals for each child, extending back to the start of the school year. Teachers were asked to complete a broadband behavioral checklist to screen for possible co-occurring problems.

Satisfied that the identified children could potentially benefit from the Anger Coping Program, Jenna began the process of enlisting the teachers as full collaborators in the skills training effort. Because there were three different teachers, she arranged to meet them all as a group one day before the start of school. At this meeting, she explained the objectives of the training, session by session, and brainstormed with the teachers how they could serve as generalization facilitators in their classrooms. Two of the teachers were receptive to this new role, but the third one clung to her belief that her student belonged in special education, and therefore she was resistant to putting forth "extra effort." Nevertheless, Jenna obtained useful information from the teachers to guide her in the goal-setting activities and scheduled times to consult with each one on a weekly basis.

A week prior to the first meeting, she and her co-leader met to discuss behavior management strategies for the group. It was agreed that Jenna would be in charge of the skills training while the guidance counselor handled the points, strikes, and other necessary behavior management responsibilities. They obtained a small budget from the school fund and purchased a number of school-related items to be used as reinforcers. A donation from the parent organization allowed them to purchase snacks as well. Jenna believed that she was ready.

(The following extract is from an e-mail that Jenna sent to one of us [Larson] after her first group meeting.)

> The first meeting was an example of worst-case scenario. I went to retrieve the five boys from their classrooms, and two took off in opposite directions down the hall. The other three walked with me down to the meeting room. I asked the guidance counselor to stay with them while I went to find the other two students. Fetching them was something of a hunting expedition. I went down to the end of one hall, where I saw the two boys together, and when I got there they were gone. I walked down the stairs and down to the other

end of the hall. Still no one. So, I went back up the stairs at the other end of the hall and repeated my pathway. This time, I noticed a head peeping out from behind the utility cabinet at the base of the stairs. I retrieved that child and asked the guidance counselor to contain him while I found the other boy. While I was looking for him, the guidance counselor got a phone call, for which he had to go to another room to answer. In the meantime, the "lost boy" came and got his runaway buddy, and off they ran.

About this time, a teacher asked what I was doing and if she could help. She suggested we look in the boys' bathroom. We did and found the two boys wetting down the Nerf ball that was a prop for our first session. After escorting them back to the group room after the 30-minute search, I was finally ready to begin Session 1. Such would not be the case.

One boy began punching at the walls and running around touching everything. He grabbed his buddy, and then he curled up in the corner with his buddy and refused to sit in his seat. His buddy just lay there sucking his thumb and saying to me, "I have ADHD, and I had sugar this morning." Then one boy called another a name, and a fistfight broke out between them. In the midst of all this, there was a breakthrough of sorts. When I was finally able to introduce the point system one boy said that after earning so many points he would like to put on a show for the group. I told him that would be a great idea except that he would have to earn some points first. We began in earnest.

Things were going better until the "lost boy" who initially didn't want to come to the meeting now did not want to leave after he had earned three strikes. He grabbed onto the table legs with his hands and feet and said, "No! I don't want to go. You can't make me go!" The principal happened by and, hearing the commotion, threatened to call the child's mother if he didn't go back to his classroom as instructed. He went. The saga continues. . . . (Jenna S., personal communication, February, 2001).

Jenna and her co-leader regrouped for the next session. They met with the most problematic boys individually and more carefully explained the group and its behavioral expectations. They also set up a "transition points" schedule to reinforce appropriate movement in and out of the classroom and practiced the behavior with the boys individually. The second meeting went much more smoothly, and the student made it through the Session 1 objectives without any major incidents. The same boy tallied three strikes again, but he returned obligingly to his room. Although he continued to be something of a challenge as the training progressed, this was his last "three strikes" removal from the group.

Jenna met with each of the teachers on a weekly basis to inform them of the progress in the group and to encourage the teachers to watch for and reinforce any incidences of anger control observed in the authentic setting. The teachers also supplied information about the behavioral and social issues currently facing the group members in the classroom so as to help her make her training efforts as relevant as possible. One teacher was especially good at suggesting relevant role plays, and another devised a system to help ensure that the Goal Sheet was signed daily and returned. Unfortunately, the teacher who started out resistant remained that way throughout the course of the intervention and used the meeting time to vent her anger about her student (and other children as well). She was a younger woman, nowhere near retirement, so Jenna decided that this relationship was an investment in possibly many children to come and dutifully kept her appointments and positive attitude. She made a mental note about working to secure classroom discipline training for the staff for next year—and possibly some stress management workshops.

As the sessions progressed, Jenna kept an ongoing record of discipline referrals for the boys in her group. She graphed them for each of the group members so she could monitor one of the outcome goals of the intervention as they progressed. Two of the teachers agreed to complete goal attainment scaling (GAS) forms for her, and she maintained those results on a line graph.

In the group, the puppet self-control sessions went very well, but once the puppets were put away in the succeeding meeting, one of the boys had a little more difficulty. During the taunting exercise, the first boy in the "safety circle" had a problem using his self-control techniques and bolted from the room. Once retrieved, he agreed to watch as the others took their turns, and they did particularly well. Jenna offered the first child another opportunity. He declined, but at the next meeting he agreed to try it again so long as Jenna and only one of the boys did the taunting. This time the exercise was somewhat more successful. Ultimately, although the other boys achieved effective self-control with the use of self-instruction, this child decided to use the technique of leaving the scene when he felt his anger aroused.

To make an effort at enhancing generalization, at the next meeting Jenna and her co-leader took the self-control exercise out of the group room and into the natural school environment. They practiced the taunting self-control exercise on the playground, at a pickup basketball game, in the hallway, and in the lunchroom. One of the boys noted the similarity with the popular "trash talking" on the basketball court and concluded that if he could handle it there he could handle it other places too. "In basketball, they just trying to get you off your game, but you don't let 'em," he said. "And in school, they're just trying to get you into trouble, and you don't let 'em do that either." "I wanted to hug him!" Jenna reported. "But, instead, I stayed the good school psychologist and enthusiastically praised his insight."

The first opportunity to cash in acquired points for school merchandise came at the fifth session. Points were tallied and exchanged for tickets taken from a ticket roll obtained by the group leaders. Because the leaders had made an effort to provide points at a generally equal rate among the children (often not an easy task), everyone was enthusiastic about participating. "I will never again underestimate the value to a fourth grader of a brand new rubber eraser!" Jenna reported.

When it eventually came time to make their video, the group was energized by the task. The group leaders taught the boys the "brainstorming" process—the free opportunity to suggest *anything*, with no criticism allowed. After their normal Goal Sheet review, they spent an entire meeting brainstorming possible scenarios, with the co-leader writing them on the chalkboard as they went along. At the next meeting, they narrowed the choices to three: a pushing incident on a basketball court, a mistaken accusation of student misbehavior by a teacher, and a tripping incident in the lunchroom that may or may not have been an accident.

The group leaders decided that the next task was script writing but soon discovered that the boys were considerably better at improvisation than they were at writing; so, the "scripts" became only general notes about who was to be in what role in each scenario. (*Note:* It has been our experience that groups can go in either direction with script writing for the video. Some want to produce complex, dialogue-driven "masterpieces," whereas others prefer to just "wing it" until it comes out right. Our advice is to follow the lead of the group members on this issue.) Each scenario was assigned a "director" from the group, whose responsibility was to organize the cast, assign roles, and be in charge of the rehearsals. Following in the Hitchcock tradition, directors were also allowed walk-on parts in their videos. Per a directive from the principal, however, the boys were not allowed to operate the school's video camera.

"By this time the boys were very attuned to the expected behaviors in the group and were virtually no management problem," Jenna reported. "Consequently, as the leaders, we had to continually remind ourselves that the video was *training*, not just a school project with a bunch of fourth graders."

If the leaders needed reminding that the boys were in need of continuing skill development, the rest of the school apparently did not. In the middle of making the video, two of the boys were suspended from school for 3 days for participating in a brawl on the school bus, and a third had an in-school suspension and parent conference for calling the art teacher "a fat hog lady" and pushing over an easel.

The video production was halted while the group addressed the particular issues surrounding the fight and the failure to maintain self-control in the art room. The Hassle Logs were used to structure the incidents and allow for self-evaluation. Role plays were then set up to re-create the events and practice anger coping responses. The group leaders sought but were denied permission to take one of the role plays onto an actual school bus for practice, so they made do by aligning chairs bus-style in the group room.

The art teacher was remarkably forgiving and professional, and she agreed to participate in a series of role plays with both the offending child and the other group members. The art room was apparently a "trigger" environment for self-control problems of many sorts, and the teacher was eager to address them in the context of the boys' training. She was also open to suggestions from Jenna about classroom management strategies.

With the latest disciplinary concerns finally addressed to the satisfaction of the group leaders and the boys, they returned to producing the video. The "tripping incident in the lunchroom" scenario was replaced with the bus fight incident. This alternative was decided upon both because of the immediate relevancy and the fact that, because of all the previous practice and repetition in the role plays, it was now "camera-ready." After five or so "takes," the group agreed on the best one and moved on to the other scenarios.

The group continued for 4 more weeks while the members completed the other video vignettes, maintaining a training focus and continuing work on the classroom goals as they progressed. When all of the videos were finally "in the can," they set a date for their graduation event. It was decided that each group member could invite parents and one adult from the school. Because of the parents' work schedules, the event was scheduled for 6:00 P.M. Each boy invited his classroom teacher (unfortunately, only two accepted), and the leaders invited the principal and the art teacher.

Everyone met in the school library, feasting on cupcakes and soda while the boys explained what they had been learning and proudly showed their videos. The leaders had prepared a Certificate of Completion for each of the children and distributed the certificates with as much pomp as the situation would allow. Certificates of Appreciation were also given to parents and teachers. It was a rare and proud moment for these high-risk children and their parents.

The group leaders scheduled booster sessions and gathered the boys together at the appointed time for problem solving and role plays. Postgroup data derived from discipline reports and GAS ratings showed a positive trend, if not necessarily a statistically significant one, for four of the boys during treatment and at booster session intervals. The fifth child (whose teacher was *you know who*) continued to struggle, but primarily in the environment of the classroom, not on the playground or the bus. All were subsequently promoted to the fifth grade, and none was referred for special education. Jenna and her co-leader made plans to reassemble the group at the start of school in September for additional booster sessions and ongoing support with their fifth-grade teachers.

Note: Appreciation is extended to the real "Jenna" and the many other practitioners and interns whose accumulated experiences with the Anger Coping Program are also represented in this case example.

CHAPTER 12

Frequently Asked Questions

Q: What about working with girls or with girls and boys together in the same group?

A: Literally all of the research on the Anger Coping Program involved boys. This decision was made in part because boys are at considerably higher risk, as a gender, for externalizing behavior problems and the subsequent mental health and legal difficulties that may follow in the developmental trajectory. That said, there is no reason that practitioners should not use the program with girls who are demonstrating anger control problems, particularly if such problems are manifested as reactive physical aggression. In other words, the more the girls' anger resembles the boys' anger, the higher the likelihood that the ACP will be an appropriate intervention. Note, however, that there is a growing body of research that suggests that girls may experience and express anger and aggression in a somewhat different manner than boys (see Crick, 1997; Crick & Bigbee, 1998; Crick & Werner, 1998; but see also Pepler & Sedighdeilami, 1998, for additional viewpoints). In general, this literature indicates that many more girls than boys may use *relational* aggression. This type is typically a nonphysical kind of aggression that often involves using social exclusion, rumor spreading, and mean-spirited teasing as forms of retaliation. There are numerous important considerations that apply in conducting anger management with young girls or with blended sex groups. See Chapter 9 for a detailed discussion of these issues.

Q: What are the upper and lower age ranges for the Anger Coping Program?

A: The bulk of the existing research on the Anger Coping Program has been done with boys in the 8- to 12-year-old range. Clinically, both of us have worked with children somewhat younger and somewhat older, and doing so can be a successful experience if the appropriate adaptations are made. For instance, with older middle school students, we have modified the puppet self-control activity, replacing it with magazine cutouts of popular culture figures pasted on cardboard and affixed to holding sticks. When working with very young children, group leaders should attend carefully to developmental variables. Younger

151

children need to "do and see" to a greater degree than their older peers, and this requirement has implications for the more cognitive aspects of the Anger Coping Program. For them, sessions need to be shorter, less didactic, and contain abundant use of manipulatives and behavioral rehearsal. Young children are quite capable of developing problem-solving skills, but, again, developmental status is a major consideration. (See Shure, 1996, for a useful research-supported guide for problem-solving work with preschool and kindergarten children.)

Q: How many children per group is an optimal number?

A: The ideal number varies, depending on a few factors, including room size and the number of leaders. With two group co-leaders and sufficient space, five to seven children is a good target. Avoid allowing the "group" to become more like a "class" with the addition of too many children, thus increasing behavioral management problems and reducing opportunities for more individualized attention. Single group leaders will find four to five children to be sufficient. This number is large enough to account for the inevitable absences and still allow for "group-type" activities.

Q: Can we meet more than once per week?

A: Certainly, but not if the goal is to rush through the sessions to meet a school deadline or some other target date. Give yourself enough time to have the children *in treatment* at least 16–18 weeks. If you are planning a second-semester group, this requirement may mean getting started with identification and parent consents before the holiday break to give yourself plenty of time.

Q: How long should each session be?

A: Forty-five minutes to an hour is a good target figure.

Q: Can I add some activities that I learned from another intervention, or must I limit myself to what is found in the Anger Coping Program manual?

A: The procedures contained in the Anger Coping Program manual are those that have been shown to be effective in our research. That said, we can think of no reason that the addition, rather than substitution, of other rationally conceived cognitive-behavioral activities that address the training objectives should not be included by experienced group leaders. The key is "flexibility in the context of fidelity." This criterion holds true for creative behavioral management procedures as well. Indeed, we would appreciate being informed of any useful modifications.

Q: I am uncomfortable with the teasing activity that goes on in the self-control sessions. Don't they do enough of that on their own without having to "practice" it in the counseling room?

A: The self-control sessions are specifically created to produce in each identified child a *need*, however artificial, to exert self-control and other anger coping strategies. We know of no other way, short of following the children around all day, to allow them to practice the skills needed. The self-control sessions are analogous to going out the first time in the driver's education car on the practice track: it's not the real condition, but it is close enough to stimulate the new driver's skill development. This simulation helps ensure that the skills needed in the eventual "real thing" are practiced and thus potentially accessible under the more highly stressful conditions of the public highways. Similarly, children who lack the skills to adaptively manage anger and aggression need to spend quality time on the therapy "practice track" before they can be expected to more skillfully navigate the higher-stress conditions of the authentic school and home environments.

Q: Can I use the Anger Coping Program in my clinical practice?

A: Certainly, although adaptations to achieve generalization will have to be made. In such cases, enlisting the parent/guardian—rather than the classroom teacher—as the principal collaborator for goals and other generalization activities makes sense. In a residential treatment setting, both house parents/unit counselors and school staff may be engaged for these purposes.

Q: How do I obtain a free DVD of the Anger Coping Video?

A: Send an e-mail with your request to author Larson at his address below.

Q: Is staff training available in the Anger Coping Program?

A: Yes. Contact either author.

Jim Larson
Department of Psychology
University of Wisconsin–Whitewater
Whitewater, WI 53190
E-mail: *larsonj@uww.edu*

John E. Lochman
Department of Psychology
University of Alabama
348 Gordon Palmer
Box 870348
Tuscaloosa, AL 35487-0348
E-mail: *jlochman@gp.as.ua.edu*

Q: Can I connect with others who are implementing the Anger Coping Program?

A: A supporting blog is available at *treatingangerinschool.blogspot.com*.

Q: Is there a similar program for high school students?

A: Anger management with older adolescents presents its own collection of challenges, and careful study and preparation beforehand is highly recommended. Consider consulting the following sources for further guidance:

Feindler, E. L., & Scalley, M. (1999). Adolescent anger-management groups for violence reduction. In T. Kratochwill & K. Stoiber (Eds.), *Handbook of group interventions for children and families* (pp. 100–119). New York: Allyn & Bacon.

Goldstein, A. P., Glick, B., & Gibbs, J. C. (1998). *Aggression replacement training: A comprehensive intervention for aggressive youth*. Champaign, IL: Research Press.

Hammond, W. R. (1991). *Dealing with anger: A violence prevention program for African-American youth*. Champaign, IL: Research Press.

Larson, J. (2005). *Think first: Addressing aggressive behavior in secondary schools*. New York: Guilford Press.

CHAPTER 13

Afterword

PROGRESS MONITORING AND POSTTREATMENT EVALUATION

In our many years of working in schools and with school personnel, we have heard both hard-working counselors and school psychologists evaluate their recently completed group counseling experience in words such as these:

"I think it went well."
"The kids seemed to enjoy it, and they worked hard."
"I think the teachers were pleased."
"The principal told me she was really glad somebody had worked with these kids."

Typically, these individuals could not produce any other useful outcome data beyond this informal adult social validation to support the efficacy of their often very considerable effort. The reasons for this lack of data were varied, but they generally boiled down to the fact that the practitioners simply failed to see the need for it. The mere fact that they had chosen to actually "do something" with some of the most disruptive children in their school often provided enough social approval from staff and parents to make any other form of data gathering seem unnecessary. Whether the children changed demonstrably in any positive fashion became almost irrelevant to the fact that at least the effort was made. We can speak from personal experience: Professional approval from teachers and administrators is powerful stuff for most supportive services staff.

Although the approval of peers and parents is often desirable and important, by itself it should be insufficient for the effective school practitioner. The need for data-based decision making in considering both the needs of children and the issues associated with professional accountability argue compellingly for the acquisition of more substantial data. Using research-supported interventions, such as the Anger Coping Program, is certainly the start, as it increases the likelihood that desired outcomes will be forthcoming. In addition, empirically validated interventions are more easily supportable in the face of outside scrutiny of accountability. Moving on to gather useful outcome data that speak to the relative effectiveness of the intervention is the next critical step.

Some practitioners may shy away from this form of outcome measurement, fearing a personal lack of knowledge in either program evaluation or research design. However, an applied evaluation of the effects of a school intervention need not be complex or rigorously designed. Face it—it isn't going to be published in the *Journal of Applied Behavioral Analysis*. What the practitioner is looking for is simply data to document that the anticipated objectives were met. Did the children achieve many or most of their classroom goals as recorded on the Goal Sheets? Are the children engaging in fewer anger-related fights or disruptions, as documented in classroom and office records? Does a teacher checklist (e.g., Dodge & Coie, 1987, App. B), completed before the group started and then repeated at postintervention, indicate positive changes in the classroom? Do the children's postintervention self-reports indicate increased understanding of problem-solving skills or anger control in comparison with preintervention levels?

Using permanent products data (e.g., attendance records, office referral counts, and the like) acquired during the identification phase can be extremely helpful in documenting clinically useful changes (as noted in Chapter 4). Baseline levels of discipline reports and other authentic school data acquired prior to the start of the intervention can serve as comparison points for similar data acquired during and following the intervention. Moreover, if these data are continuously monitored as the intervention proceeds, in the manner of a *formative evaluation*, adjustments and refinements can be made along the way. The practitioner is looking only for *positive trends*, not necessarily statistical significance. Two methods of evaluating treatment outcomes that have applicability to in-school interventions are percentage of nonoverlapping data and goal attainment scaling.

OUTCOMES ANALYSIS WITH PERCENTAGE OF NONOVERLAPPING DATA

A comparably simple method of analyzing a recurring data series, such as office referrals received by children in the Anger Coping intervention, is known as PND, or percentage of nonoverlapping data. PND is a single-subject analysis method that, in this case, is replicated for each member of the group so that a group of five children is analyzed as five individuals. (The analysis of grouped data is inappropriate, given the small size of the typical groups.) Elegant in its simplicity, PND can provide group leaders with supportable evidence of treatment outcomes. Here's how to do it:

1. Identify one or more continuing measures of treatment effects, or what is commonly referred to as the dependent variable. This is a variable that occurs regularly and one that is expected to change as a result of the child's participation in the Anger Coping group. That change may be in the form of an increase, such as with homework return, or a decrease, such as with disciplinary office referrals. Using a variable that is already being collected by

the school as a permanent product is easiest. Alternatively, the Classroom Progress Monitoring Report (CPMR; Appendix M), if completed by the classroom teacher on a regular basis, may be used as a whole by averaging each week's scores for each child or by focusing on one or more of the individual items.

2. An essential feature of a PND analysis is to acquire at least three data points as a baseline prior to the start of the group, which requires a little advanced planning. As soon as the children have been identified, group leaders should start collecting baseline data on each child (e.g., 3 weeks' worth of office referrals, absentees, homework returns, and/or 3 weeks of the CPMR). Existing permanent products data, such as office referrals or attendance records, can simply be checked retroactively for 3 weeks if this is more convenient. Three data points is the minimum; there is no maximum. Ideally, one wants to have a relatively stable baseline, that is, with all of the numbers grouped pretty closely together.

3. Once the baseline is established, enter it on any data management program that will produce a graph, such as Excel or ChartDog (available at *www.interventioncentral.com*).

4. Proceed with the Anger Coping Program, and continue to collect the data on the identified variable(s) each week, entering the data into the computer program regularly. These weekly data serve as formative progress monitoring, allowing the collaborative team of group leaders and teacher(s) to make adjustments as needed. Remember that the goal is behavior change, not intervention research integrity.

5. When the Anger Coping group has completed its last meeting, have the computer program produce a line graph of all the data (see Figure 13.1). Next, count the number of data points on your graph in the treatment phase that do not overlap the data points in the baseline phase. In the example graph in Figure 13.1, notice that in postbaseline weeks 1 and 4, the number of office referrals received by Robert overlapped the baseline, thus leaving 16 weeks of nonoverlapping data points.

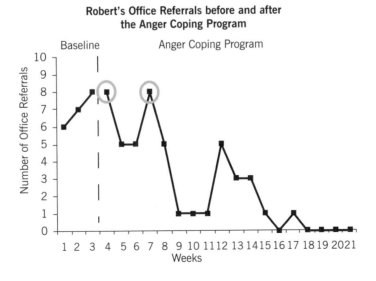

FIGURE 13.1. Using PND to evaluate treatment effectiveness.

6. To find the PND, divide the number of nonoverlapping data points (16 in our example) by the total number collected across treatment (18 in our example) and multiply by 100. The online program "ChartDog" will compute the PND for you (e.g., [16/18] × 100 = .89%).

7. The meaning of PND can be easily communicated to others when using the following descriptors suggested by Scruggs and Mastropieri (as cited in Jenson, Clark, Kircher, & Kristjansson, 2007): PND of 90% or greater is considered highly effective, 70–90% moderately effective, 50–70% questionably effective, and 50% or less ineffective. Thus, the results of the Anger Coping Program for Robert would be described as "moderately effective" (PND = .89%), as reflected by the considerable decrease in his office referrals across the 18 weeks that the program was implemented with him.

GOAL ATTAINMENT EVALUATION USING THE MODIFIED GOAL ATTAINMENT SCALING PROCEDURE

Goal attainment scaling as a procedure for monitoring progress in behavioral interventions has been widely used in community mental health programs for nearly five decades. The methodology involves (1) identification of a target behavior, (2) an objective description of the desired outcome of the proposed treatment, and (3) the development of three to five descriptions of the target behavior that approximate the desired outcome (Sladeczek, Elliott, Kratochwill, Robertson-Majaanes, & Callan-Stoiber, 2001). This procedure has applications in the Anger Coping Program with teachers who are motivated to spend a little extra time to provide the data. Appendix G provides a model GAS worksheet that we have found useful.

For example, assume that the child's goal is stated as follows: "Jason will not get out of his seat without permission during seat work time." The rating scale is as follows (refer to Appendix G):

  0 = Current level of performance, or what the child typically does during this time; the expected level of performance, perhaps 4 to 5 instances of out-of-seat behavior; this is placed in the middle of the scale. This is also known as baseline data.

Above the expected level of performance on the scale:

  +1 = Improvement over the expected level of performance, perhaps only 2 to 3 instances
  +2 = Much improvement over the expected level of performance, perhaps 0 to 1 instances

Below the expected level of performance on the scale:

  −1 = Poorer than the expected level of performance, perhaps 6 to 7 instances
  −2 = Worst possible outcome, much poorer than the expected level of performance, perhaps more than 7 instances.

These data may then be quantified and charted by the group leaders over time—perhaps every 2 weeks—to provide both a formative and summative progress measure of the effects of the intervention relative to the specified classroom goals. Readers interested in further discussion of goal attainment scaling are referred to Kiresuk, Smith, and Cardillo's volume (1994), and for more general issues in outcome measurement, to Jenson et al. (2007).

CONVERGING EVIDENCE

Examine the convergence of multiple sources of data. Data from a single source may be unimpressive when viewed alone, but when added to data from additional sources, a converging trend may be readily observable. For instance, the CPMR may show very little pre- to postintervention positive gain in the targeted behaviors. However, when these data are examined along with even modest reductions in office referrals, a majority of goals met, and an improvement in academic grades, then the converging evidence can be evaluated as clinically positive.

The information gleaned from formative and summative assessments are meant to assist the practitioner in refining later iterations of the intervention as well as to provide him or her with documentation that may be useful in subsequent school or district accountability exercises. The data may be thereafter rendered to graph form for easy dissemination to interested parties, with confidentiality maintained, of course (e.g., Child 1, Child 2, and so forth).

USING BOOSTER SESSIONS FOR MAINTENANCE OF TREATMENT GAINS

As was noted in Chapter 5, it is essential to maintenance and generalization efforts that the leaders plan for additional group meetings over the rest of the school year. As with the learning and application of other psychosocial skills, children can forget them, develop alternative but inappropriate habits, or simply fail to implement learned skills. Booster sessions can help to reinforce and strengthen previous learning and provide group members with an opportunity to address newly arising issues. A suggested schedule is as follows:

Booster 1: 2 weeks after the final session
Booster 2: 4 weeks after the final session
Booster 3: prior to summer

Use of the Hassle Log procedure at the booster sessions to help the children to maintain skills learned in the Anger Coping sessions is recommended. In addition, previous classroom goals should be reviewed, and the children should use their problem-solving skills to address any backsliding or newly emerging difficulties. These sessions should be informal, but group leaders should always remember the dictum "Practice, practice, practice." Discussion is important but insufficient. Get the group members up and immediately role playing their current concerns.

ADDITIONAL ISSUES RELATING TO MAINTENANCE AND GENERALIZATION

In addition to conducting booster sessions, the following measures are recommended to help the students maintain their skills and generalize them to authentic settings:

1. Keep in close contact with the classroom teacher(s) regarding the behavior of group members, both during and after the intervention. Use the Anger Coping Program Classroom Generalization Inservice Guide (see Appendix E) to assist the teacher. See the group members individually, as needed.

2. Consult with the teacher regarding classroom or recess discipline or behavior management programs. Encourage incentives that emphasize the anger management skills taught in the group.

3. Inform administrators of the skills learned in the Anger Coping Program and encourage them to reinforce the group members when appropriate.

4. Meet with parents to help problem-solve home difficulties that may have a direct impact on school behavior. Provide parent management training when possible (see Chapter 7).

5. Have recent "graduates" give talks to classes of younger students (e.g., K–3) about what they have learned, using role plays to demonstrate new skills.

6. Encourage teachers to place graduates in appropriate positions of responsibility, such as playground monitor, so as to allow them to exercise their newly acquired skills in a prosocial manner.

7. Engage alumni from previous Anger Coping groups to serve as "consultants" to newer groups. Allow them to explain what they have learned and provide teaching models for the younger children at selected times during the intervention. Meichenbaum and Biemiller's *Nurturing Independent Learners: Helping Students Take Charge of Their Learning* (1998) is an excellent resource on the subject of maintenance and generalization for a variety of learning tasks, including the use of the "consultant" role.

ONGOING NEEDS

Practitioners working with highly externalizing children are cautioned about a possible negative phenomenon that may arise. It had been our experience that some well-meaning but misguided teachers and administrators have unrealistic expectations about the effects of even well-designed anger control interventions. Consequently, if one or more of the children do not exhibit obvious and dramatic behavioral changes following the intervention, those children may be subject to undue punitive responses—"Well, look at all the effort we made for him, and he still chooses to act this way!"

When retributive attitudes develop among adult staff members, the potential for inappropriate educational planning and behavioral consequences escalates. Negative biases toward the child can potentially result in increased use of empirically unsupported behavioral consequences such as suspensions from school, corporal punishment, and even inappropriate referral to special education.

Practitioners should remind fellow staff members that for some individuals aggression is a very stable behavioral response, and the likelihood is high that some children who have successfully completed the entire Anger Coping Program will still need continued intervention as they progress through school. If a child does well during his participation in the group but regresses to old behavioral habits in succeeding months, practitioners should help others to *take that outcome as data, not failure.* Some children need insulin, some need psychostimulant medication, and others need hearing aids to maintain their optimal functioning in the school setting. In a similar manner, some highly externalizing children will need ongoing behavioral support to maintain their own optimal functioning, and supportive services professionals should advocate for the child's right to that support.

Appendices

Anger Coping Program Teacher Nomination Form

To the Teacher:

Please think about the pupils in your classroom, and identify those children whose circumstances seem to fit *at least three of the five statements* below to some degree. Please feel free to be "liberal" in your selection; we will narrow the list down later.

1. The child has marked difficulties with interpersonal problem solving; seems to argue or fight with other children more than most.
2. The child is prone to anger management problems and may use both physical and nonphysical aggression against peers at rates higher than most.
3. The child is frequently disruptive and gives oppositional responses to teacher directives.
4. The child seems to be rejected by the more adaptive children in the class.
5. The child is having academic failure or underachievement problems.

Please list the names below. Rank ordering or filling in all of the slots is not necessary.

_____   _____

_____   _____

_____   _____

_____   _____

_____   _____

_____   _____

_____   _____

_____   _____

Teacher's name: _____   Room: _____

Anger Coping Program Teacher Screening Scale

Child's Name _____

School _____ Teacher _____

   1. When teased, fights back*   1: Never 2 3 4 5: Almost always

   2. Blames others in fights*   1: Never 2 3 4 5: Almost always

   3. Overreacts angrily to accidents*   1: Never 2 3 4 5: Almost always

   4. Teases and name calls   1: Never 2 3 4 5: Almost always

   5. Starts fights with peers   1: Never 2 3 4 5: Almost always

   6. Gets into verbal arguments   1: Never 2 3 4 5: Almost always

   7. When frustrated, quick to fight   1: Never 2 3 4 5: Almost always

   8. Breaks rules in games   1: Never 2 3 4 5: Almost always

   9. Responds negatively when fails   1: Never 2 3 4 5: Almost always

10. Uses physical force to dominate**   1: Never 2 3 4 5: Almost always

11. Gets others to gang up on a peer**   1: Never 2 3 4 5: Almost always

12. Threatens and bullies others**   1: Never 2 3 4 5: Almost always

Global Rating _____ (sum of all items)

Reactive Aggression Rating (sum of items 1, 2, and 3): _____

*Reactive aggressive; **proactive aggressive.

Classroom Goals Interview

Student _____

Teacher _____ Date _____

Teacher Narrative of Problem Behavior: *What kinds of classroom behavior problems does the student have? When and how frequently do they occur?*

Problem Behavior Hierarchy: *Which of these problems are of greatest concern to you?*

1. _____
2. _____
3. _____

Can't Do or Won't Do: *Which problems appear to reflect lack of skill, and which appear to reflect lack of motivation?*

(cont.)

Select a "Lack of Motivation" Problem: *What specifically do you want the student to do instead of engaging in this problem behavior? What behavior will be encouraged? Is this a behavior goal in which there is a high likelihood for success?*

Behavior Goal:

Supports for New Behavior:

Group Leaders will:

Teacher will:

Explain that the goal will be monitored through the weekly Goal Sheet activity and describe the teacher's role. Make arrangements for consultation time for support or revisions.

Best time to meet: _____

Anger Coping Agreement

This AGREEMENT is entered into between _____ and the

Anger Coping group leader(s) _____

on this day, _____.

I, _____, agree to the following:

1. I will attend each Anger Coping group session unless I have a valid excuse.

2. I will participate in the group and cooperate with the group's leaders.

3. I will respect myself and my fellow group members.

4. I understand that I will be learning new skills to solve problems.

5. I agree to try hard, practice, and do my best to learn these new skills.

I understand that the Anger Coping leaders will work with me in helping me to learn and to improve my behavior in school.

I understand that there may be setbacks and mistakes, but I will do everything I can to bounce back and keep working to achieve my goals.

Our signatures below indicate our willingness to work hard together, cooperate, respect one another, and stick to this agreement.

_____   _____

Group Member   Group Leader(s)

Anger Coping Program Classroom Generalization Inservice Guide

Session 1

Get acquainted; learn the rules about points and strikes; come up with other behavioral expectations; begin learning about individual differences.

In the Classroom: Does the child know the time and date of the next meeting? Does he or she know why he or she is in the Anger Coping group? Does he or she know the rules? Does he or she enter and leave the classroom appropriately when group time arrives?

Session 2

Goal setting is explained, and initial classroom behavioral goals are determined. (Note: The child will be given a new Goal Sheet each week for the duration of the group.)

In the Classroom: Does the child spontaneously explain his or her goal to you? Does he or she demonstrate an effort to achieve this goal? Does he or she ask for your initials on his or her Goal Sheet regularly and at the appropriate time? Does he or she reference his or her goal in casual conversation with you? Is his or her goal too difficult to achieve at this time? Can it be modified to be more reasonable?

Session 3

Begin training in the use of self-instruction—talking silently to yourself—to maintain anger control; the puppet self-control exercise is used for the first time.

In the Classroom: Watch for possible excitement carried over from the group. Does the child understand the purpose of the puppet self-control exercise? Watch for the child bragging about his or her puppet's verbal taunting, and help him or her turn it around to describing the puppet's self-control instead. Does the child demonstrate an incident of anger control and, spontaneously or when queried, attribute it to self-talk? Reinforce any effort at anger control, including walking away or seeking out an adult.

Session 4

Continue training in the use of self-instruction for anger control, using direct verbal taunts.

In the Classroom: Watch for possible excitement carried over from the group. Does the child understand the purpose of the taunting exercise? Watch for the child bragging about his or her verbal taunting, and help him or her turn it around to describing his or her own self-control instead. What did he or she say to him- or herself to keep from getting angry? Would those words work in the classroom or at recess? Does the child demonstrate an instance of anger control and, spontaneously or when queried, attribute it to self-talk? Reinforce any effort at anger control. Remind the child to "Use your self-talk!" Model your own self-talk where and when appropriate.

(cont.)

Session 5

Begin training in understanding the concepts of empathy and perspective taking—for example, "Can you see why that might be fun for you but not for him [or her]?" Begin understanding problem recognition as a difference in perspective or understanding a situation from another's viewpoint.

In the Classroom: Encourage opportunities for problem recognition during conflict situations—for example, "Charles, how do you see the problem? Now, Jason, how do you see the problem?" Model individual perspective taking aloud where and when appropriate—that is, your perspective versus the child's.

Session 6

Continue training in problem recognition; assist the children in understanding the feeling of anger—the feeling they have when they think they cannot get something they want, do something they want to do, or feel provoked.

In the Classroom: Continue encouraging problem recognition. Help the child to label his or her own feelings—for example, "You seem angry [or sad, or frightened, or happy]. Tell me why." Or, "Tell me what you're feeling now." As always, reinforce evidence of anger control when observed.

Session 7

Begin training in the physiological cues to anger—how the child's body feels when he or she is getting angry; begin training in the mediating role of thoughts in anger management—how what you say to yourself can get you more angry or less angry.

In the Classroom: Assist the child in recognizing his or her own anger cues by asking the child to describe them; model aloud your own anger cues in an authentic situation—for example, "I know I'm starting to get angry because I feel my heart starting to pound, so I want you two to get to work."

Session 8

Begin training in generating alternative responses to problem situations and evaluating possible consequences.

In the Classroom: Ask for alternative responses to authentic problem situations—for example, "What else could you have done? And what else?" Help the child anticipate possible consequences in his or her response selection—for example, "What would probably happen if you did that?" This is also an excellent exercise for the class as a whole.

Session 9

Begin training in following a sequential problem-solving model: (1) What is the problem? (2) What are my feelings? (3) What are my choices? (4) What will happen if? (5) What will I do?

In the Classroom: Continue to assist the child's efforts to address ambiguous or conflict situations as problems to be addressed. When possible and safe, put the responsibility for nonaggressive conflict resolution directly on the child—for example, "Jared, I can see you're angry with William. Can you solve this problem so that it turns out best for both of you?" Consider teaching the process to the class as a whole.

(cont.)

Session 10

Continue training in the problem-solving model.

   In the Classroom: Continue as in the preceding session. The teacher should begin to communicate to the child higher expectations for anger management and problem resolution. Continue giving verbal praise for effective efforts, and openly acknowledge his or her changes for the better whenever they are demonstrated.

Session 11

Starting at about this session, group members will begin making their own videotape, in which they will demonstrate what they have learned about anger control and problem solving.

   In the Classroom: In this and subsequent sessions, inquire about the progress of the video. What scenarios have been chosen to be taped? How are things going? What skills are you practicing for the video? The teacher should continue to communicate to the child higher expectations for anger management and problem resolution. Continue to heap verbal praise on effective efforts, and avidly encourage changes for the better as they emerge.

My Goal Sheet

Name _____   Goal Sheet Number _____

Today's date _____

A goal is something I want to get or something I want to have happen, <u>and I am willing to work for it</u>.

My goal is:

for at least _____ out of five days.

Group member's signature _____

Group leader's signature _____

My teacher will write "Yes" and initial if I met my goal for the day, or "No" and initial if I did not.

	Day 1	Day 2	Day 3	Day 4	Day 5
Teacher initials	_____	_____	_____	_____	_____
Weekly goal met? (circle)	Yes!!	Not yet	Date _____		

Goal Attainment Scaling Form

Pupil: _____ Teacher: _____ Date of rating: _____

Level of possible behavior change with participation in the Anger Coping Program	Goal 1: Title	Goal 2: Title	Goal 3: Title
More than expected improvement (+2)			
Expected improvement (+1)			
Current status (baseline) (0)			
Less than expected outcome (−1)			
Much less than expected outcome (−2)			
	Rating _____	Rating _____	Rating _____

Sample Parental Consent Letter

(Use the school's letterhead, and arrange to have the Principal or Administrator sign the letter.)

Dear Parent/Guardian:

Your child, _____, is being asked to take part in a small counseling group. The group is called Anger Coping. Your child is being asked to take part in this group because the teacher and I believe that it will help in reaching one or more of these goals we have for the group:

1. Help the children improve control of their anger or tempers
2. Help the children improve their behavior in school
3. Help the children improve their problem-solving skills and set positive classroom goals

The group will meet here at school for about _____ weeks. We will meet on _____ [day or days]. The group leader in charge will be _____. He/she can be reached at _____ [phone number].

There are no foreseeable risks that come with participation in this group. Every effort will be made to see that your child misses as little classroom instruction as possible. The teacher will see to it that your child will have makeup time, if needed.

In the group, the children will use role playing to learn anger control skills, how to solve problems with other students or adults, and how to set and meet classroom goals. This is a skills group related primarily to self-control in school. Non-school-related issues are not typically addressed. A full explanation of each activity is available by calling the group leader at the number above. Please call if you have questions or to arrange a meeting here at school. Your support is very important. If, however, you decide that you do not want your child to participate, please know that we will continue to work with him or her in the classroom to be the best student possible. Similar services may be available in the community. Please call for this information if you are interested.

You, your child, and/or the teacher may be asked to complete a checklist so that the group leader can better help your child in the group. The results will be kept confidential though, as the parent or guardian, you are free to inspect them or obtain a copy if you desire. The checklists that will be used are:

_____   _____

Please sign and return the tear-off portion of this letter, below. Keep the remainder for your files.

Sincerely,

_____
(Principal/Administrator)

- -

(Check one)

_____   I give my permission for my child, _____, to take part in the Anger Coping group described above.

_____   I do NOT give my permission.

_____   _____
Signature   Date

_____

Anger Coping Program Initial Checklist

Group starting date _____   Times _____

_____ Parental consents obtained and filed

_____ Co-leader identified

_____ Pregroup assessments completed

_____ Room secured

_____ VCR/monitor reserved

_____ Camcorder reserved

_____ Teacher(s) consulted on individual classroom goals for Goal Setting in Session 2

_____ Behavior management strategies designed

_____ Reinforcers identified and obtained, if needed

_____ DUSO or *Second Step* card obtained for Sessions 1 and 5

_____ Hand puppets obtained for Session 3

_____ Dominoes and deck of cards obtained for Session 4

_____ Transition rules and behavior explained and practiced

Group members:

1. _____   Grade: _____   Room: _____
2. _____   Grade: _____   Room: _____
3. _____   Grade: _____   Room: _____
4. _____   Grade: _____   Room: _____
5. _____   Grade: _____   Room: _____
6. _____   Grade: _____   Room: _____
7. _____   Grade: _____   Room: _____

NOTES:

Hassle Log

Name _____   Date _____

WHERE WAS I?

_____ In my classroom   _____ In the gym

_____ In the hall   _____ In the lunchroom

_____ On the playground   _____ _____

WHAT HAPPENED?

_____ Someone hit or pushed me   _____ Someone teased me

_____ Someone took something of mine   _____ Someone told me to do something

_____ Someone said "No"   _____ _____

WHAT DID I DO?

_____ Used Anger Coping   _____ Hit or pushed the person

_____ Yelled and screamed   _____ Walked away, left

_____ Sulked or pouted   _____ Told an adult

HOW ANGRY WAS I? (Circle)

Furious!   Pretty Angry   Irritated   Annoyed, but okay

10 9 8   7 6 5   4 3   2 1

HOW DID I HANDLE MYSELF?

_____ Great! I really controlled my anger.

_____ Pretty well. I tried to use what I have learned.

_____ Not so well. I still had trouble with my anger.

Anger Coping Program Parent Letters

PARENT LETTER 1

Dear Parents:

Thank you for allowing your child to participate in the Anger Coping group. We are off to a very good start and look forward to helping the children to learn many new skills. Once again, we will be meeting on _____ . The members of the group have begun working on personal goals that will help them improve their schoolwork and behavior in the classroom. The group members came up with their own personal goals. Our group session always starts by reviewing these goals and encouraging the children to work hard to meet them.

Most of the goals have to do with getting along with others in school, improving class work, or listening to and obeying the teacher. Once the children have met their goals, they will begin work on new ones.

HOW YOU CAN HELP

- Ask your child to discuss his or her goal with you. Why was it important? What are the plans for meeting this goal?
- How will your child know when the goal has been met? What problems might be encountered? What are the plans for dealing with those problems?

If three or four times a week you say, "Tell me how you are doing on your Anger Coping goal," your child will understand that what is important at school is also important at home. You may also want to have your child start to set goals for behavior around the home too.

Yours sincerely,

_____

- -

Use this tear-off sheet only if you want to send back any comments or questions you have about the Anger Coping group. Be sure to leave a phone number and "best times to call" if you want me to phone you about your concern.

Your name:

_____

(cont.)

PARENT LETTER 2

Dear Parents:

We are well under way in our Anger Coping group. Recently, we have been working on ways to control the feeling of anger. Lots of children have trouble keeping their tempers under control. In our group, we have been practicing some methods for "keeping your cool." The group members are learning that *what they think or say to themselves* as they start to become angry is very important.

For instance, in our group we have worked on an activity in which the group members actually try to make one another angry. But instead of getting really upset, the children are learning to stay in control by paying attention to what they say to themselves.

HOW YOU CAN HELP

- Ask your child to discuss "The Puppet Self-Control" activity. What did the puppet in the circle do to keep from getting too angry?
- Ask your child to discuss what he or she did when he or she was in the "safety circle" without the puppet and the others tried to make your child angry. What did your child do to keep from losing his or her temper?
- Discuss with your child what you do when you want to "keep your cool" and how important that skill is for you.

Controlling anger is important at home too. Reminding your child to "use your Anger Coping" will help when problems come up at home.

Yours sincerely,

_____

Use this tear-off sheet only if you want to send back any comments or questions you have about the Anger Coping group. Be sure to leave a phone number and "best times to call" if you want me to phone you about your concern.

Your name:

_____

(cont.)

PARENT LETTER 3

Dear Parents:

We have begun to work on one of the most important skills in Anger Coping: how to solve problems with other people. This can include problems with other kids, teachers or other grown-ups, and, of course, problems with parents. To do this, the children have been learning to approach problems by asking a series of "problem-solving questions." The questions are these:

What is the problem? (Stated as *the child's* problem, not the other person's)
What are my feelings? (Is what I feel anger? Am I afraid? Am I sad?)
What are my choices? (Problems often have a number of solutions, good and bad)
What will happen? (Each solution will have consequences)

HOW YOU CAN HELP

- Ask your child to discuss his or her understanding of the problem-solving questions. Do they make sense? Are they helpful?
- See if your child can apply the questions to a problem that may be occurring at home. Was that helpful in reaching a satisfactory solution?

If your children see and hear *you* using the questions to solve a problem of your own, it may help them to learn the skill themselves. I often use this "thinking out loud" method in the group. Try it. You may like it! Call me if you would like some help with this exercise.

Yours sincerely,

_____

Use this tear-off sheet only if you want to send back any comments or questions you have about the Anger Coping group. Be sure to leave a phone number and "best times to call" if you want me to phone you about your concern.

Your name:

_____

Sample Parental Consent Letter
and Anger Coping Program Parent Letters—Spanish Versions

Estimados Padres:

Su hijo ha sido seleccionado para tomar parte en un pequeño grupo de terapía. El grupo se llama "Anger Coping" (Canalizar Enojos). Su hijo ha sido seleccionado para tomar parte de este grupo porque su maestro(a) y yo consideramos que esto le ayudará en uno o más de estos objetivos o metas:

1. Ayudará al niño a controlar mejor sus enojos y reacciones negativas.
2. Ayudará al niño a mejorar su conducta en la escuela.
3. Ayudará al niño a mejorar sus abilidades para resolver/solucionar conflictos y a seleccionar metas positivas en el salón de clases.

El grupo se reunirá en la escuela aproximadamente por _____ semanas, todos los _____. El encargado del grupo será _____, a quien usted podrá contactar llamando al _____. Se hará todo el esfuerzo posible para que el niño no pierda mucho tiempo de clase y su maestro(a) le dará tiempo adicional para terminar los trabajos, si fuera necesario.

En el grupo, los niños intractuarán para aprender cómo controlar sus enojos, cómo resolver conflictos con otros niños y adultos, y también trabajarán en el salón de clases para lograr las metas fijadas. Este es un grupo diseñado para enseñar primordialmente cómo obtener control sobre uno mismo en la escuela. Ningún tópico que no sea relacionado con la escuela será discutido en el grupo. Una explicación completa de cada actividad estará a su disposición con sólo llamar al número de teléfono antes mencionado. Por favor llame si tiene alguna pregunta o si desea hacer una cita en la escuela. Su cooperación es muy importante, si por alguna razón usted decidiera que su niño no participe en el grupo, nosotros seguiremos trabajando con él en el salón de clases para que pueda ser un buen estudiante. Servicios similares a éste pueden encontrarse en la comunidad. Siéntase en la libertad de llamar si desea más información o si esta interesado(a).

Usted, su hijo y/o el maestro de su hijo pueden ser contactados para completar un formulario para que el encargado del grupo pueda ayudar mejor a su hijo. Los resultados de éstos formularios seran guardados confidencialmente, aunque ustedes cómo padres tienen la libertad de verlos si desean. Los formularios que se utilizaran son:

_____   _____

Por favor firme y devuelva el talonario que se encuentra al final de ésta carta. Conserve la parte de arriba de ésta carta para su información.

Sinceramente,

_____
(Principal/Administrador)

(cont.)

(Escoja uno)

_____ Yo autorizo a mi hijo, _____ , para participar
en el grupo "Anger Coping" (Canalizar Enojos), descrito arriba.

_____ Yo NO autorizo.

_____   _____
Firma   Fecha

(cont.)

Carta a los Padres 1

Estimados Padres:

Gracias por permitirle a su hijo participar en el grupo "Anger Coping" (Canalizar Enojos). Hemos tenido un buen comienzo y esperamos ayudar a que su hijo aprenda nuevas habilidades. Una vez más, nos estamos reuniendo los _____ a las _____.

Los miembros del grupo han comenzado a trabajar en las metas personales que los ayudarán a mejorar sus trabajos escolares y su conducta en el salón de clases. Cada miembro del grupo fijó su propia meta. Nuestras reuniones siempre comienzan repasando esas metas y animando a que los niños trabajen duro para lograrlas.

La mayoría de las metas estan relacionadas a cómo llevarse bien con otros niños en la escuela, como mejorar el trabajo de la clase ó escuela, y a major escuchar y obedecer al maestro (a). Una vez que el niño haya realizado su meta, éste comenzara con una nueva meta.

COMO USTED PUEDE AYUDAR:

- Pídale a su hijo que le cuente/platique sus metas a usted. ¿Porqué desidió que era importante? ¿Cuáles son sus planes para realizar esa metas?
- ¿Cómo sabrá él cuándo ha realizado su meta? ¿Qué problemas podría tener él? ¿Cuáles son sus planes para enfrentarse con esos problemas?

Si de tres o cuatro veces por semana usted dice, "Dime, cómo te va con la meta de 'Anger Coping' (Canalizar Enojos)," él entenderá que lo que es importante en la escuela también es importante en casa.

Sinceramente,

_____

- -

Use la parte de abajo sólo si usted quiere enviar cualquier comentario o pregunta sobre el grupo. Esté seguro de dejar su número de teléfono y "la mejor hora para hablarle" si usted quiere que le llame con relacion a su comentario. Favor de regresar la forma con su hijo al maestro.

Su nombre: _____

(cont.)

Carta a los Padres 2

Estimados Padres:

Vamos bien en nuestro grupo de Anger Coping. Recientemente hemos estado trabajando en diversos metodos para controlar nuestros sentimientos de coraje. Muchos niños tienen problemas manteniendo su temperamento bajo control. En nuestro grupo, hemos estado practicando algunos metodos para "como mantenerse calmado." Los miembros del grupo estan aprendiendo que lo que ellos piensan y se dicen asi mismos cuando se enojan es bien importante.

Por ejemplo, en nuestro grupo hemos estado trabajando en una actividad en la cual los miembros del grupo intentan hacerce enoja unos a otros. Pero, en vez de enojarse los niño estan aprendiendo a mantenerse en control, poniendo atención a lo que se dicen asi mismos.

COMO USTED PUEDE AYUDAR:

- Pregunte a su hijo sobre la actividad "El auto-control de la Marioneta." ¿Qué hicieron las marionetas en el circulo pare evitar enojarse?
- Pregunte a su hijo lo que hizo cuando estaba dentro del "circulo de seguridad" sin su marioneta y los demas niños trataban de hacerle enojar. ¿Qué hizo para no perder el control?
- Platique con su hijo que hacer cuando el/ella quiere "mantenerse en control" y lo importante es esa abilidad para el/ella.

Controlar los enojos es algo muy importante en la casa tambien. Recuerde a su hijo de usar las abilidades aprendidas en el grupo de "Anger Coping" (Canalizando Enojos), esto lo ayudara a resolver problemas que tenga en su casa.

Sinceramente,

_____

Use la parte de abajo sólo si usted quiere enviar cualquier comentario o pregunta sobre el grupo. Este seguro de dejar su número de teléfono y á "la mejor hora para hablarle" si usted quiere que le llame con relacion a su comentario. Favor de regresar la forma con su hijo al maestro.

Su nombre: _____

(cont.)

Carta a los Padres 3

Estimados Padres:

Hemos comenzado a trabajar en una de las abilidades más importantes en "Anger Coping" (Canalizar Enojos): Cómo solucionar problemas con otras personas. Esto puede incluir problemas con otros niños, maestros o otros adultos, y por supuesto, problemas con los padres. Para lograr ésto, los niños han estado aprendiendo a enfrentar los problemas por medio de una serie de preguntas. Las preguntas son estas:

> **¿Qué/Cual es el problema?** (Exponiendolo como su problema no el de otras personas)
> **¿Cuales son mis sentimientos?** (¿Es enojo?, ¿Estoy asustado?)
> **¿Cuales son mis opciones?** (Los problemas con frequencia tienen varias soluciones, buenas y malas)
> **¿Qué podra pasar?** (Cada solución tiene una consequencia)

Si su niño lo ve y escucha utilizando éstas preguntas para resolver un problema suyo, esto podra a ayudarlo a aprender esta abilidad por si mismo. Yo uso con frequencia este proceso de pensar en voz alta en el grupo. Tratelo. Puede ser que a usted le guste!! Puede llamarme si desea alguna ayuda.

Sinceramente,

_____

Use la parte de abajo sólo si usted quiere enviar cualquier comentario o pregunta sobre el grupo. Este seguro de dejar su número de teléfono y "la mejor hora para hablarle" si usted quiere que le llame con relacion a su comentario. Favor de regresar la forma son su hijo al maestro.

Su nombre: _____

Anger Coping Program Classroom Progress Monitoring Report (CPMR)

Student's Name _____   Teacher _____

For the time period _____ to _____

PLEASE CONSIDER THE TIME PERIOD *AS A WHOLE*.

1. Adherence to classroom rules and routines

Above the class average	At the class average	Below the class average	Well below the class average
4	3	2	1

Optional Comment:

2. Self-control of vocal disruptive behavior

Above the class average	At the class average	Below the class average	Well below the class average
4	3	2	1

Optional Comment:

3. Self-control of anger

Above the class average	At the class average	Below the class average	Well below the class average
4	3	2	1

Optional Comment:

4. Homework returned

Above the class average	At the class average	Below the class average	Well below the class average
4	3	2	1

Optional Comment:

5. In-class assignment effort

Above the class average	At the class average	Below the class average	Well below the class average
4	3	2	1

Optional Comment:

6. (Optional other) _____

Above the class average	At the class average	Below the class average	Well below the class average
4	3	2	1

Optional Comment:

Teacher signature _____

Please return to _____

Anger Coping Program Intervention Integrity Checklists

SESSION 1: DATE(S) _____

- ☐ Explained the rationale and objectives of the group
- ☐ Explained meeting times, program length, and classroom pickup schedule/behavior
- ☐ Developed group rules
- ☐ Explained points and strikes
- ☐ Completed a "Get Acquainted" activity
- ☐ Completed individual picture description activity
- ☐ Explained the importance of generalizing what is learned in the group
- ☐ Provided positive feedback on meeting

Notes:

(cont.)

SESSION 2: DATE(S) _____

    ☐ Reviewed preceding meeting's content

    ☐ Defined the term *goal* so that all understood

    ☐ Introduced and explained "My Goal Sheet"

    ☐ Allowed members to discuss teacher goals

    ☐ Allowed members to complete their portion of the goal sheet

    ☐ Explained reinforcement for goal attainment

    ☐ Provided positive feedback on meeting

Notes:

(cont.)

SESSION 3: DATE(S) _____

- ☐ Reviewed goals progress
- ☐ Reviewed preceding meeting's content
- ☐ Completed the "one too few puppets" activity
- ☐ Explained the concept of self-talk to regulate anger level
- ☐ Modeled self-talk with puppet
- ☐ Allowed members to decide on own self-talk and appropriate taunts ahead of time
- ☐ Each member was in the circle a minimum of two times
- ☐ Discussed generalization activities
- ☐ Provided positive feedback on meeting

Notes:

(cont.)

SESSION 4: DATE(S) _____

    ☐ Reviewed goals progress

    ☐ Reviewed preceding meeting's content

    ☐ Each member engaged in the card memory activity and was debriefed afterward

    ☐ Each member engaged in the domino activity and was debriefed afterward

    ☐ Leader modeled anger regulation self-statements in the circle

    ☐ Allowed members to decide on own self-talk and appropriate taunts ahead of time

    ☐ Each member was in the circle a minimum of three times

    ☐ Discussed generalization activities

    ☐ Provided positive feedback on meeting

Notes:

(cont.)

SESSION 5: DATE(S) _____

    ☐ Reviewed goals progress

    ☐ Reviewed preceding meeting's content

    ☐ Each student volunteered a possible "problem" to the stimulus picture

    ☐ Perspectives of others in the picture were queried

    ☐ Role play regarding the problem was enacted

    ☐ Members were debriefed about the role play

    ☐ (Optional) Real-life problem was enacted and debriefed

    ☐ Discussed generalization activities

    ☐ Provided positive feedback on meeting

Notes:

(cont.)

SESSION 6: DATE(S) _____

- ☐ Reviewed goals progress
- ☐ Reviewed preceding meeting's content
- ☐ Role play regarding an incident involving anger (picture or real-life) was enacted
- ☐ Members were debriefed on role play
- ☐ Discussed "anger" as a human emotion that exists on a continuum
- ☐ Definition of *anger* was agreed upon
- ☐ Reasons for anger at school were elicited and discussed
- ☐ Hassle Log was introduced and explained
- ☐ Discussed generalization activities
- ☐ Provided positive feedback on meeting

Notes:

(cont.)

SESSION 7: DATE(S) _____

    ☐ Reviewed goals progress

    ☐ Reviewed preceding meeting's content

    ☐ Leader modeled cue recognition from own experience

    ☐ Each member described own physiological cues

    ☐ Each member described angry self-statements aligned with Hassle Log incident

    ☐ Discussed generalization activities

    ☐ Provided positive feedback on meeting

Notes:

(cont.)

SESSION 8: DATE(S) _____

    ☐ Reviewed goals progress

    ☐ Reviewed preceding meeting's content

    ☐ Students brainstormed choices from Hassle Log incidents

    ☐ Choices were examined for self-statements and anger control

    ☐ The term *consequences* was defined and discussed

    ☐ Consequences for earlier choices were brainstormed and rated

    ☐ Discussed generalization activities

    ☐ Provided positive feedback on meeting

Notes:

(cont.)

SESSION 9: DATE(S) _____

☐ Reviewed goals progress

☐ Reviewed preceding meeting's content

☐ Problem-solving steps were listed on poster board

☐ Each step was discussed

☐ Sample problems from members were used to provide discussion examples

☐ Each group member was able to repeat the steps from memory

☐ Discussed generalization activities

☐ Provided positive feedback on meeting

Notes:

(cont.)

SESSION 10: DATE(S) _____

    ☐ Reviewed goals progress

    ☐ Reviewed preceding meeting's content

    ☐ Members shown videotape *Anger Coping Video* from Session 10 and alternative consequences discussed

    ☐ Possible topics for group videotape discussed

    ☐ Provided positive feedback on meeting

Notes:

(cont.)

SESSIONS 11–18: VIDEO WRITING, REHEARSAL, AND PRODUCTION

11. Date: _____
    Notes:

12. Date: _____
    Notes:

13. Date: _____
    Notes:

14. Date: _____
    Notes:

(cont.)

15. Date: _____
    Notes:

16. Date: _____
    Notes:

17. Date: _____
    Notes:

18. Date: _____
    Notes:

(cont.)

Stimulus Pictures

Picture credit: Barbara Beaver.

Recommended Further Reading

Larson, J. (2008). Best practices in school violence prevention. In A. Thomas & J. Grimes (Eds.), *Best practices in school psychology V.* (pp. 1291–1307). Bethesda, MD: National Association of School Psychologists.

Helps the practitioner place the Anger Coping Program within the context of a multi-level school-based prevention program.

Larson, J. (2005). *Think first: Addressing aggressive behavior in secondary schools.* New York: Guilford Press.

A small-group, evidence-supported anger management program for older middle school and high school students.

Lochman, J. E., Powell, N. R., Clanton, N., & McElroy, H. K. (2006). Anger and aggression. In G. Bear & K. Minke (Eds.), *Children's needs III* (pp. 115–134). Bethesda, MD: National Association of School Psychologists.

A comprehensive discussion of anger and aggressive children and youth, with references to numerous school-based programs and procedures.

Lochman, J. E., FitzGerald, D. P., & Whidby, J. M. (1999). Anger management with aggressive children. In C. Schaefer (Ed.), *Short-term psychotherapy groups for children* (pp. 301–349). Northvale, NJ: Jason Aronson.

Lochman, J. E., Lampron, L. B., Gemmer, T. C., & Harris, S. R. (1987). Anger-coping interventions for aggressive children: Guide to implementation in school settings. In P. A. Keller & S. Heyman (Eds.), *Innovations in clinical practice: A source book* (Vol. 6, pp. 339–356). Sarasota, FL: Professional Resource Exchange.

Lochman, J. E., Lampron, L .B., Gemmer, T. C., Harris, S. R., & Wyckoff, G. M. (1989). Teacher consultation and cognitive-behavioral interventions with aggressive boys. *Psychology in the Schools, 26* 179–188.

Lochman, J. E., Magee, T. N., & Pardini, D. (in press). Cognitive behavioral interventions for aggressive children. In M. Reinecke & D. Clark (Eds.), *Cognitive therapy over the lifespan: Theory, research and practice.* Cambridge, UK: Cambridge University Press.

Lochman, J. E., & Szczepanski, R. G. (1999). Externalizing conditions. In V. L. Schwean & D. H. Saklofske (Eds.), *Psychosocial correlates of exceptionality* (pp. 219–246). New York: Plenum.

Lochman, J. E., Powell, N. R., Whidby, J. M., & FitzGerald, D. P. (2006). Cognitive-behavioral assessment and treatment with aggressive children. In P. C. Kendall (Ed.), *Child and adolescent therapy: Cognitive-behavioral procedures* (3rd ed., pp. 33–81). New York: Guilford Press.

Matthys, W., & Lochman, J. E. (2010). *Oppositional defiant disorder and conduct disorder in childhood.* Chichester, West Sussex, UK: Wiley-Blackwell.

These references offer further insight into both the theoretical foundation and research base for the interested practitioner or researcher.

Mayer, M. J., Van Acker, R., Lochman, J. E., & Gresham, F. M. (Eds.). (2009). *Cognitive-behavioral interventions for emotional and behavioral disorders: School-based practice.* New York: Guilford Press.

This edited volume explains the uses of cognitive-behavioral interventions in the school-based treatment of aggression, anxiety, depression, ADHD, and autism.

Meichenbaum, D. H. (2001). *Treatment of individuals with anger-control problems and aggressive behaviors: A clinical handbook.* Clearwater, FL: Institute Press. Available for purchase from the author at *dhmeich@aol.com.*

This is an essential guide for anyone doing anger and aggression management treatment with children and youth. Contains a wealth of insights, procedures, resources, and suggestions from one of the major voices in the field.

Pepler, D. J., Madsen, K. C., Webster, C., & Levene, K. S. (Eds.). (2004). *The development and treatment of girlhood aggression.* Mahwah, NJ: Erlbaum.

Moretti, M. M., Jackson, M., & Odgers, C. (Eds.). (2004). *Girls and aggression: Contributing factors and intervention principles.* Norwell, MA: Kluwer Academic.

Putallaz, M., & Beirman, K. (Eds.). (2004). *Aggression, antisocial behavior, and violence among girls: A developmental perspective.* New York: Guilford Press.

Underwood, M. K. (2003). *Social aggression among girls.* New York: Guilford Press.

Four very useful and scholarly volumes on the subject of understanding and treating aggression in girls.

References

Achenbach, T. M., & Rescorla, L. A. (2001). *Manual for ASEBA School-Age Forms and Profiles*. Burlington, VT: University of Vermont, Research Center for Children, Youth, and Families.

Adler, A. (1964). *Social interest: A challenge to mankind*. New York: Capricorn.

Alink, L. R. A., Mesman, J., van Zijl, J., Solk, M. N., Juffer, F., Koot, H. M., et al. (2006). The early childhood aggression curve: Development of physical aggression in 10- to 50-month-old children. *Child Development, 77*, 954–966.

American Guidance Service (2001). *Developing understanding of self and others (DUSO)*. Circle Pines, MN: Author.

American Psychiatric Association (1994). *Diagnostic and statistical manual of mental disorders* (4th ed.). Washington, DC: Author.

American Psychological Association. (2002a). *Ethical principles of psychologists and code of conduct 2002*. Retrieved from *www.apa.org/ethics/code2002.html*.

American Psychological Association. (2002b). *Guidelines for multicultural education, training, research, practice, and organizational change for psychologists*. Washington, DC: Author.

Ang, R. P., & Hughes, J. N. (2002). Differential benefits of skills training with antisocial youth based on group composition: A meta-analytic investigation. *School Psychology Review, 31*, 164–185.

Arnold, M. E., & Hughes, J. N. (1999). First do no harm: Adverse effects of grouping deviant youth for skills training. *Journal of School Psychology, 37*, 99–115.

Asarnow, J. R., & Callan, J. W. (1985). Boys with peer adjustment problems: Social cognitive processes. *Journal of Consulting and Clinical Psychology, 53*, 80–87.

Asher, S. R., & Renshaw, P. D. (1981). Children without friends: Social knowledge and social skills training. In S. R. Asher & J. M. Gottman (Eds.), *The development of children's friendships* (pp. 273–296). New York: Cambridge University Press.

Attar, B., Guerra, N., & Tolan, P. (1994). Neighborhood disadvantage, stressful life events, and adjustment in urban elementary school children. *Journal of Clinical Child Psychology, 23*, 391–400.

Augimeri, L. K. (2008, June). *SNAP girl connection: Basic program information*. Toronto: Centre for Children Committing Offences & Program Development, Child Development Institute.

Bandura, A. (1971). *Social learning theory*. New York: General Learning Press.

Bandura, A. (1973). *Aggression: A social learning analysis*. Englewood Cliffs, NJ: Prentice-Hall.

Bandura, A. (1983). Psychological mechanisms of aggression. In R. G. Geen & E. I. Donnerstein (Eds.), *Aggression: Theoretical and empirical reviews* (Vol. 1, pp. 1–40). San Diego, CA: Academic Press.

Bandura, A., & Barab, P. (1973). Processes governing disinhibitory effects through symbolic modeling. *Journal of Abnormal Psychology, 82*, 1–9.

Bandura, A., & Walters, R. H. (1959). *Adolescent aggression*. New York: Ronald Press.

Barkley, R. A. (1998). *Attention-deficit hyperactivity disorder: A handbook for diagnosis and treatment* (2nd ed.). New York: Guilford Press.

Barry, T. D., Thompson, A., Barry, C. T., Lochman,

J. E., Adler, K., & Hill, K. (2007). The importance of narcissism in predicting proactive and reactive aggression in moderately to highly aggressive children. *Aggressive Behavior, 33,* 185–197.

Barth, J. M., Dunlap, S. T., Dane, H., Lochman, J. E., & Wells, K. C. (2004). Classroom environment influences on aggression, peer relations, and academic focus. *Journal of School Psychology, 42,* 115–133.

Bierman, K. L. (1986). Process of change during social skills training with preadolescents and its relation to treatment outcome. *Child Development, 57,* 230–240.

Bierman, K. L. (2007). Anger and aggression: A developmental perspective. In T. A. Cavell & K. T. Malcom (Eds.), *Anger, aggression, and interventions for interpersonal violence* (pp. 215–238). Mahwah, NJ: Erlbaum.

Bloomquist, M. L., August, G. J., Cohen, C., Doyle, A., & Everhart, K. (1997). Social problem solving in hyperactive-aggressive children: How and what they think in conditions of automatic and controlled processing. *Journal of Clinical Psychology, 26*(2), 172–180.

Boivin, M., Dodge, K. A., & Coie, J. D. (1995). Individual-group behavioral similarity and peer status in experimental play groups of boys: The social misfit revisited.*Journal of Personality and Social Psychology, 69,* 269–279.

Boxmeyer, C. L., Lochman, J. E., Powell, N. R., Windle, M., & Wells, K. (2008). School counselors' implementation of Coping Power in a dissemination field trial: Delineating the range of flexibility within fidelity. *Report on Emotional and Behavioral Disorders in Youth, 8,* 79–95.

Boxmeyer, C. L., Lochman, J. E., Powell, N., Yaros, A., & Wojnaroski, M. (2007). A case study of the Coping Power Program for angry and aggressive youth. *Journal of Contemporary Psychotherapy, 37,* 165–174.

Brestan, E. V., & Eyberg, S. M. (1998). Effective psychosocial treatment of conduct-disordered children and adolescents: 29 years, 82 studies, and 5,272 kids. *Journal of Clinical Child Psychology, 27,* 180–189.

Broidy, L. M., Nagin, D. S., Tremblay, R. E., Bates, J. E., Brame, B., Dodge, K. A., et al. (2003). Developmental trajectories of childhood disruptive behaviors and adolescent delinquency: A six-site, cross-national study. *Developmental Psychology, 2,* 222–245.

Brown, D., Pryzwansky, W. B., & Schulte, A. C. (1995). *Psychological consultation: Introduction to theory and practice* (2nd ed.). New York: Allyn & Bacon.

Busse, R. T., & Beaver, B. R. (2000). Informant report:

Parent and teacher interviews. In E. S. Shapiro & T. R. Kratochwill (Eds.), *Conducting school-based assessments of child and adolescent behavior* (pp. 235–273). New York: Guilford Press.

Charlebois, P., LeBlanc, M., Gagnon, C., & Larivee, S. (1994). Methodological issues in multiple-gating screening procedures for antisocial behaviors in elementary students. *Remedial and Special Education, 15,* 44–54.

Chassin, L., Curran, P. J., Hussong, A. M., & Colder, C. R. (1996). The relation of parent alcoholism to adolescent substance use: A longitudinal follow-up study. *Journal of Abnormal Psychology, 105,* 70–80.

Coie, J. D., Lochman, J. E., Terry, R., & Hyman, C. (1992). Predicting early adolescent disorder from childhood aggression and peer rejection. *Journal of Consulting and Clinical Psychology, 60* 783–792.

Coie, J. D., Terry, R., Zakriski, A., & Lochman, J. E. (1995). Early adolescent social influences on delinquent behavior. In J. McCord (Ed.), *Coercion and punishment in long-term perspectives* (pp. 229–244). Cambridge, UK: Cambridge University Press.

Coie, J. D., Underwood, M., & Lochman, J. E. (1991). Programmatic intervention with aggressive children in the school setting. In D. J. Pepler & K. H. Rubin (Eds.), *Development and treatment of childhood aggression* (pp. 389–445). Hillsdale, NJ: Erlbaum.

Committee for Children. (2001). *Second step violence prevention curriculum.* Seattle, WA: Author.

Conduct Problems Prevention Research Group. (1992). A developmental and clinical model for the prevention of conduct disorder: The Fast Track Program. *Development and Psychopathology, 4,* 509–527.

Conduct Problems Prevention Research Group. (1999a). Initial impact of the Fast Track prevention trial for conduct problems: I. The high-risk sample. *Journal of Consulting and Clinical Psychology, 67,* 631–647.

Conduct Problems Prevention Research Group. (1999b). Initial impact of the Fast Track prevention trial for conduct problems: II. Classroom effects. *Journal of Consulting and Clinical Psychology, 67,* 648–657.

Conduct Problems Prevention Research Group. (2004). The effects of the Fast Track program on serious problem outcomes at the end of elementary school. *Journal of Clinical Child and Adolescent Psychology, 33,* 650–661.

Conoley, J. C., & Conoley, C. W. (1992). *School consultation: Practice and training* (2nd ed.). Boston: Allyn & Bacon.

Council of National Psychological Associations for the

Advancement of Ethnic Minority Interests. (2009). *Psychology education and training from culture-specific and multiracial perspectives: Critical issues and recommendations.* Washington, DC: American Psychological Association.

Crick, N. R. (1997). Engagement in gender normative versus non-normative forms of aggression: Links to social-psychological adjustment. *Developmental Psychology, 33,* 610–617.

Crick, N. R., & Bigbee, M. A. (1998). Relational and overt forms of peer victimization: A multi-informant approach. *Journal of Consulting and Clinical Psychology, 66,* 337–347.

Crick, N. R., Casas, J. F., & Ku, H. (1999). Relational and physical forms of peer victimization in preschool. *Developmental Psychology, 35,* 376–385.

Crick, N. R., & Dodge, K. A. (1994). A review and reformulation of social information-processing mechanisms in children's social adjustment. *Psychological Bulletin, 115,* 74–101.

Crick, N., & Grotpeter, J. (1995). Relational aggression, gender, and social-psychological adjustment. *Child Development, 66,* 710–722.

Crick, N., & Grotpeter, J. (1996). Children's treatment by peers: Victims of relational and overt aggression. *Development and Psychopathology, 8,* 367–380.

Crick, N. R., & Werner, N. E. (1998). Response decision processes in relational and overt aggression. *Child Development, 69,* 1630–1639.

Cummings, E. M., Iannotti, R. V., & Zahn-Waxler, C. (1985). Influence of conflict between adults on the emotions and aggression of young children. *Developmental Psychology, 21,* 495–507.

Curran, P. J., Stice, E., & Chassin, l. (1997). The relation between adolescent alcohol use and peer alcohol use: A longitudinal random coefficients model. *Journal of Consulting and Clinical Psychology, 65,* 130–140.

Day, D. M., Golench, C. A., MacDougall, J., & Beals-Gonzalez, C. A. (1995). School-based violence prevention in Canada: Results of a national survey of policies. Retrieved from *www.publicsafety.gc.ca/serv/srch/search-eng.aspx?q=school-based+violence+prevention.*

Deluty, R. H. (1983). Children's evaluation of aggressive, assertive, and submissive responses. *Journal of Consulting and Clinical Psychology 51,* 124–129.

DeRubeis, R. J., Tang, T. Z., & Beck, A. T. (2001). Cognitive therapy. In K. S. Dobson (Ed.), *Handbook of cognitive-behavioral therapies* (2nd ed., pp. 349–392). New York: Guilford Press.

Dishion, T. J., & Andrews, D. W. (1995). Preventing escalation in problem behaviors with high-risk young adolescents: Immediate and 1-year outcomes. *Journal of Consulting and Clinical Psychology, 63,* 538–548.

Dishion, T. J., & Dodge, K. A. (2006). Deviant peer contagion in interventions and programs: An ecological framework for understanding influence mechanisms. In K. A. Dodge, T. J. Dishion, & J. E. Lansford (Eds.), *Deviant peer influences in programs for youth* (pp. 14–43). New York: Guilford Press.

Dishion, T. J., Dodge, K. A., & Lansford, J. E. (2006). Findings and recommendations: A blueprint to minimize deviant peer influence in youth interventions and programs. In K. A. Dodge, T. J. Dishion, & J. E. Lansford (Eds.), *Deviant peer influences in programs for youth: Problems and solutions* (pp. 366–394). New York: Guilford Press.

Dishion, T. J., Eddy, J. M., Haas, E., Li, F., & Spracklen, K. (1997). Friendships and violent behavior during adolescence. *Social Development, 6,* 207–223.

Dishion, T. J., McCord, J., & Poulin, F. (1999). When interventions harm: Peer groups and problem behavior. *American Psychologist, 54,* 755–764.

Dishion, T. J., Poulin, F., & Burraston, B. (2001). Peer group dynamics associated with iatrogenic effects in group interventions with high-risk young adolescents. In D. W. Nangle, & C. A. Erdley (Eds.), *The role of friendship in psychological adjustment* (pp. 79–92). San Francisco: Jossey-Bass.

Dishion, T. J., Reid, J. B., & Patterson, G. R. (1988). Empirical guidelines for a family intervention for adolescent drug use. *Journal of Chemical Dependency Treatment, 1,* 189–224.

Dodge, K. A. (1980). Social cognition and children's aggressive behavior. *Child Development, 51,* 162–170.

Dodge, K. A. (1986). A social information processing model of social competence in children. In M. Perlmutter (Ed.), *Cognitive perspectives on children's social and behavioral development: The Minnesota Symposium on Child Psychology* (Vol. 18, pp. 77–125). Hillsdale, NJ: Erlbaum.

Dodge, K. A. (1991). The structure and function of reactive and proactive aggression. In D. J. Pepler & K. H. Rubin (Eds.), *Development and treatment of childhood aggression* (pp. 201–218). Hillsdale, NJ: Erlbaum.

Dodge, K. A. (1993a). Social-cognitive mechanisms in the development of conduct disorder and aggression. *Annual Review of Psychology, 44,* 559–584.

Dodge, K. A. (1993b). The future of research on the treatment of conduct disorder. *Development and Psychopathology, 5,* 311–319.

Dodge, K. A. (1999). Cost-effectiveness of psychotherapy for child aggression: First, is there effectiveness? Comment on Schectman and Ben-David. *Group Dynamics, 3,* 275–278.

Dodge, K. A., Bates, J. E., & Pettit, G. S. (1990).

Mechanisms in the cycle of violence. *Science, 250,* 1678–1683.

Dodge, K. A., & Coie, J. D. (1987). Social information processing factors in reactive and proactive aggression in children's peer groups. *Journal of Personality and Social Psychology, 53,* 1146–1178.

Dodge, K. A., Coie, J. D., & Lynam, D. (2006). Aggression and antisocial behavior in youth. In W. Damon & R. M. Lerner (Series Eds.) & N. Eisenberg (Vol. Ed.), *Handbook of child psychology: Vol. 3. Social, emotional, and personality development* (6th ed., pp. 719–788). New York: Wiley.

Dodge, K. A., Dishion, T. J., & Lansford, J. E. (2006). *Deviant peer influences in programs for youth: Problems and solutions.* New York: Guilford Press.

Dodge, K. A., & Frame, C. L. (1982). Social cognitive biases and deficits in aggressive boys. *Child Development, 53,* 620–635.

Dodge, K. A., Laird, R., Lochman, J. E., Zelli, A., & Conduct Problems Prevention Research Group. (2002). Multi-dimensional latent construct analysis of children's social information processing patterns: Correlations with aggressive behavior problems. *Psychological Assessment, 14,* 60–73.

Dodge, K. A., Lochman, J. E., Harnish, J. D., Bates, J. E., & Pettit, G. S. (1997). Reactive and proactive aggression in school children and psychiatrically impaired chronically assaultive youth. *Journal of Abnormal Psychology, 106,* 37–51.

Dodge, K. A., Murphy, R. R., & Buchsbaum, K. (1984). The assessment of intention-cue detection skills in children: Implications for developmental psychopathology. *Child Development, 55,* 163–173.

Dodge, K. A., & Newman, J. P. (1981). Biased decision-making processes in aggressive boys. *Journal of Abnormal Psychology, 90,* 375–379.

Dodge, K. A., & Pettit, G. S. (2003). A biopsychosocial model of the development of chronic conduct problems in adolescence. *Developmental Psychology, 39,* 349–371.

Dodge, K. A., Pettit, G. S., & Bates, J. E. (1997). How the experience of early physical abuse leads children to become chronically aggressive. In D. Cicchetti & S. L. Toth (Eds.), *Rochester Symposium on Developmental Psychopathology, Vol. 8. Developmental perspectives on trauma: Theory, research and intervention* (pp. 263–288). Rochester, NY: University of Rochester Press.

Dodge, K. A., Pettit, G. S., McClaskey, C. L., & Brown, M. M. (1986). Social competence in children. *Monographs of the Society for Research in Child Development, 51*(2, Serial No. 213).

Dollard, J., Doob, L. W., Miller, N. E., Mowrer, O. H., & Sears, R. R. (1939). *Frustration and aggression.* New Haven, CT: Yale University Press.

Donnerstein, E. I., Slaby, R. G., & Eron, L. D. (1994). The mass media and youth aggression. In L. D. Eron, J. H. Gentry, & P. Schlegel (Eds.), *Reason to hope: A psychological perspective on violence and youth* (pp. 383–404). Washington, DC: American Psychological Association.

Duncan, G. J., Brooks-Gunn, J., & Klebanov, P. K. (1994). Economic deprivation and early childhood development. *Child Development, 65,* 296–318.

Dunn, S. E., Lochman, J. E., & Colder, C. R. (1997). Social problem-solving skills in boys with conduct and oppositional disorders. *Aggressive Behavior, 23,* 457–469.

Eber, L., Sugai, G., Smith, C. & Scott, T. M. (2002). Wraparound and positive behavioral Interventions and supports in the schools. *Journal of Emotional and Behavioral Disorders, 10,* 136–173.

Eisenberg, N., Fabes, R. A., Nyman, M., Bernzweig, J., & Pinuelas, A. (1994). The relations of emotionality and regulation to children's anger-related reactions. *Child Development, 65,* 109–128.

Elliott, S. N., & Gresham, F. M. (1991). *Social skills intervention guide: Practical strategies for social skills training.* Circle Pines, MN: American Guidance Service.

Elliott, S. N., Witt, J. C., Galvin, G., & Peterson, R. (1984). Acceptability of behavior interventions: Factors that influence teachers' decisions. *Journal of School Psychology, 22,* 353–360.

Erdley, C. A. (1990). *An analysis of children's attributions and goals in social situations: Implications of children's friendship outcomes.* Unpublished manuscript, University of Illinois, Champaign.

Eron, L. D., Huesmann, L. R., Dubow, E., Romanoff, R., & Yarmel, P. W. (1987). Aggression and its correlates over 22 years. In D. Crowell, E. Evans, & C. O'Donnell (Eds.), *Aggression and violence: Sources of influence, prevention, and control* (pp. 249–262). New York: Plenum Press.

Eron, L. D., & Slaby, R. G. (1994). Introduction. In L. D. Eron, J. H. Gentry, & P. Schlegel (Eds.), *Reason to hope: A psychological perspective on violence and youth* (pp. 1–22). Washington, DC: American Psychological Association.

Eyberg, S. M., Nelson, M. N., & Boggs, S. R. (2008). Evidence-based psychosocial treatments for children and adolescents with disruptive behavior. *Journal of Clinical Child and Adolescent Psychology, 37,* 215–237.

Falender, C. A., & Shafranske, E. P. (2004). *Clinical supervision: A competency-based approach.* Washington, DC: American Psychological Association.

Federal Bureau of Investigation. (2006). *Crime in the United States, 2005: Uniform Crime Reports.* Washington, DC: U.S. Department of Justice, FBI.

Feindler, E. L., Adler, N., Brooks, D., & Bhumitra, E. (1993). The development of the Children's Anger Response Checklist (CARC). In L. VanderCreek (Ed.), *Innovations in clinical practice* (Vol. 12, pp. 337–362). Sarasota, FL: Professional Resources Press.

Feindler, E. L., & Ecton, R. B. (1986). *Adolescent anger control: Cognitive-behavioral techniques.* New York: Allyn & Bacon.

Feldman, E., & Dodge, K. A. (1987). Social information processing and sociometric status: Sex, age, and situational effects. *Journal of Abnormal Child Psychology, 15,* 211–227.

Feldman, R. A., Caplinger, T. E., & Wodarski, J. S. (1983). *The St. Louis conundrum: The effective treatment of antisocial youths.* Englewood Cliffs, NJ: Prentice-Hall.

Fenning, P., & Rose, J. (2007). Overrepresentation of African American students in exclusionary discipline: The role of school policy. *Urban Education, 42,* 536–559.

Fergusson, D. M., & Horwood, L. J. (2002). Male and female offending trajectories. *Developmental and Psychopathology, 14,* 159–177.

Fiske, S. T., & Taylor, S. E. (1984). *Social cognition.* Reading, MA: Addison-Wesley.

Fite, P. J., Colder, C. R., Lochman, J. E., & Wells, K. C. (2007). Pathways from proactive and reactive aggression to substance use. *Psychology of Addictive Behaviors, 21,* 355–364.

Fite, P. J., Colder, C. R., Lochman, J. E., & Wells, K. C. (2008a). Developmental trajectories of proactive and reactive aggression from 5th to 9th grade. *Journal of Clinical Child and Adolescent Psychology, 37,* 412–421.

Fite, P. J., Colder, C. R., Lochman, J. E., & Wells, K. C. (2008b). The relation between childhood proactive and reactive aggression and substance use initiation. *Journal of Abnormal Child Psychology, 36* 261–271.

Flannery-Schroeder, E. C., & Kendall, P. C. (2000). Group and individual cognitive-behavioral treatments for youth with anxiety disorders: A randomized clinical trial. *Cognitive Therapy and Research, 24,* 251–278.

Forehand, R. L., & McMahon, R. J. (1981). *Helping the noncompliant child: A clinician's guide to parent training.* New York: Guilford Press.

Forum on Child and Family Statistics (2009). *America's children: Key national indicators of well-being.* Retrieved from *www.childstats.gov/.*

Freeman, A., & Leaf, R. C. (1989). Cognitive therapy applied to personality disorders. In A. Freeman, K. M. Simm, L. E. Beutler, & H. Arkowitz (Eds.), *Comprehensive handbook of cognitive therapy* (pp. 403–433). New York: Plenum Press.

Fuchs, L. S. (1995). Defining student goals and outcomes. In A. Thomas & J. Grimes (Eds.), *Best practices in school psychology III* (pp. 539–546). Bethesda, MD: National Association of School Psychologists.

Furlong, M. J., & Smith, D. C. (Eds.). (1994). *Anger, hostility, and aggression: Assessment, prevention, and intervention strategies for youth.* Brandon, VT: Clinical Psychology.

Garbarino, J. (2006). *See Jane hit: Why girls are growing more violent and what we can do about it.* New York: Penguin Press.

Goetz, E. T., Hall, R. J., & Fetsco, T. G. (1989). Information processing and cognitive assessment I: Background and overview. In J. N. Hughes & R. J. Hall (Eds.), *Cognitive-behavioral psychology in the schools: A comprehensive handbook* (pp. 87–115). New York: Guilford Press.

Goleman, D. (1995). *Emotional intelligence.* New York: Bantam Books.

Gottfredson, D. C. (1997). School-based crime prevention. In L. Sherman, D. Gottfredson, D. Mackenzie, J. Eck, P. Reuter, & S. Bushway (Eds.). *Preventing crime: What works, what doesn't and what's promising.* College Park, MD: Department of Criminology and Criminal Justice.

Gouze, K. R. (1987). Attention and social problem solving as correlates of aggression in preschool males. *Journal of Abnormal Child Psychology, 15,* 181–197.

Guerra, N. G., & Slaby, R. G. (1989). Evaluative factors in social problem solving by aggressive boys. *Journal of Abnormal Child Psychology 17,* 277–289.

Handwerk, M. L., Field, C. E., & Friman, P. C. (2000). The iatrogenic effects of group intervention for antisocial youth: Premature extrapolations? *Journal of Behavioral Education, 10,* 223–238.

Henggeler, S. W., Melton, G. B., & Smith, L. A. (1992). Family preservation using multisystemic therapy: An effective alternative to incarcerating serious juvenile offenders. *Journal of Consulting and Clinical Psychology, 60,* 953–961.

Henington, C., Hughes, J. N., Cavell, T. A., & Thompson, B. (1998). The role of relational aggression in identifying aggressive boys and girls. *Journal of School Psychology, 36,* 457–477.

Higgins, E. T., King, G. A., & Marvin, G. H. (1982). Individual construct accessibility and subjective impressions and recall. *Journal of Personality and Social Psychology, 43,* 35–47.

Hoagwood, K., & Johnson, J. (2003). School psychology: A public health framework: From evidence-based practices to evidence-based policies. *Journal of School Psychology, 41,* 3–21.

Holmes, K. J., & Lochman, J. E. (2009). Ethnic identity in African American and European American preadolescents: Relation to self-worth, social goals, and aggression. *Journal of Early Adolescence, 29,* 476–496.

Horton, C. B., & Cruise, T. K. (2001). *Child abuse and neglect: The school's response.* New York: Guilford Press.

Hughes, J. N., & Clavell, T. A. (1995). Cognitive-affective approaches: Enhancing competence in aggressive children. In G. Cartledge & J. F. Miburn (Eds.), *Teaching social skills to children and youth: Innovative approaches* (3rd ed., pp. 199–236). Boston: Allyn & Bacon.

Hughes, J. N., & Hall, R. J. (1987). A proposed model for the assessment of children's social competence. *Professional School Psychology, 2,* 247–260.

Hyman, I. A. (1997). *School discipline and school violence: The teacher variance approach.* Boston: Allyn & Bacon.

Ikeda, M. J., Grimes, J., Till, W. D., III, Allison, R., Kurns, S., & Stumme, J. (2002). Implementing an intervention-based approach to service delivery: A case example. In M. R. Shinn, H. M. Walker, & G. Stoner (Eds.). *Interventions for academic and behavior problems II: Preventive and remedial approaches.* Bethesda, MD: National Association of School Psychologists.

Ingram, R. E., & Kendall, P. C. (1986). Cognitive clinical psychology: Implications of an informational processing perspective. In R. E. Ingram (Ed.), *Information processing approaches to clinical psychology* (pp. 3–21). New York: Academic Press.

Jacob-Timm, S., & Hartshorne, T. (2007). *Ethics and law for school psychologists* (5th ed.). New York: Wiley.

Jenson, W. R., Clark, E., Kircher, J. C., & Kristjansson, S. D. (2007). Statistical reform: Evidence-based practice, meta-analyses, and single subject designs. *Psychology in the Schools, 44,* 483–493.

Jimerson, S. R., Swearer, S. S., & Espelage, D. L. (Eds.). (2010). *Handbook of bullying in schools: An international perspective.* New York: Routledge.

Joffe, R. D., Dobson, K. S., Fine, S., Marriage, K., & Haley, G. (1990). Social problem-solving in depressed, conduct-disordered, and normal adolescents. *Journal of Abnormal Child Psychology, 18,* 565–575.

Jones, R. T., Kephart, C., Langley, A. K., Parker, M. N., Shenoy, U., & Weeks, C. (2001). Cultural and ethnic diversity issues in clinical child psychology. In C. E. Walker & M. C. Roberts (Eds.), *Handbook of clinical child psychology* (3rd ed., pp. 955–973). New York: Wiley.

Jones, R. N., Sheridan, S. M., & Binns, W. R. (1993). Schoolwide social skills training: Providing preventative services to students at risk. *School Psychology Quarterly, 8,* 58–80.

Katsurada, E., & Sugawara, A. I. (1998). The relationship between hostile attributional bias and aggressive behavior in preschoolers. *Early Childhood Research Quarterly, 13,* 623–636.

Kaufman, J. M. (2005). *Characteristics of emotional and behavioral disorders of children and youth* (8th ed.). Upper Saddle River, NJ: Pearson.

Kazdin, A. E. (1982). Symptom substitution, generalization and response covariation: Implications for psychotherapy outcome. *Psychological Bulletin, 91,* 349–365.

Kazdin, A. E. (1987a). Treatment of antisocial behavior in children: Current status and future directions. *Psychological Bulletin, 102,* 187–203.

Kazdin, A. E. (1987b). *Conduct disorders in childhood and adolescence* (Vol. 9). Beverly Hills, CA: Sage.

Kazdin, A. E. (1995). Interventions for aggressive and antisocial children. In L. D. Eron, J. H. Gentry, & P. Schlegel (Eds.), *A reason to hope: A psychosocial perspective on violence and youth* (pp. 341–382). Washington, DC: American Psychological Association.

Kazdin, A. E. (1998). Conduct disorder. In R. J. Morris & T. R. Kratochwill (Eds.), *The practice of child therapy* (3rd ed., pp. 199–230). Boston: Allyn & Bacon.

Kazdin, A. E. (2001). *Behavior modification in applied settings* (6th ed.). Belmont, CA: Wadsworth/Thomson Learning.

Kazdin, A. E., Siegel, T. C., & Bass, D. (1992). Cognitive problem-solving skills training and parent management training in the treatment of antisocial behavior in children. *Journal of Consulting and Clinical Psychology, 60,* 733–747.

Kazdin, A. E., & Weisz, J. R. (1998). Identifying and developing empirically supported child and adolescent treatments. *Journal of Consulting and Clinical Psychology, 66,* 19–36.

Keane, S. P., & Parrish, A. E. (1992). The role of affective information in the determination of intent. *Developmental Psychology, 28,* 159–162.

Kellam, S. G., Ling, X., Mersica, R., Brown, C. H., & Ialongo, N. (1998). The effect of the level of aggression in the first grade classroom on the course of malleability of aggressive behavior into middle school. *Development and Psychopathology, 10,* 165–185.

Kelly, G. A. (1955). *The psychology of personal constructs.* New York: Norton.

Kendall, P. C. (1982). Individual versus group cognitive-behavioral self-control training: 1-year follow-up. *Behavior Therapy, 13,* 241–247.

Kendall, P. C. (2000). Guiding theory for therapy with children and adolescents. In P. C. Kendall (Ed.), *Child and adolescent therapy: Cognitive-behavioral procedures* (2nd ed., pp. 3–27). New York: Guilford Press.

Kendall, P. C., Ronan, K. R., & Epps, J. (1991). Aggression in children/adolescents: Cognitive-behavioral treatment perspectives. In D. J. Pepler & K. H. Rubin (Eds.), *Development and treatment of childhood aggression* (pp. 341–360). Hillsdale, NJ: Erlbaum.

Kendall, P. C., & Zupan, B. A. (1981). Individual versus group application of cognitive-behavioral self-control procedures with children. *Behavior Therapy, 12*, 344–359.

Kiresuk, T. J., Smith, A., & Cardillo, J. E. (Eds.). (1994). *Goal attainment scaling: Application, theory, and measurement.* Hillsdale, NJ: Erlbaum.

Kratochwill, T. R., & Bergan, J. R. (1990). *Behavioral consultation in applied settings.* New York: Plenum Press.

Landau, S., Milich, R., & Diener, M. B. (1998). Peer relations of children with attention-deficit hyperactivity disorder. *Reading and Writing Quarterly: Overcoming Learning Difficulties, 14*, 83–105.

Larson, J. (1994). Violence prevention in the schools: A review of selected programs and procedures. *School Psychology Review, 23*, 151–164.

Larson, J. (2005). *Think first: Addressing aggressive behavior in secondary schools.* New York: Guilford Press.

Larson, J., & Lochman, J. E. (2002). *Helping schoolchildren cope with anger: A cognitive-behavioral intervention.* New York: Guilford Press.

Larson, J., Lochman, J. E., & McBride, J. A. (1996). *The Anger Coping Video.* Whitewater, WI: Author.

Larson, J., Smith D. C., & Furlong, M. J. (2002). Best practices in school violence prevention. In A. Thomas & J. Grimes (Eds.), *Best practices in school psychology IV* (pp. 1081–1097). Bethesda, MD: National Association of School Psychologists.

Lavallee, K. L., Bierman, K. L., Nix, R. L. & Conduct Problems Prevention Research Group. (2005). The impact of first-grade "Friendship Group" experiences on child social outcomes in the Fast Track Program. *Journal of Abnormal Child Psychology, 33*, 307–324.

Leschied, A., Cummings, A., Van Brunschot, M., Cunningham, A., & Saunders, A. (2000). *Female adolescent aggression: A review of the literature and the correlates of aggression* (User Report No. 2000-04). Ottawa, CA: Solicitor General Canada.

Letendre, J., & Davis, K. (2004). What really happens in violence prevention groups? A content analysis of leader behaviors and child responses in a school-based violence prevention project. *Small Group Research, 35*, 367–387.

Levene, K. S., Walsh, M. M., Augimeri, L. K., & Pepler, D. J. (2004). Linking identification and treatment of early risk factors for female delinquency. In R. Roesch (Series Ed.), M. M. Moretti, C. L. Odgers, & M. A. Jackson (Vol. Eds.), *Perspectives in law and psychology: Vol. 19. Girls and aggression: Contributing factors and intervention principles* (pp. 147–163). New York: Kluwer Academic/Plenum.

Lipsey, M. W. (2006). The effects of community-based group treatment for delinquency: A meta-analytic search for cross-study generalizations. In K. A. Dodge, T. J. Dishion, & J. E. Lansford (Eds.), *Deviant peer influences in programs for youth: Problems and solutions* (pp. 162–184). New York: Guilford Press.

Lo, Y., & Cartledge, G. (2007). Office disciplinary referrals in an urban setting. *Multicultural Learning and Teaching, 2*, 20–28.

Lochman, J. E. (1984). Psychological characteristics and assessment of aggressive adolescents. In C. R. Keith (Ed.), *The aggressive adolescent: Clinical perspectives* (pp. 17–62). New York: Free Press.

Lochman, J. E. (1985). Effects of different treatment lengths in cognitive-behavioral interventions with aggressive boys. *Child Psychiatry and Human Development, 16*, 45–56.

Lochman, J. E. (1987). Self and peer perceptions and attributional biases of aggressive and non-aggressive boys in dyadic interactions. *Journal of Consulting and Clinical Psychology, 55*, 404–410.

Lochman, J. E. (1990). Modification of childhood aggression. In M. Hersen, R. Eisler, & P. M. Miller (Eds.), *Progress in behavior modification* (Vol. 2., pp. 47–85). Newbury Park, CA: Sage.

Lochman, J. E. (1992). Cognitive-behavioral interventions with aggressive boys: Three-year follow-up and preventive effects. *Journal of Consulting and Clinical Psychology, 60*, 426–432.

Lochman, J. E. (2000a). Parent and family skills training in targeted prevention programs for at-risk youth. *Journal of Primary Prevention, 21*, 253–265.

Lochman, J. E. (2000b). Theory and empiricism in intervention research: A dialectic to be avoided. *Journal of School Psychology, 38*, 359–368.

Lochman, J. E. (2000c). Conduct disorder. In W. E. Craighead & C. B. Nemeroff (Eds.), *The Corsini encyclopedia of psychology and neuroscience* III. New York: Wiley.

Lochman, J. E. (2003). Preventive intervention with precursors to substance abuse. In W. J. Bukoski &

Z. Sloboda (Eds.), *Handbook of drug abuse theory, science, and practice* (pp. 307–326). New York: Plenum Press.

Lochman, J. E., Boxmeyer, C., Powell, N., Qu, L., Wells, K., & Windle, M. (2009). Dissemination of the Coping Power Program: Importance of intensity of counselor training. *Journal of Consulting and Clinical Psychology, 77*, 397–409.

Lochman, J. E., Boxmeyer, C., Powell, N., Wojnaroski, M., & Yaros, A. (2007). The use of the Coping Power Program to treat a 10-year-old girl with disruptive behaviors. *Journal of Clinical Child and Adolescent Psychology, 36*, 677–687.

Lochman, J. E., Burch, P. P., Curry, J. F., & Lampron, L. B. (1984). Treatment and generalization effects of cognitive-behavioral and goal setting interventions with aggressive boys. *Journal of Consulting and Clinical Psychology, 52*, 915–916.

Lochman, J. E., Coie, J. D., Underwood, M., & Terry, R. (1993). Effectiveness of a social relations intervention program for aggressive and nonaggressive rejected children. *Journal of Consulting and Clinical Psychology, 61*, 1053–1058.

Lochman, J. E., & Curry, J. F. (1986). Effects of social problem-solving training and self-instruction training with aggressive boys. *Journal of Consulting and Clinical Psychology, 63*, 549–559.

Lochman, J. E., Dane, H. E., Magee, T. N., Ellis, M., Pardini, B. A., & Claton, N. R. (2001). Disruptive behavior disorders: Assessment and intervention. In B. Vance & A. Pumareigal (Eds.), *The clinical assessment of child and youth behavior: Interfacing intervention with assessment* (pp. 231–262). New York: Wiley.

Lochman, J. E., & Dodge, K. A. (1994). Social-cognitive processes of severely violent, moderately aggressive, and nonaggressive boys. *Journal of Consulting and Clinical Psychology, 62*, 366–374.

Lochman, J. E., & Dodge, K. A. (1998). Distorted perceptions in dyadic interactions of aggressive and nonaggressive boys: Effects of prior expectations, context, and boys' age. *Development and Psychopathology, 10*, 495–512.

Lochman, J. E., FitzGerald, D. P., Gage, S. M., Kannaly, M. K., Whidby, J. M., Barry, T. D., et al. (2001). Effects of social-cognitive intervention for aggressive deaf children: The Coping Power Program. *Journal of the American Deafness and Rehabilitation Association, 35*, 39–61.

Lochman, J. E., FitzGerald, D. P., & Whidby, J. M. (1999). Anger management with aggressive children. In C. Schaefer (Ed.), *Short-term psychotherapy groups for children* (pp. 301–349). Northvale, NJ: Jason Aronson.

Lochman, J. E., Holmes, K., & Wojnaroski, M. (2008). Children and cognition: Development of

social schema. In J. K. Asamen, M. L. Ellis, & G. L. Berry (Eds.), *Handbook of child development, multiculturalism, and media* (pp. 33–46). Thousand Oaks, CA: Sage.

Lochman, J. E., & Lampron, L. B. (1986). Situational social problem-solving skills and self-esteem of aggressive and nonaggressive boys. *Journal of Abnormal Child Psychology 14*, 605–617.

Lochman, J. E., & Lampron, L. B. (1988). Cognitive behavioral intervention for aggressive boys: Seven month follow-up effects. *Journal of Child and Adolescent Psychotherapy, 5*, 15–23.

Lochman, J. E., Lampron, L. B., Burch, P. R., & Curry, J. E. (1985). Client characteristics associated with behavior change for treated and untreated boys. *Journal of Abnormal Child Psychology, 13*, 527–538.

Lochman, J. E., Lampron, L. B., Gemmer, T. C., & Harris, S. R. (1987). Anger coping intervention with aggressive children: A guide to implementation in school settings. In P. A. Keller & S. R. Heyman (Eds.), *Innovations in clinical practice: A source book* (Vol. 6, pp. 339–356). Sarasota, FL: Professional Resources Exchange.

Lochman, J. E., Lampron, L. B., Gemmer, T. C., Harris, S. R., & Wyckoff, G. M. (1989). Teacher consultation and cognitive-behavioral interventions with aggressive boys. *Psychology in the Schools, 26*, 179–188.

Lochman, J. E., Lampron, L. B., & Rabiner, D. L. (1989). Format and salience effects in the social problem-solving of aggressive and nonaggressive boys. *Journal of Clinical Child Psychology 18*, 230–236.

Lochman, J. E., & Lenhart, L. (1995). Cognitive behavioral therapy of aggressive children: Effects of schemas. In H. P. G. van Bilsen, P. C. Kendall, & J. H. Slavenburg (Eds.), *Behavioral approaches for children and adolescents: Challenges for the next century* (pp. 145–166). New York: Plenum Press.

Lochman, J. E., Magee, T. N., & Pardini, D. (2003). Cognitive behavioral interventions for aggressive children. In M. Reinecke & D. Clark (Eds.), *Cognitive therapy over the lifespan: Theory, research and practice*. Cambridge, UK: Cambridge University Press.

Lochman, J. E., Meyer, B. L., Rabiner, D. L., & White, K. J. (1991). Parameters influencing social problem-solving of aggressive children. In R. Prinz (Ed.), *Advances in behavioral assessment of child and families* (Vol. 5, pp. 31–63). Greenwich, CT: JAI Press.

Lochman, J. E., Nelson, W. M., & Sims, J. P. (1981). A cognitive behavioral program for use with aggressive children. *Journal of Clinical Child Psychology 13*, 146–148.

Lochman, J. E., Powell, N., Boxmeyer, C., Qu, L., Wells, K., & Windle, M. (2009). Implementation of a school-based prevention program: Effects of counselor and school characteristics. *Professional Psychology: Research and Practice, 40,* 476–497.

Lochman, J. E., Powell, N., Clanton, N., & McElroy, H. (2006). Anger and aggression. In G. Bear & K. Minke (Eds.), *Children's Needs III: Development, prevention, and intervention* (pp. 115–133). Washington D. C.: National Association of School Psychologists.

Lochman, J. E., Powell, N. R., Whidby, J. M., & FitzGerald, D. P. (2006). Cognitive-behavioral assessment and treatment with aggressive children. In P. C. Kendall (Ed.), *Child and Adolescent Therapy: Cognitive-Behavioral Procedures* (3rd ed., pp. 33–81). New York: Guilford Press.

Lochman, J. E., Powell, N. R., Whidby, J. M., & FitzGerald, D. P. (in press). Aggressive children: Cognitive-behavioral assessment and treatment. In P. C. Kendall (Ed.), *Child and adolescent therapy: Cognitive-behavioral procedures* (4th ed.). New York: Guilford Press.

Lochman, J. E., Rahmani, C. H., Flagler, S. L., Nyko-Silva, I., Ross, J. J., & Johnson, J. L. (1998). [Untitled]. Unpublished manuscript, University of Alabama, Tuscaloosa, AL.

Lochman, J. E., & Szczepanski, R. G. (1999). Externalizing conditions. In V. L. Schwean & D. H. Saklofske (Eds.), *Psychosocial correlates of exceptionality* (pp. 219–246). New York: Plenum Press.

Lochman, J. E., & Wayland, K. K. (1994). Aggression, social acceptance, and race as predictors of negative adolescent outcomes. *Journal of the Academy of Child and Adolescent Psychiatry, 33,* 1026–1035.

Lochman, J. E., Wayland, K. K., & White, K. K. (1993). Social goals: Relationship to adolescent adjustment and to social problem solving. *Journal of Abnormal Child Psychology, 21,* 135–151.

Lochman, J. E., & Wells, K. C. (1996). A social-cognitive intervention with aggressive children: Prevention effects and contextual implementation issues. In R. D. Peters & R. J. McMahon (Eds.), *Prevention and early intervention: Childhood disorders, substance use and delinquency* (pp. 111–143). Thousand Oaks, CA: Sage.

Lochman, J. E., & Wells, K. C. (1999c, April). *Reactive and proactive aggression in children: Associated child, peer, family and community characteristics.* Paper presented at the biennial meeting of the Society for Research in Child Development, Albuquerque, NM.

Lochman, J. E., & Wells, K. C. (2002a). Contextual social-cognitive mediators and child outcome: A test of the theoretical model in the Coping Power Program. *Development and Psychopathology, 14,* 971–993.

Lochman, J. E., & Wells, K. C. (2002b). The Coping Power Program at the middle school transition: Universal and indicated prevention effects. *Psychology of Addictive Behaviors, 16,* S40–S54.

Lochman, J. E., & Wells, K. C. (2003). Effectiveness study of Coping Power and classroom intervention with aggressive children: Outcomes at a one-year follow-up. *Behavior Therapy, 34,* 493–515.

Lochman, J. E., & Wells, K. C. (2004). The Coping Power program for preadolescent aggressive boys and their parents: Outcome effects at the one-year follow-up. *Journal of Consulting and Clinical Psychology, 72,* 571–578.

Lochman, J. E., Wells, K. C., & Colder, C. (1999, September). *Influence of social competence, child, parent, and neighborhood variables on patterns of reactive and proactive aggression in children.* Paper presented at the Life History Research Society annual conference, Kauai, HI.

Lochman, J. E., Wells, K. C., & Lenhart, L. A. (2008a). *Coping Power child group program: Facilitator guide.* New York, NY: Oxford University Press.

Lochman, J. E., Wells, K. C., & Lenhart, L. A. (2008b). *Coping Power child group program: Workbook.* New York: Oxford University Press.

Lochman, J. E., Whidby, J. M., & FitzGerald, D. P. (2000). Cognitive-behavioral assessment and treatment with aggressive children. In P. C. Kendall (Ed.), *Child and adolescent therapy: Cognitive-behavioral procedures* (2nd ed., pp. 31–87). New York: Guilford Press.

Lochman, J. E., White, K. J., Curry, J. F., & Rumer, R. (1992). Antisocial behavior. In V. B. Van Hasselt & D. J. Kolko (Eds.), *Inpatient behavior therapy for children and adolescents* (pp. 277–312). New York: Plenum Press.

Lochman, J. E., White, K. J., & Wayland, K. K. (1991). Cognitive-behavioral assessment and treatment with aggressive children. In P. C. Kendall (Ed.), *Child and adolescent therapy: Cognitive-behavioral procedures* (pp. 25–65). New York: Guilford Press.

Loeber, R. (1990). Development and risk factors of juvenile antisocial behavior and delinquency. *Clinical Psychology Review, 10,* 1–41.

Loeber, R., & Dishion, T. J. (1983). Early predictors of male delinquency: A review. *Psychological Bulletin, 94,* 68–99.

Loeber, R., Dishion, T. J., & Patterson, G. R. (1984). Multiple-gating: A multi-stage assessment procedure for identifying youth at risk for delinquency. *Journal of Research in Crime and Delinquency, 21,* 7–32.

Loeber, R., & Schmalling, K. B. (1985). Empirical evidence for overt and covert patterns of antisocial conduct problems: A meta-analysis. *Journal of Abnormal Child Psychology, 13,* 337–352.

Losen, D., & Orfield, G. (Eds.). (2002). *Racial inequality in special education.* Cambridge, MA: Harvard Educational Publishing Group.

Mager, W., Milich, R., Harris, M. J., & Howard, A. (2005). Intervention groups for adolescents with conduct problems: Is aggregation harmful or helpful? *Journal of Abnormal Child Psychology, 33,* 349–362.

Manassis, K., Mendlowitz, S. L., Scapillato, D., Avery, D., Fiksenbaum, L., Freire, M., et al. (2002). Group and individual cognitive-behavioral therapy for childhood anxiety disorders: A randomized trial. *Journal of the American Academy of Child and Adolescent Psychiatry, 41,* 1423–1431.

Marks, E. S. (1995). *Entry strategies for school consultation.* New York: Guilford Press.

Martens, B. K., & Meller, P. J. (1990). The application of behavioral principles to applied settings. In T. B. Gutkin & C. R. Reynolds (Eds.), *The handbook of school psychology* (2nd ed., pp. 612–634). New York: Wiley.

Mayer, M. J., & Van Acker, R. (2009). Historical roots, theoretical and applied developments, and critical issues in cognitive-behavior modification. In M. J. Mayer, R. Van Acker, J. E. Lochman, & F. M. Gresham (Eds.), *Cognitive-behavioral interventions for emotional and behavioral disorders: School-based practice* (pp. 3–28). New York: Guilford Press.

McConaughy, S. H., & Skiba, R. J. (1993). Comorbidity of externalizing and internalizing problems. *School Psychology Review, 22,* 421–436.

McKinnon, C. E., Lamb, M. E., Belsky, J., and Baum, C. (1990). An affective-cognitive model of mother–child aggression. *Development and Psychopathology 2,* 1–13.

McMahon, R. J., & Estes, A. M. (1997). Conduct problems. In E. J. Mash & L. G. Terdal (Eds.), *Behavioral assessment of childhood disorders* (3rd ed., pp. 130–193). New York: Guilford Press.

McMahon, R. J., & Wells, K. C. (1998). Conduct problems. In E. J. Mash & R. A. Barkley (Eds.), *Treatment of childhood disorders* (2nd ed., pp. 111–207). New York: Guilford Press.

Meichenbaum, D. H. (2006, May). Comparison of aggression in boys and girls: A case for gender-specific interventions. Paper presented at the 10th annual conference of the Melissa Institute for Violence Prevention and Treatment, Miami, Fl. Retrieved from *www.melissainstitute.org/documents/2006/Meich_06_genderdifferences.PDF.*

Meichenbaum, D. H., & Biemiller, A. (1998). *Nurturing independent learners: Helping students take charge of their learning.* Cambridge, MA: Brookline Books.

Mendez, L. M., & Knoff, H. (2003). Who gets suspended from school and why: A demographic analysis of schools and disciplinary infractions in a large school district. *Education and Treatment of Children, 26,* 30–51.

Milich, R., & Dodge, K. A. (1984). Social information processing in child psychiatric populations. *Journal of Abnormal Child Psychology 12,* 471–490.

Miller-Johnson, S., Coie, J. D., Maumary-Gremaud, A., Lochman, J., & Terry, R. (1999). Relationship between childhood peer rejection and aggression and adolescent delinquency severity and type among African American youth. *Journal of Emotional and Behavioral Disorders, 7,* 137–146.

Miltenberger, R. G. (1997). *Behavior modification: Principles and procedures.* Pacific Grove, CA: Brooks/Cole.

Mischel, W. (1990). Personality disposition revisited and revised: A view after three decades. In L. Pervin (Ed.), *Handbook of personality: Theory and research* (pp. 111–134). New York: Guilford Press.

Moffitt, T. E., Caspi, A., Rutter, M., & Silva, P. A. (2001). *Sex differences in antisocial behavior.* Cambridge, UK: Cambridge University Press.

Moretti, E. (2007). Crimes and the cost of criminal justice. In C. Belfield & H. M. Levin (Eds.), *The price we pay: Economic and social consequences of inadequate education.* New York: Brookings Institution.

National Association of School Psychologists. (1984). *Principles for professional ethics.* Bethesda, MD: Author.

National Center for Education Statistics. (2009). *Indicators of school crime and safety: 2009.* Retrieved from *nces.ed.gov/pubs2010/2010012.pdf.*

Nelson, W. M., III, & Finch, A. J. (2000). *Children's inventory of anger.* Los Angeles: Western Psychological Services.

Nolan, M., Carr, A., Fitzpatrick, C., O'Flaherty, A., Keary, K., Turner, R., et al. (2002). A comparison of two programmes for victims of child sexual abuse: A treatment outcome study. *Child Abuse Review, 11,* 103–123.

Novaco, R. W. (1978). Anger and coping with stress: Cognitive-behavioral intervention. In J. P. Foreyet & D. P. Rathjen (Eds.), *Cognitive behavioral therapy: Research and application* (pp. 135–173). New York: Plenum Press.

O'Donnell, C. R. (2001). Trends, risk factors, prevention, and recommendations. *Law and Policy, 23,* 409–416.

O'Neill, R. E., Horner, R. H., Albin, R. W., Sprague,

J. R., Storey, K., & Newton, J. S. (1997). *Functional assessment and program development for problem behavior: A practical handbook* (2nd ed.). Pacific Grove, CA: Brooks/Cole.

Olweus, D. (1993). *Bullying at school: What we know and what we can do.* Cambridge, MA: Blackwell.

OSEP Technical Assistance Center on Positive Behavioral Interventions and Supports (2009). Retrieved from *www.pbis.org/school/what_is_swpbs.aspx.*

Pardini, D. A., Lochman, J. E., & Frick, P. J. (2003). Callous/unemotional traits and social cognitive processes in adjudicated youth. *Journal of the American Academy of Child and Adolescent Psychiatry, 42,* 364–371.

Park, R. D., & Slaby, R. G. (1983). The development of aggression. In E. M. Hetherington (Ed.), *Handbook of child psychology: Vol. 4. Socialization, personality, and social development* (pp. 547–641). New York: Wiley.

Parron, D. L. (1994). DSM-IV: Making it culturally relevant. In S. Friedman (Ed.), *Anxiety disorders in African Americans* (pp. 149–165). New York: Springer.

Patterson, G. R. (1982). *Coercive family process.* Eugene, OR: Castalia.

Patterson, G. R. (1993). Orderly change in a stable world: The antisocial trait as a chimera. *Journal of Consulting and Clinical Psychology, 61,* 911–919.

Patterson, G. R., DeBaryshe, B. D., & Ramsey, E. (1989). A developmental perspective on antisocial behavior. *American Psychologist, 44,* 329–335.

Patterson, G. R., Dishion, T. J., & Yoerger, K. (2000). Adolescent growth in new forms of problem behavior: Macro- and micro-peer dynamics. *Prevention Science, 1,* 3–13.

Patterson, G. R., Reid, J. B., & Dishion, T. J. (1992). *Antisocial boys.* Eugene, OR: Castalia.

Patterson, G. R., Reid, J. B., Jones, R. R., & Conger, R. E. (1975). *A social learning approach to family intervention: Families with aggressive children* (Vol. 1). Eugene, OR: Castalia.

Pepler. D. J., & Craig, W. M. (2005). Aggressive girls on troubled trajectories: A developmental perspective. In D. J. Pepler, K. C. Madsen, C. Webster, & K. S. Levine (Eds.), *The development and treatment of girlhood aggression* (pp. 3–27). Mahwah, NJ: Erlbaum.

Pepler, D. J., Craig, W. M., & Roberts, W. I. (1998). Observations of aggressive and nonaggressive children on the school playground. *Merrill-Palmer Quarterly 44*(1), 55–76.

Pepler, D. J., King, G., & Byrd, W. (1991). A social-cognitively based social skills training program for aggressive children. In D. J. Pepler & K. H. Rubin (Eds.), *Development and treatment of childhood aggression* (pp. 361–379). Hillsdale, NJ: Erlbaum.

Pepler, D. J.., Levene, K., & Walsh, M. (2004). Interventions for aggressive girls: Tailoring and measuring the fit. In R. Roesch (Series Ed.), & M. M. Moretti, C. L. Odgers, & M. A. Jackson (Vol. Eds.), *Perspectives in law and psychology: Vol. 19. Girls and aggression: Contributing factors and intervention principles* (pp. 41–56). New York: Kluwer Academic/Plenum.

Pepler, D. J., & Sedighdeilami, F. (1998, October). *Aggressive girls in Canada* (Report No. W-98–30E). Applied Research Branch, Strategic Policy, Human Resources Development Canada, Hull, Quebec, Canada. [Online]. Available at *www.hrdc-drhc.gc.ca/stratpol/arb/publications/research/abw-98–30e.shtml.*

Pepler, D. J., & Slaby, R. G. (1994). Theoretical and developmental perspectives on youth and violence. In L. D. Eron, J. H. Gentry, & P. Schlegel (Eds.), *Reason to hope: A psychological perspective on violence and youth* (pp. 27–58). Washington, DC: American Psychological Association.

Pepler, D. J., Waddell, J., Jiang, D., Craig, W., Connolly, J., & Lamb, J. (2006). Aggressive girls' health & parent–daughter conflict. *Women's Health and Urban Life, 5,* 25–41.

Pepler, D. J., Walsh, M. M., & Levene, K. (2004). Interventions for aggressive girls: Tailoring and measuring the fit. In M. M. Moretti, M. Jackson, & C. Odgers (Eds.), *Girls and aggression: Contributing factors and intervention principles.* Norwell, MA: Kluwer Academic.

Perry, D. G., Perry, L. C., & Rasmussen, P. (1986). Cognitive social learning mediators of aggression. *Child Development, 57,* 700–711.

Pettit, G. S. (1997). Aggressive behavior. In G. C. Bear, K. M. Minke, & A. Thomas (Eds.), *Children's needs II: Development, problems, and alternatives* (pp. 135–148). Bethesda, MD: National Association of School Psychologists.

Poulin, F., Dishion, T. J., & Burraston, B. (2001). 3-year iatrogenic effects associated with aggregating high-risk adolescents in cognitive-behavioral interventions. *Applied Developmental Science, 5,* 214–224.

Powell, N. P., Lochman, J. E., Boxmeyer, C. L., Barry, T. D., & Young, L. (2010). Anger and aggression in children: The role of arousal and cognition. In W. Arsenio & E. Lemerise (Eds.), *Emotions, aggression, and moral development* (pp. 239–258). Washington, DC: American Psychological Association.

Prinstein, M. J., & La Greca, A. M. (2004). Childhood peer rejection and aggression as predictors of adolescent girls' externalizing and health risk behaviors: A 6-year longitudinal study. *Journal of Consulting and Clinical Psychology, 72,* 103–112.

Putnam, R. F., Luiselli, J. K., Handler, M. W., & Jefferson, G. L. (2003). Evaluating student discipline practices in a public school through behavioral assessment of office referrals. *Behavior Modification, 27*, 505–523.

Rabiner, D. L., Lenhart, L., & Lochman, J. E. (1990). Automatic vs. reflective problem solving in relation to children's sociometric status. *Developmental Psychology, 71*, 535–543.

Rausch, M. K., & Skiba, R. (2004, July). *Disproportionality in school discipline among minority students in Indiana: Description and analysis* (Children Left Behind Policy Briefs, Supplementary Analysis 2-A). Bloomington, IN: Center for Evaluation and Policy.

Redding, R. E., & Shalf, S. M. (2001). The legal context of school violence: The effectiveness of federal, state, and local law enforcement efforts to reduce gun violence. *Law and Policy, 23*, 297–344.

Reid, J. B., & Patterson, G. R. (1991). Early prevention and intervention with conduct problems: A social interactional model for the integration of research and practice. In G. Stoner, M. R. Shinn, & H. M. Walker (Eds.), *Interventions for achievement and behavior problems* (pp. 715–739). Bethesda, MD: National Association of School Psychologists.

Reynolds, C., & Kamphaus, R. W. (2005). *Behavior assessment system for children* (2nd ed.) San Antonio, TX: Pearson.

Roff, J. D. (1986). Identification of boys at high risk for delinquency. *Psychological Reports, 58*, 615–618.

Rones, M., & Hoagwood, K. (2000). School-based mental health services: A research review. *Clinical Child and Family Psychology Review, 3*, 223–241.

Rotter, J. B., Chance, J. E., & Phares, E. J. (1972). *Applications of a social learning theory of personality*. New York: Holt, Rinehart & Winston.

Rubin, K. H., Bream, L. A., & Rose-Krasnor, L. (1991). Social problem solving and aggression in childhood. In D. J. Pepler & K. H. Rubin (Eds.), *The development and treatment of childhood aggression* (pp. 219–248). Hillsdale, NJ: Erlbaum.

Sancilio, M., Plumert, J. M., & Hartup, W. W. (1989). Friendship and aggressiveness as determinants of conflict outcomes in middle childhood. *Developmental Psychology, 25*, 812–819.

Sandomierski, T., Kincaid, D., & Algozzine, B. (2007). Response to intervention and positive behavior support: Brothers from different mothers or sisters with different misters? *Positive Behavioral Interventions and Supports Newsletter, 4*(2), 1–4.

Scelfo, J. (2005, June 13). *Bad girls go wild: A rise in girl-on-girl violence is making headlines and prompting scientists to ask why*. Newsweek. Retrieved from *www.newsweek.com/id/50082*.

Schaeffer, C. M., Petras, H., Ialongo, N., Masyn, K. E., Hubbard, S., Poduska, J., et al. (2006). A comparison of girls' and boys' aggressive-disruptive behavior trajectories across elementary school: Prediction to young adult antisocial outcomes. *Journal of Consulting and Clinical Psychology, 74*, 500–510.

Schechtman, Z. (2003). Therapeutic factors and outcomes in group and individual therapy of aggressive boys. *Group Dynamics, 7*, 225–237.

Schechtman, Z. (2004). Client behavior and therapist helping skills in individual and group treatment of aggressive boys. *Journal of Counseling Psychology, 51*, 463–472.

Schechtman, Z., & Ben-David, M. (1999). Individual and group psychotherapy of childhood aggression: A comparison of outcomes and processes. *Group Dynamics, 3*, 263–274.

Shannon, M. M., & McCall, D. S. (2003). Zero tolerance policies on context: A preliminary investigation to identify actions to improve school discipline and school safety. Retrieved from *www.safehealthyschools.org/whatsnew/capzerotolerance.htm*.

Shure, M. (1996). *I can problem-solve: An interpersonal cognitive problem-solving program*. Champaign, IL: Research Press.

Simmons, R. (2002). *Odd girl out: The hidden culture of aggression in girls*. San Diego: Harcourt.

Sinclair, E., Del'Homme, M., & Gonzalez, G. (1993). Systematic screening for preschool behavioral disorders. *Behavioral Disorders, 18*, 177–188.

Skiba, R., & Peterson, R. (2000). School discipline at a crossroads: From zero tolerance to early response. *Exceptional Children, 32*, 200–216.

Slaby, R. G., & Guerra, N. G. (1988). Cognitive mediators of aggression in adolescent offenders: An assessment. *Developmental Psychology, 24*, 580–588.

Sladeczek, I. E., Elliott, S. N., Kratochwill, T. R., Robertson-Majaanes, S., & Callan-Stoiber, K. (2001). Application of goal attainment scaling to a conjoint behavioral consultation. *Journal of Educational and Psychological Consultation, 12*, 45–48.

Smith, C. A., & Lazarus, R. W. (1990). Emotion and adaptation. In L. Pervin (Ed.), *Handbook of personality: Theory and research* (pp. 609–637). New York: Guilford Press.

Smith, D. C., Larson, J. D., DeBaryshe, B. D., & Salzman, M. (2000). Anger management for youth: What works and for whom? In D. S. Sandhu (Ed.), *Violence in American schools: A practical guide for counselors* (pp. 217–230). Reston, VA: American Counseling Association.

Stein, R. P., Richin, R. A., Banyon, R., Banyon, F., & Stein, M. F. (2000). *Connecting content to character: Helping students do the right thing*. Alexandria, VA: Association for Curriculum Development.

Steinberg, M. E., & Dodge, K. A. (1983). Attributional bias in aggressive adolescent boys and girls. *Journal of Social and Clinical Psychology, 1,* 312–321.

Stormshak, E. A., Bierman, K. L., Bruschi, C., Dodge, K. A., Coie, J. D., & Conduct Problems Prevention Research Group (1999). The relation between behavior problems and peer preference in different classroom contexts. *Child Development, 70,* 169–182.

Striepling, S. H. (1997). The low aggression classroom: A teacher's view. In A. P. Goldstein & J. C. Conoley (Eds.). *School violence intervention: A practical handbook* (pp. 23–45). New York: Guilford Press.

Sutherland, E. (1939). *Principles of criminology.* Philadelphia: Lippincott.

Tangney, J. P., Wagner, P. E., Hansbarger, A., & Gramzow, R. (1991). *The Anger Response Inventory for Children (ARI-C).* Fairfax, VA: George Mason University Press.

Tharinger, D., & Stafford, M. (1996). Best practices in individual counseling of elementary-age students. In A. Thomas & J. Grimes (Eds.), *Best practices in school psychology III* (pp. 893–907). Bethesda, MD: National Association of School Psychologists.

Thelen, M. H., Fry, R. A., Feherenbach, P. A., & Frautschi, N. M. (1979). Therapeutic videotape and film modeling: A review. *Psychological Bulletin, 86,* 701–720.

Thornberry, T. P., & Krohn, M. D. (1997). Peers, drug use, and delinquency. In D. M. Stoff, J. Breiling, & J. D. Maser (Eds.), *Handbook of antisocial behavior* (pp. 218–233). New York: Wiley.

Thornberry, T. P., Krohn, M. D., Lizotte, A. J., Smith, C. A., & Tobin, K. (2003). *Gangs and delinquency in developmental perspective.* New York: Cambridge University Press.

Tillitski, C. J. (1990). A meta-analysis of estimated effect sizes for group versus individual versus control treatments. *International Journal of Group Psychotherapy, 40,* 215–224.

Tremblay, R. E., Kurtz, L., Masse, L. C., Vitaro, F., & Pihl, R. O. (1995). A bimodal preventive intervention for disruptive kindergarten boys: Its impact through mid-adolescence. *Journal of Consulting and Clinical Psychology, 63,* 560–568.

U.S. Department of Education. (1998). *Early warning, timely response: A guide to safe schools.* Washington, DC: Author.

U.S. Department of Health and Human Services. (1999). *Mental health: A report of the Surgeon General—Executive summary.* Retrieved from *www.surgeongeneral.gov/library/mentalhealth/ home.html.*

Van de Wiel, N. M. H., Matthys, W., Cohen-Kettenis, P. T., Maassen, G. H., Lochman, J. E., & van Engeland, H. (2007). The effectiveness of an experimental treatment when compared with care as usual depends on the type of care as usual. *Behavior Modification, 31,* 298–312.

Van de Wiel, N. M. H., Matthys, W., Cohen-Kettenis, P., & van Engeland, H. (2003). Application of the Utrecht Coping Power program and care as usual to children with disruptive behavior disorders in outpatient clinics: A comparative study of cost and course of treatment. *Behavior Therapy, 34,* 421–436.

Vitaro, F., Tremblay, R. E., Kerr, M., Pagani, L., & Bukowski, W. M. (1997). Disruptive friends' characteristics and delinquency in early adolescence: A test of two competing models of development. *Child Development, 68,* 676–689.

Waas, G. A. (1988). Social attributional biases of peer-rejected and aggressive children. *Child Development, 59,* 969–975.

Waas, G. A., & French, D. C. (1989). Children's social problem solving: Comparison of the open middle interview and children's assertive behavior scale. *Behavioral Assessment, 11,* 219–230.

Walker, H. M., Colvin, G., & Ramsey, E. (1995). *Antisocial behavior in schools: Strategies and best practices.* Pacific Grove, CA: Brooks-Cole.

Walker, H. M., Homer, R. H., Sugai, G., Bullis, M., Sprague, J. R., Bricker, D., et al. (1996). Integrated approaches to preventing antisocial behavior patterns among school-age children and youth. *Journal of Emotional and Behavioral Disorders, 4,* 194–209.

Walker, H. M., Ramsey, E., & Gresham, F. M. (2004). *Antisocial behavior in school* (2nd ed.). Belmont, CA: Wadsworth/Thomson Learning.

Walker, H. M., Severson, H. H., Stiller, B., Williams, G., Haring, N., Shinn, M., et al. (1988). Systematic screening of pupils in the elementary age range at risk for behavior disorders: Development and trial testing of a multiple gating model. *Remedial and Special Education, 9,* 8–14.

Walsh, M. M., Pepler, D. J., & Levene, K. S. (2002). A model intervention for girls with disruptive behaviour problems: The Earlscourt Girls Connection. *Canadian Journal of Counselling, 36,* 297–311.

Watson, T. S., & Steege, M. W. (2009). *Conducting school-based functional behavioral assessments: A practitioner's guide* (2nd ed.). New York: Guilford Press.

Weaver, B. (2000, July/August). *APS Observer.* (Available from the American Psychological Society, 1010 Vermont Avenue, NW, Suite 1100, Washington, DC 20005-4907.)

Webster-Stratton, C., & Hammond, M. (1997). Treating children with early-onset conduct problems: A comparison of child and parent training interventions. *Journal of Consulting and Clinical Psychology, 65*, 93–109.

Weiner, B., & Graham, S. (1999). Attribution in personality psychology. In L. A. Pervin & O. P. John (Eds.), *Handbook of personality: Theory and research* (2nd ed., pp. 605–628). New York: Guilford Press.

Weiss, B., Caron, A., Ball, S., Tapp, J., Johnson, M., & Weisz, J. R. (2005). Iatrogenic effects of group treatment for antisocial youths. *Journal of Consulting and Clinical Psychology, 73*, 1036–1044.

Weisz, J. R., Donenberg, G. R., Han, S. S., & Kauneckis, D. (1995). Child and adolescent psychotherapy outcomes in experiments versus clinics: Why the disparity? *Journal of Abnormal Child Psychology, 23*, 83–106.

Wells, K. C., Lochman, J. E., & Lenhart, L. A. (2008a). *Coping Power parent group program: Facilitator guide.* New York: Oxford University Press.

Wells, K. C., Lochman, J. E., & Lenhart, L. A. (2008b). *Coping Power parent group program: Workbook.* New York: Oxford University Press.

Whebby, J. H., Dodge, K. A., Valente, E., Jr., Bierman, K., Coie, J. D., Greenburg, M., et al. (1993). School behavior of first grade children identified as at-risk for development of conduct problems. *Behavioral Disorders, 19*, 67–78.

Williams, S. C., Lochman, J. E., Phillips, N. C., & Barry, T. D. (2003). Aggressive and nonaggressive boys' physiological and cognitive processes in response to peer provocations. *Journal of Clinical Child and Adolescent Psychology, 32*, 568–576.

Wills, T. A., McNamara, G., Vaccaro, D., & Hirkey, A. E. (1996). Escalated substance use: A longitudinal grouping analysis from early to middle adolescence. *Journal of Abnormal Child Psychology, 105*, 166–180.

Wiseman, R. (2003). *Queen bees and wannabes: Helping your daughter survive cliques, gossip, boyfriends, and other realities of adolescence.* New York: Three Rivers Press.

Wright, J. C., Giammarino, M., & Parad, H. W. (1986). Social status in small groups: Individual-group similarity and the social "misfit." *Journal of Personality and Social Psychology, 50*, 523–536.

Xie, H., Farmer, T. W., & Cairns, B. D. (2003). Different forms of aggression among inner-city African-American children: Gender configurations and school social networks. *Journal of School Psychology, 41*, 355–375.

Young, E. L., Boye, A., & Nelson, D. (2006). Relational aggression: Understanding, identifying, and responding in the schools. *Psychology in the Schools, 43*, 297–312.

Young, E. L., Nelson, D. A., Hottle, A. B., Warburton, B., & Young, B. K. (2009, December). Relational aggression in schools: Information for Educators. *Communiqué, 38*(4), 24.

Yung, B. R., & Hammond, W. R. (1998). Breaking the cycle: A culturally sensitive violence prevention program for African-American children and adolescents. In A. Lutzker (Ed.), *Handbook of child abuse research and treatment* (pp. 319–340). New York: Plenum Press.

Zahn, M. A., Brumbaugh, S., Steffensmeier, D., Feld, B. C., Morash, M., Chesney-Lind, M., et al. (2008). *Violence by teenage girls: Trends and context.* Washington, DC: Office of Juvenile Justice and Delinquency Prevention. Retrieved December 15, 2009, from *www.ncjrs.gov/pdffiles1/ojjdp/218905.pdf.*

Zelli, A., Dodge, K. A., Lochman, J. E., Laird, R. D., & the Conduct Problems Prevention Research Group. (1999). The distinction between beliefs legitimizing aggression and deviant processing of social cues: Testing measurement validity and the hypothesis that biased processing mediates the effects of beliefs on aggression. *Journal of Personality and Social Psychology, 77*, 150–166.

Zins, J. E., & Elias, M. J. (2006). Social and emotional learning. In G. G. Bear & K. M. Minke (Eds.), *Children's needs III: Development, prevention, and intervention* (pp. 1–13). Bethesda, MD: National Association of School Psychologists.

Zonnevylle-Bender, M. J. S., Matthys, W., van de Wiel, N. M. H., & Lochman, J. (2007). Preventive effects of treatment of DBD in middle childhood on substance use and delinquent behavior. *Journal of the American Academy of Child and Adolescent Psychiatry, 46*, 33–39.

Index

f following a page number indicates a figure.